BUCKNELL REVIEW

The Arts and Their Interrelations

STATEMENT OF POLICY

Bucknell Review is a scholarly interdisciplinary journal. Each issue will be devoted to a major theme or movement in the humanities or sciences, or to two or three closely related topics. The editors invite heterodox, orthodox, and speculative ideas and welcome manuscripts from any enterprising scholar in the humanities and sciences.

BUCKNELL REVIEW

A Scholarly Journal of Letters, Arts and Sciences

Contributors should send manuscripts with a self-addressed stamped envelope to the Editor, Bucknell University, Lewisburg, Pennsylvania 17837. Subscription, $12.00 per volume of two issues; single copy, $7.50.

BUCKNELL REVIEW

The Arts and Their Interrelations

Edited by
HARRY R. GARVIN

Special Associate Editor This Issue
JAMES M. HEATH

LEWISBURG
BUCKNELL UNIVERSITY PRESS
LONDON: ASSOCIATED UNIVERSITY PRESSES

Cranbury, New Jersey 08512

Associated University Presses
Magdalen House
136-148 Tooley Street
London SE1 2TT, England

Library of Congress Cataloging in Publication Data
Main entry under title:

The Arts and their interrelations.

(Bucknell review ; v. 24, no. 2)
Includes bibliographical references.
1. Arts—Addresses, essays, lectures. I. Garvin, Harry Raphael, 1917- II. Heath, James M. III. Series.
AP2.B887 vol. 24, no. 2 [NX60] 051s [700] 78-62038
ISBN 0-8387-2355-1

Fall 1978
(Volume XXIV, Number 2)

Printed in the United States of America

Contents

Notes on Contributors

JAMES A. W. HEFFERNAN: Teaches at Dartmouth College. Author of *Wordsworth's Theory of Poetry*. Project: a full-length study on the relations between English Romantic poetry and landscape painting.

GERALD P. TYSON: Currently at the National Endowment for the Humanities. Forthcoming book: *Joseph Johnson, A Liberal Publisher*. Articles in *Ariel, Studies in Bibliography, Eighteenth-Century Studies*, and *Computers and the Humanities*.

BARTON L. ST. ARMAND: Teaches at Brown University. Publications: *The Roots of Horror in the Fiction of H. P. Lovecraft*; articles on Poe, Hawthorne, Frost, Whitman, and Jewett in such journals as *American Quarterly, Criticism, American Literature, Journal of American Folklore, Emerson Society Quarterly, American Transcendental Quarterly*, and *Michigan Quarterly Review*.

ROBERT S. FREDRICKSON: Teaches at Gettysburg College. Professional interests: nineteenth-century American literature, literature in relation to film and psychology.

LAURA RICE-SAYRE: Teaches at Wake Forest University. Publications on Michel Butor and René Char. Professional interests: literature and the plastic arts, and contemporary literature (Spanish, French, American). Projects: books on the poetics of parody and, in collaboration with Henry M. Sayre, on the odalisque as a model in art and literature (a phenomenological approach to women's studies).

HENRY M. SAYRE: Teaches at Wake Forest University. Publications on Gertrude Stein and Juan Gris, William Carlos Williams, and Marcel Duchamp. Projects: a book-length study of William Carlos Williams; research on the transcience of the art object (1955 to present); and, in collaboration with Laura Rice-Sayre, a book on the odalisque as a model in art and literature (a phenomenological approach to women's studies).

FRED M. ROBINSON: Teaches at University of Massachusetts, Amherst. Major fields of interest: modern literature and comedy. Has published short fiction, and is fiction editor of *The Massachusetts Review*. Project: a book on modern comic literature.

JOHN N. SERIO: Teaches at Clarkson College of Technology. Publications on Stevens, Whitman, Dickinson, Poe, Marvell. Project: the poetics of place in modern American poetry.

LEE W. GIBBS: Teaches at Cleveland State University. Publications in history of Christian thought, systematic theology, myth, and ritual. Current projects: the mystery of evil, myth and the experience of transcendent mystery, and Hooker's *The Laws of Ecclesiastical Policy*.

F. DAVID MARTIN: Teaches at Bucknell University. Books: *Art and the Religious Experience* and *The Humanities through the Arts* (with Lee A. Jacobus). Articles published in *The Journal of Aesthetic Education, The Art Journal, The Journal of Aesthetics and Art Criticism, The Journal of Philosophy, The British Journal of Aesthetics, Leonardo, Dialectics and Humanism, AAUP, Christian Scholar, Religious Studies.* Forthcoming book: *The Aesthetics of Sculpture*.

JOSEPH GRANGE: Teaches at University of Southern Maine. Professional interests: philosophy in relation to psychiatry, religion, society; the relationships between technology and culture.

Introduction

The purpose of this issue of *Bucknell Review* is to further studies in the interrelations among the arts by exploring recent developments in that area.

Of course, the search for parallels and divergences in the arts is an old one, with a kind of cyclical history from Plato, Aristotle, and Horace to the present. An innovating aesthetician or critic opens up a new road that others excitedly explore and widen until unexpected obstacles loom; and then repetition, skepticism, and timidity complete the cycle and, for the time being, stultify the enterprise. But the problems in interrelating the arts remain intrinsic, ever-beckoning. Furthermore, the contemporary interest gives evidence of responsible enthusiasm and professional rigor and deserves encouragement by editors, publishers, and universities.

Some caveats are appropriate at this point, if the enterprise is to nurture its promise. Pleasant excursions into parallels between arts won't do. Some recent papers have laboriously developed easy generalizations on peripheral issues. Some critics, in working out their independent intuitions, end up enthusiastically and innocently propounding long-accepted or long-known positions. Others are satisfied to emphasize surface similarities between two arts when the differences at deeper levels are crucial. Terms common to two or more arts are often used loosely to cover up entreating questions rather than to reveal fundamental matters. If we are to achieve something large and substantial in this enterprise, we shall need to know how not to play the game of art parallels.

The new enthusiasts should be more aware of the best work already done by aestheticians and literary and art historians, to appropriate and add to the open legacy of insights, and to discard some grand and third-rate heirlooms. Independent intuitions are not enough. Substantive knowledge has a historical base and can become cumulative—not only in the sciences but in the humanities.

The fresh explorations today are theoretical and practical. For example, phenomenologists, structuralists, and semiologists are still vigorously expanding their interdisciplinary insights into the arts. There is a high need for practical critics, with skills in close analysis, to compare and contrast the treatment of the "same" subject matter by a poet and a composer or a painter, by a novelist and film director or sculptor. Such critics should be able to tell us more about what we think we knew about different materials and forms. Some critics and aestheticians are now inquiring closely into what is going on in a consciousness while one is actually reading a poem or novel, actually listening to a madrigal, actually looking at a framed painting or a statue in the round (in a museum or outside). And the profession may soon grasp the radical significance of the distinction between a physical artifact (a canvas, for example) and a viewer's feelings in consciousness while the viewer is concentratedly looking at the canvas. For this crucial distinction, lip service becomes a mumble. The term *aesthetic experience* will take on some new meanings.

Regarding the creative processes of artists, a number of revelations should also be forthcoming if we can learn what is going on in a consciousness while a poet is actually composing his lines, while a painter is actually putting brush to canvas, while a composer is actually writing his score.

Perhaps in the future even the terms *meaning* and *knowledge* in the nonverbal as well as verbal arts will have some commonly accepted significations. When a large enterprise can nurture enthusiasm, sophistication, and niceness in thought and feeling, neither scope nor precision need be sacrificed.

The editors hope that the essays in this book will suggest some next steps in the exploration of the arts.

Harry R. Garvin
Editor

BUCKNELL REVIEW

The Arts and Their Interrelations

Literature and Painting

Reflections on Reflections in English Romantic Poetry and Painting

James A. W. Heffernan

Dartmouth College

IN aesthetic theory, the word *reflection* has long been used as a metaphor for the representation of "life" or "nature" in works of graphic and verbal art. But this metaphor is very nearly dead, and while theoreticians have long recognized that *reflection* is a problematic word for the re-*creation* of reality in art, the visible process of reflection is usually taken for granted. It is curious, in fact, that speculation about the way art "reflects" life should have generated so little reflection on the process of reflection itself, or that such speculation should have been confined to the *speculum*, or mirror, which offers only one kind of reflection. In this essay, I would like to consider how another kind of reflection is itself reflected—or represented—in the landscape paintings of Turner and Constable and in the poetry of Wordsworth, Coleridge, and Shelley. The richness of the water-borne reflections represented in the poetry and painting of these men will compel us, I think, to consider anew the very meaning of the word *reflection*.

I

The history of this word is complicated. It made its first recorded appearance about 1386, and the *OED* informs us that by 1430 it was being used to mean "the action of a mirror or other polished surface in exhibiting or reproducing the image of an object." By the middle of the sixteenth century, it had come to mean also the reflected image itself, which is what it still means—in its primary sense. But by the end of the seventeenth century, reflection had acquired a secondary sense. In his *Essay Concerning Human Understanding* (1690), Locke defined it as "that notice which the mind takes of its own operations, and the manner of them."[1] Such a "notice" is plainly an analytical activity of the mind, as the *Essay* itself abundantly illustrates, and whatever the object of this analysis, reflection itself came to denote intellectual action. In the very title of Edmund Burke's *Reflections on the Revolution in France*, published one hundred years after Locke's *Essay*, the use of the preposition *on* promises that these reflections will constitute a mental performance. Burke does not offer simply to mirror the events of the Revolution, to reproduce its images, to show us unadorned reflections *of* them; he aims rather to set his mind to work *upon* them, to consider their causes and infer their consequences.

We are still using reflection in this secondary sense. But the primary sense has persevered, and it is precisely this primary sense that makes reflection such a problematic metaphor for artistic representation. In the Renaissance, critics of art and literature alike firmly established the commonplace that both of these arts should reflect reality, and in the eighteenth century Samuel Johnson intended the highest praise when he said that Shakespeare's plays hold up "a faithful mirrour of manners and of life."[2] Yet ever since Plato, reflection has been a hazardous paradigm for the representation of reality in art. In Plato's analysis of what men see when newly released from the cave of shadowy appearances, the reflection of an object is little better than its shadow, an empty substitute from which men should turn to the thing itself, and thence to the source of all reflected light: from the sun reflected in the moon, in water, or in "any alien medium" to the sun "as it is in itself."[3] For Plato, one of the greatest obstacles to our perception of reality is the danger of mistaking a reflected object for a real one, and the danger has been almost universally recognized. It is pointedly dramatized in the enduring myth of Narcissus, who fell in love with his own reflection, and in the autobiography of Milton's Eve, whose very first act was to do the same. As she herself tells Adam in book 4 of *Paradise Lost*, she awakened to find herself

> Under a shade on flow'rs, much wond'ring where
> And what I was, whence thither brought, and how.
> Not distant far from thence a murmuring sound
> Of waters issued from a Cave and spread
> Into a liquid plain, then stood unmov'd

Pure as th'expanse of Heav'n; I thither went
With unexperienc't thought, and laid me down
On the green bank, to look into the clear
Smooth Lake, that to me seem'd another Sky.
(ll. 451-59)[4]

Coming out of the shade "with unexperienc't thought," Eve is initially drawn to waters flowing from a cave. Born (like Eve herself) in a world of shadowy appearances, the waters form a lake that seems "another Sky," a sky which Eve prefers to the real and heavenly one it reflects. This first error leads at once to a second. Though created as the "image" or reflection of Adam, who is himself the image of God, she immediately becomes entranced with her own reflection. "There," she says, "I had fixt / Mine eyes till now, and pin'd with vain desire," had she not been led away by God to Adam. But even then, she is at first repelled by one "less fair / Less winning soft, less amiably mild, / Than that smooth watery image," and she must be persuaded that her watery image is really no match for the "Substantial Life" embodied in Adam (*PL* 4.465-91). In this brief autobiographical narrative, Eve's fascination with reflections is used to reveal her fatal tendency toward self-infatuation. Shortly after this narrative, in fact, Satan begins to exploit this tendency by telling her in a dream how beautiful she looks beneath the moon, which "with more pleasing light / Shadowy sets off the face of things" (*PL* 5.42-43). The shadowy light of the moon is of course merely a reflection of the sun, and at sunrise the next day, when Even turns to Adam with her story of the dream, she is also turning from the shadowy light of self-delusion to the bright, clear sun of Adam's reason. Milton would have us do likewise. In his opinion, reflections are both philosophically insubstantial and morally dangerous.

Like beauty, however, moral danger lies in the eyes of the beholder. In the landscapes of English Romantic poetry and painting, this moral and philosophical distrust of reflections gives way to outright admiration. Wordsworth was unapologetically fascinated with them, and in his own autobiography they play a part significantly different from the one they play in Eve's. Coincidentally, his most suggestive treatment of them appears in book 4 of *The Prelude*, where he compares the difficulty of recovering his past with the difficulty of seeing into the depths of a body of water.

As one who hangs down bending from the side
Of a slow moving Boat, upon the breast

> Of a still water, solacing himself
> With such discoveries as his eye can make,
> Beneath him, in the bottom of the deeps,
> Sees many beauteous sights, weeds, fishes, flowers,
> Grots, pebbles, roots of trees, and fancies more;
> Yet often is perplex'd, and cannot part
> The shadow from the substance, rocks and sky,
> Mountains and clouds, from that which is indeed
> The region, and the things which there abide
> In their true dwelling; now is cross'd by gleam
> Of his own image, by a sunbeam now,
> And motions that are sent he knows not whence,
> Impediments that make his task more sweet.[5]

It is not easy to say just where this simile leads us—or leaves us. To some extent, Wordsworth's attitude toward reflection seems traditional: he implies that he is trying to part the shadow from the substance, even as Plato separates his Ideal Forms from the transitory objects that reflect them, or even as Milton's God takes the newly created Eve from shadow to substance, from the empty image of her face in the water to the substance of the man whom she herself reflects. Yet if Wordsworth is in fact attempting to part the shadow from the substance, to separate the reflection of clouds and mountains from the reality of underwater pebbles and roots, he is at once distracted and fascinated by the reflections, by the gleam of his own image, by sunbeams, by motions that are sent he knows not whence. The reflections get between his eye and the depths of his past experience, but they are nonetheless "impediments that make his task more sweet," and they are so interesting in themselves that he does not bother to tell us precisely just what element of himself they represent. The reference to a "gleam / Of his own image" may imply that the reflections correspond to his present feelings, and that Wordsworth is symbolically describing the autobiographer's tendency to confound his present feelings with the past—the tendency he speaks of at the end of "Nutting." But we cannot be sure about this correspondence. Indeed, looking through the reflected images of this simile, we ourselves have trouble seeing precisely just what its double tenor is, and we find ourselves increasingly perplexed by the task of parting shadow from substance, vehicle from tenor, visible reflection from intellectual reflection. Perhaps just one thing is clear: whatever their significance might be, Wordsworth was captivated by the sheer complexity of reflections in water.

Reflections of this kind were a source of consuming interest to J. M. W. Turner. The fifth of his Royal Academy lectures, which he extensively revised in 1818, is on reflection, and Turner begins by saying that a knowledge of this subject is indispensable to the painter: "Nothing is so difficult and undefined as the Theory of Reflexies and yet they are absolutely necessary to the Painters persuit. . . ."[6] Turner believed that we live in a world of reflected light, that every color in a scene is modified by reflections from every other color in it, and that so long as there is any light at all in the air, reflections will be everywhere, even in shadows.[7] But what is particularly interesting about Turner's lecture on reflection is that it dwells at length on the reflective properties of water. For purposes of reflection, he says, water cannot simply be regarded as a polished body or a mirror: "It is quite different first from color secondly from motion and thirdly its reflexies which admits of such endless variety incomprehensible contrarieties and phenomena that it imperiously demands more attention than its dismissal it has generally received" (TMS O f6). Taking these three points of difference in reverse order, the "contrarieties" of reflections in water apparently spring from the fact that, as Wordsworth also notices (with perplexity), water is both transparent and reflective, admitting light as well as returning it. Turner himself goes on to say that a mirror "repels the immediate ray while [water] absorbs it the one transparent while mirror is opaque how can they appear the same [?]" Second, water and mirrors differ "from motion," for Turner points out that water is subject to breezes and currents which make of its surface an *undulating* mirror that congregates forms.[8] Finally (or "first"), water and mirrors differ in color:

> Water often possesses color but color is not imparted to its reflections or refractions like as a colored glass when every thing seen is viciated by that color even the purest mirrour gives a tone to the sky and as the color is increased it destroys all the color of nature to its own dullness while water often seems to challenge the sky for brightness. (TMS O f6-6[v])

The mirror that Turner here describes is probably the Claude-glass, which was normally not (as is sometimes thought) a tinted lens, but rather a slightly convex blackened mirror.[9] Enthusiastically used in the eighteenth century by tourists, artists, and peripatetic poets such as Thomas Gray, it enabled the viewer to see an actual landscape as if it had been already reflected in a somber-toned canvas by Claude Lorrain. The Claude-glass thus at once reflected and beautified nature, and constituted, in fact, an objective correlative for the neoclassical theory that art should reflect not nature as it is, but nature improved, heightened, or refined—what the influential French critic Charles Batteux called "la belle nature." Johnson himself declared that it would "be as safe to turn the eye immediately upon mankind, as upon a mirrour which shows all that presents itself without discrimination."[10] Literature, then, was asked to behave like a special *kind* of mirror: like a Claude-glass, reflecting only what is beautiful and morally edifying. And it was by this theory, as M. H. Abrams observes, that Augustan critics tried to solve the problems arising from the definition of art as reflection.

But Turner's comments on reflection exacerbate these problems. If the Claude-glass symbolized the theory that art should refine what it reflects, this kind of reflection casts a shadow of its own, for as Turner suggests, the Claude-glass eclipses the brilliance of landscape. "It destroys," he says, "all the color of nature to its own dullness while water often seems to challenge the sky for brightness."

The last part of Turner's statement is the most provocative thing in it. Plainly contrasting two different *kinds* of reflection, Turner makes us realize that a mirror provides only one of them. And the fact that mirrors provide only one kind of reflection calls into question the commonplace equation of reflection with mirrors. Taking this equation for granted, Abrams has argued at length that *mirror* and *lamp* are antithetical metaphors in the history of criticism, that up to the eighteenth century the mind of the artist is "a reflector of external objects," while in the Romantic period it becomes "a radiant projector which makes a contribution to the objects it perceives."[11] The problem with this convenient formulation is that it takes no account of the differences between kinds of reflective surfaces, specifically between mirrors and bodies of water. In the landscapes of English Romantic poetry and painting, reflection is no longer simply a weary and faded metaphor for the representation of nature in the works of literature or art. Instead, reflections themselves become an integral part of what is being represented, and when seen in water they assume a kind of brilliance that makes them shadows no more. No longer are they morally, philosophically, or even aesthetically inferior to the things they reflect, and no longer do they "refine" the colors of nature by reducing them to monochromatic dullness. In Turner's eyes, the reflected sky is bright enough to challenge the real one, and the water mirror thus becomes a new kind of lamp.

This is the lamp that repeatedly illuminates Turner's paintings. In *Fishing upon Blythe Sand*, exhibited 1809 (Tate Gallery), the brightest light is not in the sky but on the horizon, where the waves both catch and intensify the light of a sun we cannot directly see. In

The Harbour of Dieppe, exhibited 1825 (Frick Collection, New York), the yellowed puff of wispy clouds in a pale blue sky encloses a hard white disc, but the hazy glow it lends to the clouds is overpowered by the shimmering white gold of the water beneath it. In *Norham Castle, Sunrise*, painted after 1830 (Tate), the ball of yellow in the clouds is matched if not surpassed by the columns of reflected yellow that radiate across the river. And in *Keelmen Heaving in Coals by Night*, exhibited 1835 (fig. 1), the grimness of an industrial subject is transfigured by reflected moonlight. Ships are densely ranged along both banks of the River Tyne, and within the shadows of the ships at lower right, where darkened figures toil away in a small inferno of red and yellow flame, the water has a cast of red. But a white moon beams down the middle of the river, and the sparkling tints of yellow-green that it reflects unmistakably rival the moonlit sky for brilliance.

An equal sensitivity to the power of reflected light is evident in the work of Turner's great contemporary, John Constable. In the oil-on-millboard version of *Waterloo Bridge from Whitehall Stairs*,

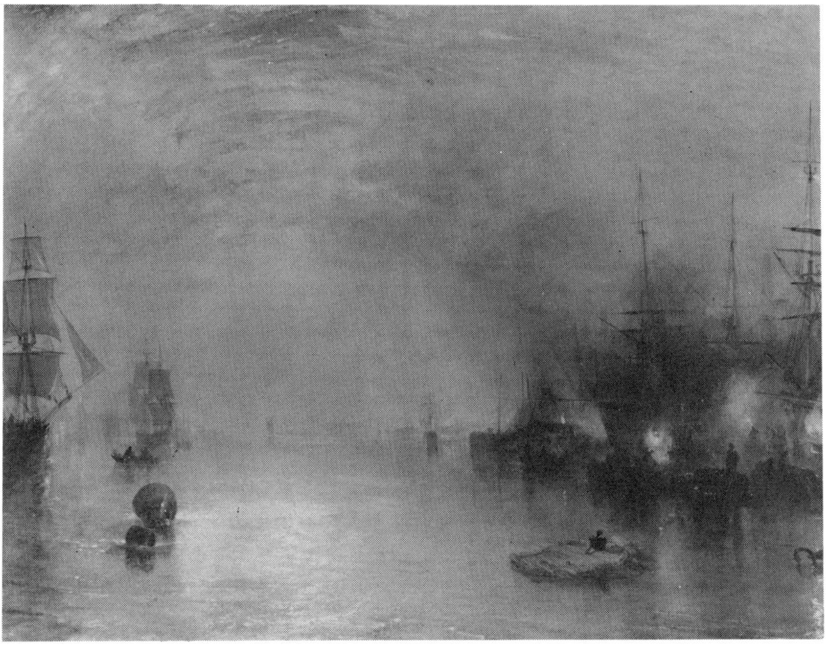

Fig. 1. Joseph Mallord William Turner, *Keelmen Heaving in Coals by Night* (682). FROM THE WIDENER COLLECTION, NATIONAL GALLERY OF ART, WASHINGTON, D.C. REPRINTED BY PERMISSION.

painted about 1819 (Victoria and Albert Museum), the light that is diffused and scattered through a cloudy sky is brilliantly condensed on the patch of water near the bridge at right, where the Thames becomes—as in Turner's *Dieppe*—a river of gold. And if Turner makes the horizon shimmer in *Blythe Sand*, Constable does likewise in *Hadleigh Castle*. Successive versions of this picture actually show that he increased the brilliance of the sea as he proceeded. In the full-sized oil sketch believed to have been made in 1828-29 (fig. 2), the slender and broken streaks of white on the distant waves are barely a match for the intensity of the swirling white clouds above; but in the finished version exhibited in 1829 (fig. 3), the clouds have been darkened, and the sea beneath them—which reflects the unseen sun behind them—has now become a sheet of shining light.

Watery mirrors could likewise turn into lamps for Wordsworth and Coleridge. In Wordsworth's account of the stolen boat in *The Prelude*, the lake on which he rowed was "shining clear" under the moon, and as he rowed the drops that fell from the tips of his oars whenever he lifted them out of the water left

> Small circles glittering idly in the moon,
> Until they melted all into one track
> Of sparkling light.
> (*Prelude* 1.383-94)

Later in book 1, the "shining water" of the moonlit sea off Westmoreland appears as a "field of light" (11. 606-7); and in book 5, in the dream of an Arabian desert doomed to inundation, the distant sea advances as "a bed of glittering light" (1850 *Prelude* 5.129). Comparable sights get into the notebooks of Coleridge. In an entry of September 1803, he speaks of a lake as "a mass of molten silver."[12] In a later entry (from the autumn of 1806), he writes: "—like a lake beneath the Sun seemed to possess in its own right and prodigally give the fiery Light, which by not receiving it flashed forth" (*NC* 2:2936). In this description, as in Turner's *Dieppe* and Constable's *Waterloo*, the reflected sunlight is so brilliant that it seems to emanate from the water itself.

But it is in his poetry that Coleridge represents most vividly the power of reflected light. In "The Rime of the Ancient Mariner," the moonlit scene that ends part 4 is strikingly similar to what we find in Turner's *Keelmen*. Like the shadows of the ships in the picture, the shadow of the mariner's ship reflects its redness:

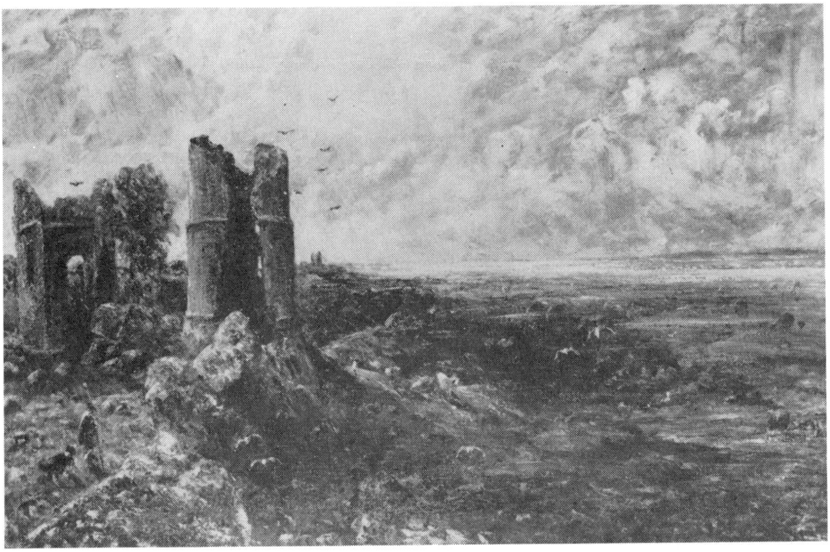

Fig. 2. Constable, *Sktetch for Hadleigh Castle.* THE TATE GALLERY, LONDON. REPRINTED BY PERMISSION.

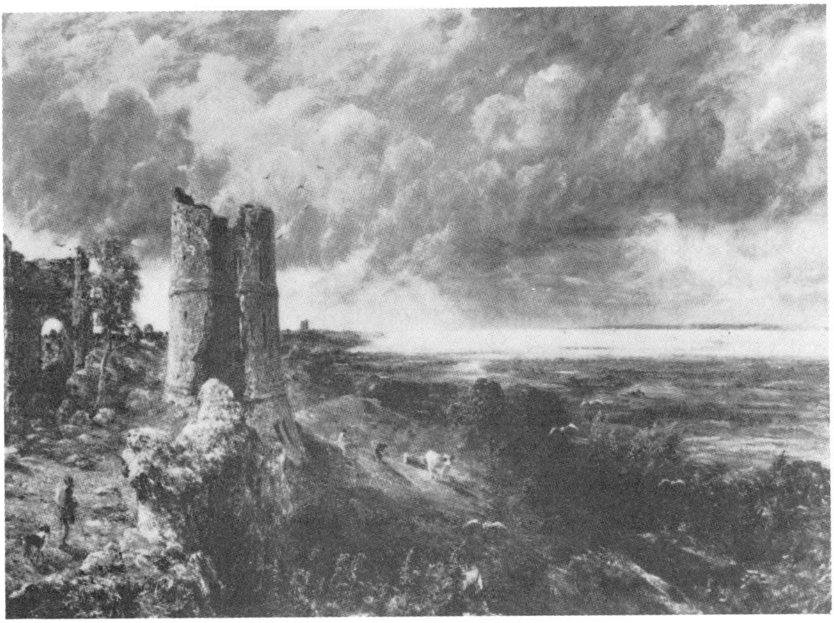

Fig. 3. Constable, *Hadleigh Castle.* COLLECTION OF MR. AND MRS. PAUL MELLON. REPRINTED BY PERMISSION.

where the ship's huge shadow lay,
The charmed water burnt alway
A still and awful red
(ll. 269-71)[13]

But beyond this reddened shadow, the moon creates a field of reflected light, and even as the reflected light in *Keelmen* transfigures the industrialized and no doubt polluted River Tyne, here it transfigures the water snakes. Hitherto ugly, they now seem beautiful, for they move in tracks of shining white and golden fire. The mariner's sudden impulse to bless them, therefore, comes not from the moon itself, but from the reflection of its light upon the water.[14] Since the only word applied to the moon is *moving* (l. 263), the moonlit sea in this passage clearly exudes a brilliance that the moon itself lacks. Yet the moon itself reflects the light of the sun, and if the moon in this poem reveals to the imagination what the sun paradoxically conceals, as Robert Penn Warren has argued, the whole structure of projected and reflected light has been inverted.

II

The treatment of reflections in English Romantic poetry and painting goes well beyond the simple observation of brilliant light upon water. But what these examples already begin to suggest is that in the Romantic period, reflections are more than empty images of real objects, images we are supposed to turn away from. The moon is no longer a weak substitute for the sun, and the reflection is no longer simply inferior to the thing it reflects. Aesthetically, at least, it becomes superior, for its greater brilliance and greater softness make it more ideal. So it seemed to Shelley one day in 1821. Gazing on an Italian scene, he wrote in his notebook: "Why is the reflection in that canal far more beautiful than the objects it reflects? The colours more vivid yet blended with more harmony; the openings from within into the soft and tender colours of the distant wood and the intersection of the mountain lines surpass and misrepresent truth."[15] The philosopher in Shelley sees truth misrepresented, but the poet in him sees truth surpassed. Two years earlier, in fact, when he wrote "Ode to the West Wind," he envisioned "palaces and towers / Quivering within the wave's intenser day." And in act 3 of *Prometheus Unbound*, written just a few months before the "Ode," he used the beauty of reflections to symbolize the beauty of a renovated earth. After Prometheus is released, the Spirit of the Earth explains to Asia that while he lay within a public fountain, "like the reflex of the moon / Seen in a wave under green leaves," he saw that all things had shed their evil natures. What epitomizes this regeneration is the loveliness of two reflected birds. "I cannot tell my joy," the Spirit says,

> when o'er a lake
> Upon a drooping bough with nightshade twined,
> I saw two azure halcyons clinging downward
> And thinning one bright branch of amber berries,
> With quick long beaks, and in the deep there lay
> Those lovely forms imaged as in a sky.[16]

When objects imaged in water are seen as thus transfigured or regenerated, the concept of reflection gains a new significance. Coleridge is thinking specifically about reflections in water when, in the *Biographia Literaria*, he defines the relation between nature and Wordsworth's poetry. Among the "excellences" he finds in this poetry, he says, is "the perfect truth of nature in his images and descriptions, as taken immediately from nature. . . . Like a green field reflected in a calm and perfectly transparent lake, the image is distinguished from the reality only by its greater softness and lustre."[17] Coleridge trips on his own language here, for if the lake were indeed perfectly transparent, it would reflect nothing at all. But he is clearly enough describing the difference between a real object and its reflection in terms of gain rather than loss. The reflected object is not a feeble approximation of the original, but an intensified and idealized version of it, and the dead or at least moribund metaphor that art is a reflection of nature gains new life from a new way of looking—of actually *looking*—at reflected objects.

Wordsworth's poetry shows us this way. It not only reflects nature as a lake reflects a field; it also bears witness to the "greater softness and lustre" of reflections themselves. In book 1 of *The Recluse*, Wordsworth writes of birds flying over a lake, and their reflections call to mind the renovated beauty of Shelley's azure halcyons:

> They tempt the sun to sport among their plumes;
> Tempt the smooth water, or the gleaming ice,
> To shew them a fair image,—'tis themselves,
> Their own fair forms, upon the glimmering plain,
> Painted more soft and fair as they descend,
> Almost to touch . . .[18]

Even as the ice gleams and the water glimmers with a light that seems almost their own, the birds are at once softened and beautified in reflection, and significantly, the beauty of the reflection suggests the heightened radiance of a painting.

Wordsworth did not always view reflections with simple admiration. The lines above date from 1800, and in "Elegiac Stanzas Suggested by a Picture of Peele Castle, in a Storm" (*PWW*, 4:258-60), written five years later, the tranquillity of a reflection is ruefully remembered as one of the things that locked the poet into a state of delusion. "Thy Form," he says to the castle,

> was sleeping on a glassy sea.
> . . . .
> Whene'er I looked, thy Image still was there;
> It trembled, but it never passed away.
> (ll. 4-8)

There was just enough motion to distinguish the surface of the sea from the surface of a mirror, but hardly enough to prefigure the stormy violence that would later take the life of his brother, who now, of course, *has* passed away. Nevertheless, the tranquillity of the reflected castle still has a hold on Wordsworth's memory. Paradoxically, even as he denies the moral permanence of this scene, its very evanescence gives it an aesthetic permanence. It remains as permanent and as ideal as the picture he *would have* painted of this reflected castle: a reflection *of* a reflection in which he would have included

> the gleam,
> the light that never was, on sea or land,
> The consecration and the poet's dream.
> (ll. 14-16)

These lines constitute the crux of the poem. Do they describe an act of self-delusion or an act of imaginative transfiguration? Though he ends the poem by stoically saying farewell to the "blind" happiness with which he beheld the tranquillity of the castle, Wordsworth does not resolve our perplexity here. When the artistic reflection of nature in poetry or painting is brighter than the thing it reflects, or when the visible reflection of light upon water is brighter than the sky it reflects, we have trouble invoking the old Platonic distinction between "substance" and "shadow." And a reflection which "trembled, but never passed away" is at once ephemeral and enduring. The past tense relegates it to the Platonic cave of passing shadows, but what is recalled from the past is precisely an image of indestructibility, of oxymoronically *trembling* steadfastness. When Shelley later echoes this line in his *Ode to Liberty* (1820), he converts the past tense to an eternal present, and the trembling reflection of Athens becomes an unequivocal sign of permanence:

> Within the surface of Time's fleeting river
> Its wrinkled image lies, as then it lay
> Immovably unquiet, and for ever
> It trembles, but it cannot pass away!
> (ll. 76-79; *PWS*, p. 600)

No longer a passing shadow, the reflection becomes a thing of enduring brilliance. Indeed, five years after "Peele Castle," where he sems to dismiss reflections for their impermanence, Wordsworth himself speaks eloquently of their power to symbolize just the opposite. In the first version of *A Guide through the District of the Lakes*, which appeared as an introduction to Joseph Wilkinson's *Select Views* in 1810, he says that a calm lake in the midst of a landscape is the embodiment of perfect tranquillity. In it, he says,

> the heavens are not only brought down into the bosom of the earth, but . . . the earth is mainly looked at, and thought of, through the medium of a purer element. . . . All . . . speaks of tranquillity . . . except the clouds gliding in the depths of the lake, or the traveller passing along, an inverted image, whose motion seems governed by the quiet of a time, to which its archetype, the living person, is, perhaps, insensible:—or it may happen, that the figure of one of the larger birds . . . is crossing silently among the reflected clouds, while the voice of the real bird, from the element aloft, gently awakens in the spectator the recollection of appetites and instincts . . . that deform and agitate the world,—yet have no power to prevent nature from putting on an aspect capable of satisfying the most intense cravings for the tranquil, the lovely, and the perfect, to which man, the noblest of her creatures, is subject.[19]

We are a long way from Plato and from Milton. Here, even as the passing traveler is turned upside down in his reflection, the traditional subordination of reflected object to real object is likewise inverted. The voice of the real bird speaks of fleeting agitation; the silent image of the reflected bird speaks of tranquillity and permanence. Contemplating the reflection, the spectator finds his imagination carried into a world where clouds pass silently beneath him, where the way up and the way down become one, where actual objects mildly distract him, but the reflection of those objects satisfies his cravings for the tranquil, the lovely, and the perfect. What the spectator sees here is in fact something like what Wordsworth himself sees in a seldom-noticed but singuarly remarkable sonnet of 1807:

Clouds, lingering yet, extend in solid bars
Through the grey west; and lo! these waters, steeled
By breezeless air to smoothest polish, yield
A vivid repetition of the stars;
Jove, Venus, and the ruddy crest of Mars
Amid his fellows beauteously revealed
At happy distance from earth's groaning field,
Where ruthless mortals wage incessant wars.
Is it a mirror?—or the nether Sphere
Opening to view the abyss in which she feeds
Her own calm fires?—But list! a voice is near;
Great Pan himself low-whispering through the reeds,
"Be thankful, thou; for if unholy deeds
Ravage the world, tranquillity is here!"
(*PWW*, 5:127)

Wordsworth here exploits Petrarchan structure to brilliant effect. Using the sestet to reflect upon the reflection described in the octave, he turns the polished steel of the water's surface into a two-way mirror. What vividly repeats the stars of outer space may be seen as a window that reveals the fires of inner space: the "calm fires" far removed from the turbulence of a warring earth, like ruddy Mars, the unmoved mover. There is a hint of subtle terror in this vision of a Pascalian abyss, and the hint is not entirely dispelled by the tidy contrast of the last two lines. Nevertheless, what this reflection on a reflection finally opens to view is the transcendent "tranquillity" of eternal fire.

A similar pattern is at work in a passage from book 5 of *The Prelude*, but here Wordsworth turns a tranquil reflection into a window on the inner space of a boy's mind.[20] This is the boy who stood beside the glimmering Lake of Winander and

Blew mimic hootings to the silent owls
That they might answer him.—And they would shout
Across the watry Vale, and shout again,
Responsive to his call, with quivering peals,
And long halloos, and screams, and echoes loud
Redoubled and redoubled; concourse wild
Of mirth and jocund din! And when it chanced
That pauses of deep silence mock'd his skill,
Then sometimes, in that silence, while he hung
Listening, a gentle shock of mild surprize
Has carried far into his heart the voice
Of mountain torrents; or the visible scene
Would enter unawares into his mind
With all its solemn imagery, its rocks,
Its woods, and that uncertain Heaven, receiv'd
Into the bosom of the steady Lake.
(*Prelude* 5.398-414)

I do not know just what "uncertain Heaven" means. It may refer to the movement of stars in the actual sky—mentioned in lines 391-93—or to the trembling of the reflected sky on the surface of the water. But even if the surface is lightly rippled, the lake itself is essentially "steady," and the reflections of the solemn imagery around it are carried far into the bosom of its depths, just as the voice of mountain torrents is carried far into the heart of the listening boy. The clamorous echo of sound thus gives way to the silent echo of sight, and the doubling of the "solemn imagery" in the depths of the lake is redoubled in the depths of the boy's mind. Once again, as in the sonnet and the passage from the *Guide*, the fleeting tumult of the actual world is surpassed by the permanence and tranquillity of the reflected one.

Both this passage and the one from the *Guide* may be revealingly set beside Turner's *Fighting Téméraire* (fig. 4). First exhibited in 1838, this painting of a grand old warship being tugged away for demolition hardly seems—at first—to illustrate either passage. Yet if we compare the actual tugboat at left with the reflection just

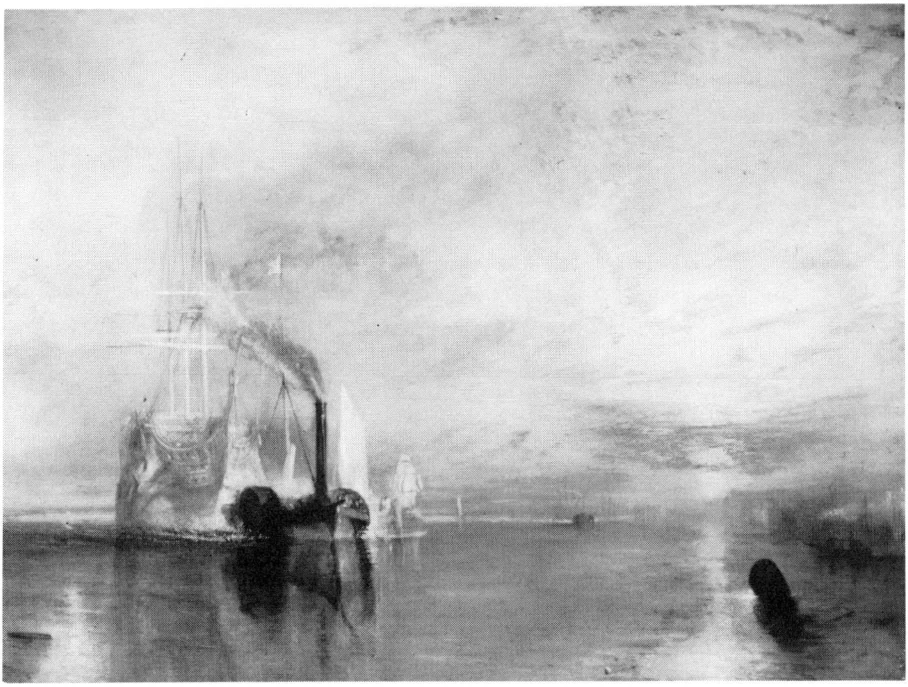

Fig. 4. Turner, *The Fighting Téméraire.* THE NATIONAL GALLERY, LONDON. REPRINTED BY PERMISSION.

beneath it, I think we can find something analogous to the contrast between the real bird and the reflected bird in the passage from the *Guide*. The real tugboat throws a plume of smoke and fire from its smokestack, and we can almost hear it chugging away. The reflected boat is more lustrous and more tranquil. With its smokestack quietly dissolving in the water, with its colors heightened and its prow delicately elongated, the boat is quite simply repeated—in a finer tone. And the same, I think, can be said of the setting sun at right. The actual sun is sinking, and its descent, as Graham Reynolds suggests, clearly symbolizes the end of the day for the *Téméraire*.[21] But like the solemn imagery reflected in the Lake of Winander, the delicately shimmering reflection of the sun is received into the bosom of a steady river. While the actual streaks of red massed just above the sun seem to be almost forcing it down, the reflected reds are spread out on a cloth of liquid gold, and the harshness of time relentlessly passing gives way—in reflection—to something that "speaks of tranquillity."

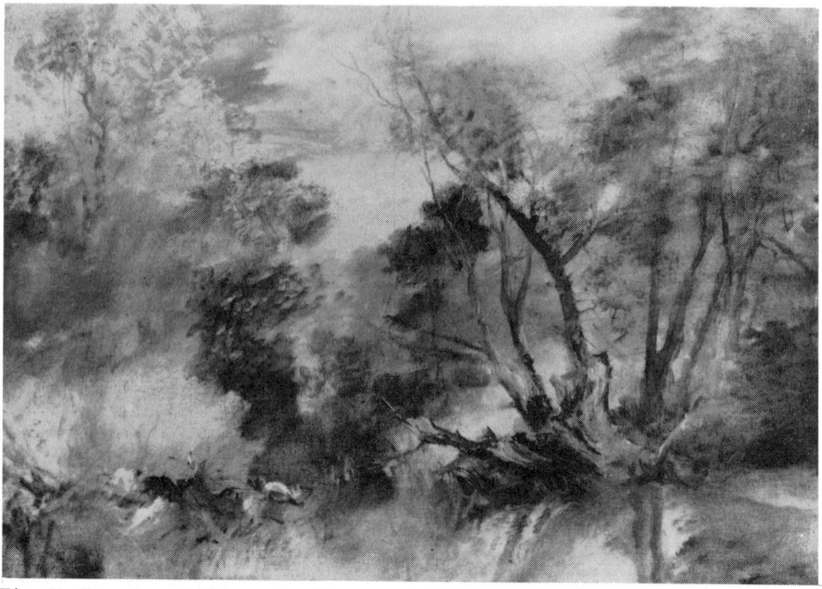

Fig. 5. Turner, *Willows beside a Stream*. THE TATE GALLERY, LONDON. REPRINTED BY PERMISSION.

III

In the face of the Platonic tradition, then, Romantic poets and painters tend to regard reflections not as inferior but as superior to the objects they reflect. Turner says that reflected light on water may rival the sky for brilliance, and both he and Constable demonstrate this effect in their work. Coleridge says that reflections have a greater softness and luster than actual objects; Wordsworth says they can better satisfy our need for loveliness, tranquillity, and perfection; Shelley says they are far more beautiful, and in the wave's intenser day he finds emblems of both renovation and permanence. Regarded in this way, water-borne reflections may embody an ideal world. As Coleridge implies, they may actually constitute a model of authentic idealization in poetry and painting, for unlike the Claude-glass, which "refines" the landscape by dulling its light, water-borne reflections intensify its light.

Nevertheless, Romantic poets and painters did not always choose to emphasize the difference between reality and reflection. In the oil painting *Willows beside a Stream* (fig. 5), done about 1807, Turner does quite the reverse. Most of the lines in this picture dissolve in its atmosphere, and it is difficult to see any line between the actual trees and the reflection of them. In the air as in the water, the foliage has a fluid delicacy set off only by the bare and spiky branches of the blasted tree at right, and the visible limbs of the other trees grow down as well as up. In this case, what the reflection conveys is not so much intensification as completion: together with the trees on the bank, the reflected trees create a harmonious, homogeneous—indeed almost *rounded*—whole. And this particular effect was something repeatedly noticed by both Wordsworth and Coleridge. Here is Coleridge, for instance, in a notebook entry of November 1799: "Monday Morning—sitting on a tree stump at the brink of the Lake by Mr. Clarkson's—perfect serenity / that round fat backside of a Hill with its image in the water made together *one* absolutely undistinguishable Form . . . the road appeared a sort of suture" (*NC*, 1:555). And here is Coleridge again, in an entry of 1804:

> Images of Calmness on Rydale Lake, Jan. 14 . . . An islet Stone, at the bottom of the Lake, the reflection so bright as to be heaved up out of the water/the Stone & its reflection looked so completely one, that Wordsworth remained for more than 5 minutes trying to explain why that stone had no reflection & at last found it out by me. (*NC*, 2:1844)

Wordsworth should have known better. Some four years before this conversation, he himself had captured a similar effect in the first book of *The Recluse*, where he describes not only the beauty of reflected birds but also the harmonious integration of a radiantly wooded hillside with its reflection in a lake:

> Behold the universal imagery
> Inverted, all its sun-bright features touched
> As with the varnish, and the gloss of dreams;
> Dreamlike the blending also of the whole
> Harmonious landscape; all along the shore

The boundary lost, the line invisible
That parts the image from reality;
And the clear hills, as high as they ascend
Heavenward, so piercing deep the lake below.
(*PWW*, 5:332)

Wordsworth is conscious of a line that parts the image from reality: he knows the difference between the sun-bright features of the actual trees and the delicate shimmer of their reflection, touched as with the varnish, and the gloss of dreams. And Turner knows the difference too: at the lower right side of his *Willows* we can barely discern a part of the waterline, a suture between reality and reflection. But in each of these landscapes the waterline is virtually erased, and the total effect is one of integration rather than division. Catching both parts of a landscape in a single, comprehensive vision, poet and painter alike transcend the difference between the trees and their reflection. In Turner's picture, as in Wordsworth's poem, we have a dreamlike blending of the "whole / Harmonious landscape," and in both cases it is nearly true to say that "all along the shore" we see "the boundary lost, the line invisible / That parts the image from reality."

Willows beside a Stream is a fair sample of what Turner characteristically did with reflection. Throughout his work, from the lake-district paintings of the 1790s to the shimmering Venetian scenes of the 1830s and 40s, he used reflection as a means of integration. In *Buttermere Lake*, exhibited 1798 (fig. 6), the arc of a rainbow joins the inverted arc of its reflection to form a ring of light: a ring that delicately binds together the lake, the mountains, and the disintegrating clouds. In *The Dogano . . . from the Steps of the Europa*, exhibited 1842 (fig. 7), reflection turns the water into an extension of the sky. The circular swirling of the clouds at upper left distinguishes them from the horizontal plane of the canal, but sky and water alike are permeated with white and blue. Paradoxically resting on their reflections, on foundations made of airy nothing, the buildings seem suspended in a substance that is neither air nor water, but a perfectly harmonious blending of the two.

Turner's blending of reflection and reality provoked some criticism. Commenting on his Venetian scenes at the exhibition of 1842, the *Art Union* declared: "A great error in Mr. Turner's smooth water pictures is, that the reflection of colours in the water are painted as strongly as the substance themselves, a treatment which diminishes the value of objects."[22] This criticism is highly revealing—though not quite in the way intended. On the one hand, it conveys the traditional assumption that reflections are inferior

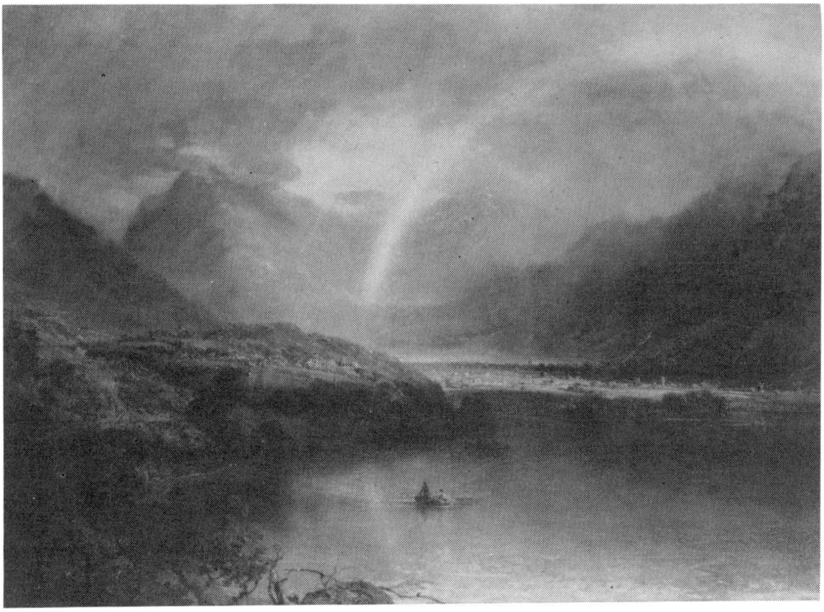

Fig. 6. Turner, *Buttermere Lake.* THE TATE GALLERY, LONDON. REPRINTED BY PERMISSION.

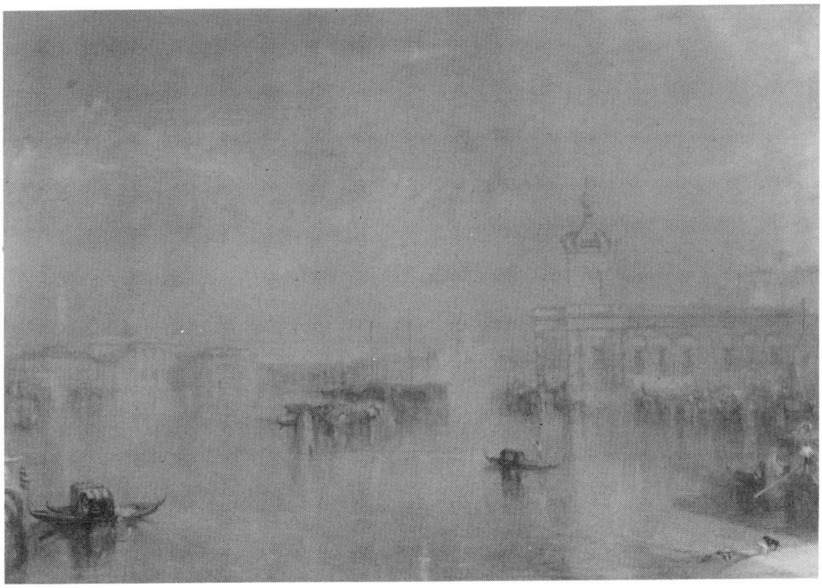

Fig. 7. Turner, *The Dogana, San Giorgio Citella, from the Steps of Europa.* THE TATE GALLERY, LONDON. REPRINTED BY PERMISSION.

"shadows" of what they reflect and should be represented as such; on the other hand, it recognizes Turner's challenge to that assumption, his deliberate attack on the traditional barrier between reflection and reality. But the critic of the *Art Union* was a little imprecise. By acting on the principle that water could rival the sky for brilliance, by raising the tone of reflected colors to the tone of the colors they reflect, Turner did not diminish the value of objects. He diminished their separateness. He made them collaborate with their reflections to produce an intradependent, integrated, harmonious whole.

To suppress the line between reflection and reality is of course to undermine or redefine the very notion of reality itself. When reflection makes the sea and the sky virtually indistinguishable, it can prompt the deepest kind of metaphysical speculation, and this is what we find in a notebook passage written by Coleridge in 1807. Thinking of Malta, where he had spent much of the year 1804, Coleridge writes:

> The Sky, o rather say, the Aether, at Malta, with the Sun apparently suspended in it, the Eye seeming to pierce beyond, & as it were, behind it and below the aetherial Sea, so blue, so [a] zerflossenes Eins, the substantial Image, and fixed real Reflection of the Sky—O I could annihilate in a deep moment all possibility of the needlepoint pinshead System of the *Atomists* by one submissive Case! Λoyos ab *Ente*—at once the existent Reflexion, and the Reflex Act—at once actual and real & therefore, filiation not creation / (*NC*, 2:3159 f.52^{v})

As Kathleen Coburn observes, Coleridge goes on to speculate on the process by which thought moves from existence (*Ente*) to Λoyos, the creative Word (*NC*, 2:3159). But the starting point for this speculation is the memory of what he had seen at Malta: the sea reflecting the sky so perfectly that it becomes at once "aetherial" and "substantial." No *insubstantial* image of a real object, it is itself a "real Reflection of the Sky," a "filiation" consubstantial with it, bound up with it in an all pervading oneness: *zerflossenes Eins*.

The sense of metaphysical oneness that Coleridge felt when he contemplated the sky and its reflection at Malta is, I think, altogether comparable to the union of sky and water expressed by the late Venetian paintings of Turner. In Turner's work, however, one of the finest examples of the way in which reflection can fuse contradictory elements is a picture not of Venice but of London: *The Burning of the Houses of Parliament*, exhibited in 1835 (fig. 8). The effect of this picture is triumphantly visual. Just as the pathetic plight of the drowning men in Turner's *Slavers* (Boston Museum of Fine Arts) is overpowered by the searing brilliance of its sunset, so the magnitude of the destruction wrought by fire in the very seat of British government is overpowered here by the magnificence of the fire itself. At left and right, the blue-green tones of the river Thames reflect the hues of the sky, and at right, the spectral towers of the Abbey and their reflection have the cool delicacy of Turner's Venice. But there is nothing cool about the center of this picture. While a massive tongue of flame takes possession of the sky, its equally massive reflection turns the river into liquid fire, and in this fusion of fire and water reflection paradoxically becomes the means by which Turner approaches the Platonic "one."

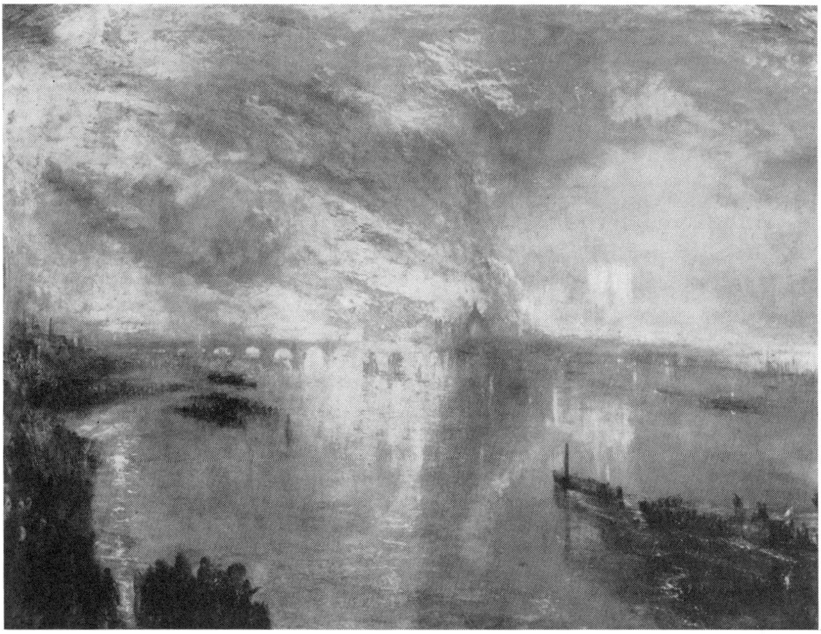

Fig. 8. Turner, *Burning of the Houses of Parliament*. THE CLEVELAND MUSEUM OF ART, BEQUEST OF JOHN L. SEVERANCE. REPRINTED BY PERMISSION.

The liquid fire of the Thames, in fact, vividly illustrates a key passage in Shelley's intensely Platonic *Adonais* (1821)—the stanza in which Shelley's grief over Keats's death changes to joy because he perceives that Keats's spirit will flow

> Back to the burning fountain whence it came,
> A portion of the Eternal, which must glow
> Through time and change, unquenchably the same.
> (ll. 338-41; *PWS*, p. 435)

Turner's Thames is itself a burning fountain. Challenging the laws of elemental contradiction even as it challenges the sky for brightness, the reflected and liquefied fire assumes a kind of transcendent radiance that the actual fire churning above it significantly lacks. It is striking to note that in the penultimate stanza of *Adonais* Shelley speaks of "man and beast and earth and air and sea" as "mirrors of / The fire for which all thirst" (ll. 483-85; *PWS*, p. 438). Had Shelley lived to see this picture, which was painted thirteen years after his death, he might well have seen its mirrored fire as an emblem of that unquenchable fire for which he thirsted.

In the landscapes of Wordsworth, Coleridge, Shelley, Turner, and Constable, water-borne reflections assume a variety of roles. Challenging the sky for brightness, as Turner says, they may visibly embody ideal brilliance. Representing sights but not sounds in a medium that trembles but does not pass away, as Wordsworth says, they may symbolize the tranquillity of ideal permanence. And finally, as agents of integration between earth, air, water, and sky, they may enable the poet and painter to represent the life of nature as an indissoluble whole, a *zerflossenes Eins*. All of these effects enrich the impact of reflection when it is metaphorically used for the representation of nature in poetry and painting. To understand what reflection really means for the Romantic poets and painters is to understand why, in what is commonly regarded as the manifesto of English Romanticism, Wordsworth defines the mind of man not as a lamp but as a special kind of mirror: "the mirror of the fairest and most interesting properties of nature" (*PrW*, 1:140). When reflections are no longer insubstantial copies of real things, when they become instead embodiments of brilliance, symbols of tranquillity, and agents of elemental integration, they assume a life and power of their own. The study of them is undeniably complicated. A poet or painter who wishes to see what is actually present in the depths of a still water may well be distracted—as Wordsworth was—by the reflection "of his image, by a sunbeam now, / And motions that are sent he knows not whence." But if these things are indeed impediments to the perception of one kind of reality, they may at last turn into windows for the perception of another.

1. *An Essay Concerning Human Understanding*, 19th ed. (London: T. Longman, 1793), 1:78.

2. Preface to Shakespeare, in *The Yale Edition of the Works of Samuel Johnson*, vol. 7 (New Haven, Conn.: Yale University Press, 1968), p. 62.

3. Plato, *Republic* 516B, trans. Francis MacDonald Cornford (New York: Oxford University Press, 1945), pp. 229-30.

4. *John Milton: Complete Poems and Major Prose*, ed. Merritt Hughes, (New York: Odyssey Press, 1957); hereafter cited in the text as *PL*.

5. I quote from the 1805-6 version of *The Prelude* 4.247-61, in *The Prelude: or, Growth of a Poet's Mind*, ed. Ernest de Selincourt, 2d ed. rev. by Helen Darbishire (Oxford: Oxford University Press, 1959), p. 122; hereafter cited in the text as *Prelude*.

6. I quote MS. O fl from British Museum (Additional) MS. 46151 (Turner manuscripts); hereafter cited in the text as TMS.

7. TMS O f3^{V}. See also Lawrence Gowing, *Turner: Imagination and Reality* (New York: Museum of Modern Art, 1966), p.21, and Turner's Sketch Books in the British Museum Print Room, CII, f15; hereafter cited as TSB.

8. TMS 0 f6. I am also drawing on a separate note made about 1808 in TSB CV, inside cover.

9. The Claude-glass is discussed and illustrated in Deborah Jean Warner, "The Landscape Mirror and Glass," *Antiques* 105 no. 1 (January 1974): 158-59. The Claude-glass could be a colored lens instead of a mirror, but the mirror seems to have been more commonly used.

10. Both Batteux and Johnson are quoted in M. H. Abrams, *The Mirror and the Lamp: Romantic Theory and the Critical Tradition* (New York: W. W. Norton, 1958), pp. 12, 35-36.

11. Abrams, *The Mirror and the Lamp*, p.vi.

12. *The Notebooks of Samuel Taylor Coleridge*, ed. Kathleen Coburn, 3 vols. (Princeton, N.J.: Princeton University Press, 1957-73), 1: 1465 f.68^{V}; hereafter cited in the text as *NC*.

13. *Coleridge: Poetical Works*, ed. Ernest Hartley Coleridge (New York: Oxford University Press, 1969), p. 197.

14. The brilliance of the snakes in this passage may be partly due to phosphorescence, a light that naturally emanates *from* them. But Coleridge's own marginal gloss tells us that the mariner sees the snakes "by the light of the Moon."

15. Quoted in Shelley, *Collected Poems*, ed. Neville Rogers (Boston: Houghton Mifflin Co., 1968), p. 485.

16. *Prometheus Unbound* 3.4. 63-83, in *The Complete Poetical Works of Percy Bysshe Shelley*, ed. Thomas Hutchinson (London: Oxford University Press, 1912), pp. 246-47; hereafter cited in the text as *PWS*.

17. *Biographia Literaria*, ed. J. Shawcross, 2 vols. (London: Oxford University Press, 1907), 2: 121.

18. *The Poetical Works of William Wordsworth*, ed. Ernest de Selincourt and Helen Darbishire, 5 vols. (Oxford: Clarendon Press, 1940-49), 5: 321; hereafter cited in the text as *PWW*.

19. *The Prose Works of William Wordsworth*, ed. W. J. B. Owen and Jane Worthington Smyser, 3 vols. (Oxford: Clarendon Press, 1974), 2:192; hereafter cited in the text as *PrW*.

20. For the use of the term *inner space* in connection with this passage, I am indebted to Eugene L. Stelzig, *All Shades of Consciousness: Wordsworth's Poetry of the Self in Time* (The Hague: Mouton, 1975), p. 162.

21. Graham Reynolds, *Turner* (New York: Abrams, 1968), p. 178.

22. Quoted in Martin Butlin et al., *Turner 1775-1851* (London: Tate Gallery Publications, 1974), p. 152.

The Rococo Style of *Tristram Shandy*

Gerald P. Tyson

R. F. Brissenden has tentatively claimed that *Tristram Shandy* approximates the "satiric rococo" of William Hogarth's art. He demurs, though, because, "the value of extending to literary forms a term normally applied only to other arts is perhaps questionable."[1] On the contrary, literary criticism has recently been moving away form its former provincialism, and for good reason, since much can be gained toward understanding the function of form and content in Sterne's novel by precisely this sort of connection. This essay, then, will concentrate on tracing the relations between rococo style in the visual arts and the rococo style of this novel in the hope that such an inquiry can offer a fuller and deeper knowledge of the work's technique and help explain some of the problems readers encounter when trying to "pull together" a central meaning for Tristram's "Life and Opinions."

To begin understanding the close relationship between the aesthetics of art and literature in the eighteenth century it is helpful to remember that from at least Horace onward writers had taken rather literally the maxim *ut pictura poesis*, and however they construed the precise link between the plastic arts and the verbal, literature (especially poetry) was generally regarded as "painting" with words. Indeed, studies like Chester Chapin's *Personification in Eighteenth-Century English Poetry* have shown that poetry was considered superior to the visual arts because a single word could evoke an image in the imagination that rivaled the best efforts of the artist. Furthermore, the similarity between poetry and art was intensified by empirical philosophy that tended to reduce sense perception to variations of sight, for example, the blind man who "saw" scarlet when he heard the sound of a trumpet. Such theoreticians as Locke and Hartley, as well as a follower like

Addison, all regarded the operations of the mind in a language borrowed from the observation of *visible* phenomena. Not surprisingly was sight considered the primary sense. Now in relating *Tristram Shandy* to the visual arts two factors must be considered. The narrower of the two concerns the author's explicit interest in art and its more or less direct impact on his novel. The second factor is more vague but no less important. This is the gestalt of rococo art, implying a characteristic ontology shared both by the artists who created this style and the audience that embraced it.

To begin with the more obvious of these two elements, instances of Sterne's interest in art have been abundantly recorded by biographers and critics. His one extant painting; his wheedling letter (via Richard Berenger) to Hogarth begging an illustration for *Tristram Shandy*; his frequent references in the novel to art, connoisseurs, and the like; flattering references to Reynolds; his delight at posing for artists; and above all his admiration for the genius of Hogarth—all reflect Sterne's preoccupation with visual art. Amid this Hogarth emerges if not as Sterne's master at least as offering him a model and an aesthetic that could express his particular vision.[2]

Hogarth presented his theories in 1753 with the *Analysis of Beauty*. That the appearance of this book coincided with the height of the rococo vogue in England is no accident, for his notions follow largely from the practice of earlier French painters and designers who established this taste, and their English imitators. The theoretical foundation is the "line of beauty," an anti-Baroque and empirical attempt to formalize the common element in all "agreeable" works of art. The serpentine line offers variety through movement and asymmetry, avoiding the stasis of the straight line or the circle.

> The serpentine line, by its waving and winding at the same time different ways, leads the eye in a pleasing manner along the continuity of its variety, if I may be allowed the expression; and which by its twisting so many different ways, may be said to inclose (tho' but a single line) varied contents; and therefore all its variety cannot be expressed on paper by one continued line without the assistance of the imagination, or the help of a figure.[3]

The line of beauty possesses not only the property of space, but also the additional one of duration ("continuity") since one's eye must take time to follow the course of its undulations. Hogarth's assertion may have had its foundation in his experience as an engraver, for in this craft even form and mass are but an aggregate of individual lines, each having its own space as well as duration in the tedious process of engraving. In any case, Hogarth emphasizes at various points in his *Analysis* the presence of temporal and spatial elements in the line of beauty. In this connection his account of the discovery of the line of beauty is especially revealing:

> I can never forget my frequent strong attraction to it [the serpentine line in motion], when I was very young, and that its beguiling movement gave me the same kind of sensation then, which I since have felt at seeing a country-dance; tho' perhaps the latter might be somewhat more engaging; particularly when my eye eagerly pursued a favorite dancer, through all the windings of the figure, who then was bewitching to the sight. . . .
>
> This single example might be sufficient to explain what I mean by *the beauty of a composed intricacy of form*; and how it may be said, with propriety, to *lead* the eye a *kind of chace.*[4]

It is significant that the theory of the serpentine line is expressed in the "organic" terms of dance and chase, while its artistic application is always given a human or "natural" form.

Just as dance suggested to Hogarth the origin of his line of beauty and consequently occupies an important place in his aesthetic theory, so too is Sterne sometimes preoccupied with this temporal and spatial art form. Specifically, his interest in dance moves from the aesthetic to the thematic, for it is associated in the novel with love and death. What is significant, though, is the obvious sensual delight both men take in the frolic and "play" of dance. The clearest example of Sterne's fascination with dance comes in volume 7 when Tristram meets Nannette, the young peasant with a slit in her petticoat. Their dance on the field in France conduces to the larger dances of the novel:

> Just disposer of our joys and sorrows, cried I, why could not a man sit down in the lap of content here— —and dance, and sing, and say his prayers, and go to heaven with this nut brown maid? Capriciously did she bend her head on one side, and dance up insiduous— —Then 'tis time to dance off, quoth I; so changing only partners and tunes, I danced it away from *Lunel* to *Montpellier*— —from thence to *Pesçnas, Beziers*— —I danced it along through *Narbonne, Carcasson,* and *Castle Naudairy,* till at last I danced myself into *Perdrillo*'s pavillion, where pulling a paper of black lines, that I might go on straight forwards, without digression or parenthesis, in my uncle *Toby's* amours— — I began thus— —
>
> END of the SEVENTH VOLUME.[5]

Like Hogarth eschewing the rigid straight line or circle as antithetical to true beauty, so Sterne resists the beaten path of conventional narrative. Writing of his dance with Nannette, Tristram is put in mind of the authorial dance he performs against which he places the demands of linear plot. But the typical method of telling a story succumbs once again to the whim of his errant hobbyhorse, which can never quite keep on the King's highway. The digressions, jerks and starts, aposiopeses, meanderings, and deflections show on the one hand Tristram's comic inability to marshal narrative, and on the other Sterne's own distrust of the conventions of fiction. Both ends are served by the serpentine plot, which also provides the sort of variety Hogarth claimed was central to beauty.

In addition to its implications for plot and style, the dance metaphor, so appealing to Hogarth and Sterne, offers a special quality that is explicitly sensuous, indeed sexual. This quality operates actively in the Nannette episode and is latently present in the artist's description of the "line of beauty," as this statement by Hogarth indicates. Note again the reference to "chace":

> Intricacy in form, therefore, I shall define to be that peculiarity in the lines, which compose it, that leads the eye a *wanton kind of chace*, and from the pleasure that gives the mind, intitles it to the name of beautiful.[6]

Joseph Burke's introduction to the Oxford edition of the *Analysis* makes a point of explaining that the artist did not mean *wanton* as "dissolute," but rather as "free and frolicksome."[7] But the sexual implication is clearly present and it is this one on which Sterne focuses. The more provocative connotation of the word provides a kind of energy that finds vent in the novel through bawdy language and sexual innuendo. A possible basis for Sterne's inference may be located in Hogarth's reference, already quoted, to the "beguiling movement" of the country-dance and its direct relationship to the line of beauty. Certainly the sexual content of Hogarth's dance analogy has been recognized by other critics, one of whom had discovered in it "the erotic origin of his [Hogarth's] taste for the sinuous line. The grace and dignity of the undulation suggest the swaying movement of a dancing form and so reveal its feminine essence."[8] This remark pertains with equal accuracy to both the dance and the line of beauty.

Hogarth's frequent comparison of the serpentine line to the dance and chase makes it impossible to ignore a special property of the line referred to previously. This is the phenomenon of the single, unbroken line possessing a certain temporal quality—the capacity to exist in both space and time. Through his training and experience

Hogarth recognized the effect of a line on the spectator's observation: it was to be perceived in a *coup d'oeil* as well as experienced in time as the eye traveled its length. These dual characteristics were identified in modern prose fiction by Joseph Frank, whose term *spatial form* has been a staple of much recent criticism. A narrative held together by a series of elements in a spatial relationship to one another suggests a situation not unlike the "line of beauty" in Hogarth's art. In both cases time and space collaborate to help complete the "experience" of the work and provide a meaning for it. Our grasp, however, of a Hogarth print does not entirely depend upon the recognition of its temporal aspects, nor does our enjoyment of a modern novel rest on our awareness of its "dimensionality." Nevertheless, to ignore either part in these situations is to miss a significant portion of the work's meaning. But spatial form is not restricted to the twentieth century, nor was Sterne unaware of its ability to thicken the mixture of his fiction.

Now *Tristram Shandy* has always roused the interest of critics by its temporal concerns. Not only is its protagonist obsessed with time, but it is also an experiment in opposing conventional chronological time with the felt time of the character's mind. Structurally, plot gives way to Tristram's spontaneous discourse. So the temporal nature of Sterne's fiction has its counterpart in Hogarth's line of beauty insofar as the serpentine line possesses a type of duration. And equally true is the converse: the notion that *Tristram Shandy* occupies space, both as a physical book, and in terms of its very content. Spatial form involves the "continual reference and cross-reference of images and symbols which must be referred to each other spatially throughout the time-act of reading."[9] The meaning accruing to a work through its spatial form depends on "reflexive reference" instead of the temporal relationship of syntactical sequence.[10] Sterne establishes spatial form not so much through interconnected images as through the meandering of the narrative stream turning back on itself to events preceding Tristram's birth, and often by way of synaptic recollection, projecting forward into the hero's later life. As far as chronology itself is concerned, the first volume of *Tristram Shandy* spans from 1690 to 1760, with some chapters treating as many as five distinct time periods in the space of nine pages.

The absence of normal chronology in the sequence of events in *Tristram Shandy* is compensated for somewhat by Sterne's humorous treatment of causality. Whereas in most other novels events move in an orderly succession operating by the rules of cause and effect, Tristram's world is far less predictable. In fact, Sterne's theory of causality would seem to involve ultimate rather than proximate cause, the search for which is at best (in Toby) a source of constant endeavor, and at worst (in Walter) a stream of endless frustration. To better see Sterne's treatment of causality, recall Tristram's encounter with the window sash. The proximate cause for the accident is the absence of counterweights in the window frame. They have been removed by Corporal Trim for use as field pieces in Uncle Toby's fortifications. But the chain of action-reaction does not stop here. Tristram's accident can be traced ultimately back to the wound Toby receives at the battle of Namur. Though at first sight this might appear to be a reductio ad absurdum of a "first cause" theory, it is not, for Sterne makes it quite clear through the spatial connection of the events leading up to Tristram's circumcision that they all cluster around Toby's obsession with the arts of war, the hobbyhorse he mounts as a consequence of his injury.

The language Tristram uses to describe his unfortunate accident also has certain elements that suggest Frank's theory of spatial form:

> The chamber-maid had left no ******* *** under the bed:—Cannot you contrive, master, quoth *Susannah*, lifting up the sash with one hand, as she spoke, and helping me up into the window seat with the other,—cannot you manage, my dear, for a single time to **** *** ** *** ******?
>
> I was five years old.—*Susannah* did not consider that nothing was well hung in our family,—so slap came the sash down like lightening upon us;—Nothing is left,—cried *Susannah*,—nothing is left —for me, but to run my country. (P. 376)

The phrase "well hung" refers directly to the window sash, but indirectly to Toby's injured groin, Grandfather Shandy, and Walter's bull. In this instance, though, the sash's descent "like lightening" recalls or implies the swiftness of a cannon ball and one's shock at its speed. Ultimately, of course, Tristram's injury is of a piece with Toby's wound, thematically related to Walter's philosophical impotence, and lastly through heredity to Grandfather Shandy's puny nose.

A second spatial device resides in the novel's physical appearance: black pages, marbled pages, blank pages, missing pages, and chapters transposed. All these call attention to the book as object: its palpable form allows the rearrangement of its parts. So the preface comes in volume 3, when Tristram can manage the time to write it. On a smaller scale the text itself is replete with dashes, asterisks, and printer's devices, all giving the impression of lightness, space, and expansiveness.[11] They also invite the reader to join Sterne in his play with language (or its absence), to indulge in the frolic through conventional narrative and typography. All the elements so far considered—suspension of conventional plot and narrative, physical appearance, imaginative use of causality, and style itself—link *Tristram Shandy* with an aesthetic tradition and a philosophic attitude that can be identified by the term *rococo*.

In considering the significance of the rococo for typifying a characteristic mode of thought in early eighteenth-century France and mid-century England, we are concerned more with the context of this artistic movement—a matrix composed of philosophy, history, science, and literature—than with the purity of the term's use in art history, though no great distortion occurs when the term is taken out of its usual setting and used in this way. But let it be understood that the word *rococo* is to some extent being appropriated to refer to a historical and cultural era rather than to the period in art history immediately following the Baroque. The justifications for such a borrowing are that others have established (albeit tentatively) this connection before, and that Sterne's novel gains considerable coherence when read along these lines.

The rococo style lent itself more to decoration than to "pure" art, presenting its content chiefly through surface features; however, this is not to say that it was primarily superficial or laid-on.[12] Historically, the rococo arose in France at a time when the values and influence of the court of Louis Quatorze had reached their fullest ripeness and were starting to decay. No longer would the luxury and ostentation of the Baroque be accepted by the *citoyen* as essential to the notion of royalty or divine right, for in his eyes the king was less and less the driving force of the state. Jean Starobinski has characterized the situation in these terms:

> Though belief in divine right was unshakable in men like Louis XIV, the eighteenth century saw the gradual disintegration of the tacit and unstable solidarity between the authoritarian king and the bemused subjects, based on royal conviction and popular submission. The military defeats of the Roi Soleil, the scandals of the [French] Regency, . . . marked the beginning of an age during which the ritual and majesty of the monarchy were to be supplanted by mere pretense.[13]

In turn, the grandiose public displays of the ruler's prerogative shifted to more intimate and personal expressions, characterized by hedonism and sensuality. Because it did not demand reverence of the spectator, because it was unimposing, the rococo style was adopted by the middle class, who used it not only for interior decor but also to adorn common household objects they had come to count on for ease and pleasure.[14]

The rococo in France emerged in the late seventeenth century after the architectural "rules" of proportion had been settled on and the design of buildings became more or less regularized. *Hôtels* and *petites maisons* consisted of spatial modules that allowed very little variety in themselves and, without the intervention of decor, tended to be predictable and monotonous. Designers like Pierre Lapautre countered with unrestrained rococo decorations. Wylie Sypher has described the relationship of space and decoration thus: "Having simplified and regularized the fabric of their walls to a framework of symmetrical planes, [Rococo architects] embroidered decorative fields on these neutral surfaces by C-curves, reverse curves, interlaces, and swirls. Thus the face of the wall became organic although the architecture was basically a geometric abstraction of uncomplicated rectangles and cubes."[15] The Rococo artist regarded the skeleton of the room as the foundation upon which his decorations rested and out of which they arose, but the room also represented an order that was abstract, "cold," and unyielding. So the architectural fixity provoked an opposite response, a sort of Dionysian exuberance countering Apollonian restriction:

> In rococo the firm, thin architectural skeleton, which almost vanished, was like a Newtonian world-order erected by mathematical concepts, those colorless mental fictions behind the intricate appearance of things; or, perhaps, like Locke's idea of a state of Nature as the invisible design beneath the social order.[16]

Consequently, the rococo strove to make a room anything but that—to defy the rules. As Fiske Kimball and Sypher have shown, rococo designs were organic: tendrils, occasional shell-work, sprays, flowers, acanthus scrolls, leafage, and palm branches.[17] It was stylized nature brought indoors. But this opposition did more than pit the "natural" against the "artificial." For instance, François de Cuvillies the Elder's "Hall of the Mirrors of the Amalienburg" (1734) uses organic forms reaching upward and giving way gradually to what by contrast seems a vast open space approaching in its blankness and extent the sublime. Similarly, the mirrors around the walls are placed to reflect the doors and windows that lead the eye outside, so giving the illusion that both the room and the world beyond are part of the same "space." Thus the geometrical limits of the hall are transcended by the rococo decoration.

At the same time such decoration added variety to the underlying structure of the room, it also reflected by its sinuousness and an evocation of the sensual the visual equivalent of the hedonism and loose morality of the court. In this it is a Cavalier form par excellence, expressing freedom and carelessness. The sensuality observed by Starobinski in Hogarth's "line of beauty" is present, too, not only in rococo designs but also in the art of the period, and, taking a more erotic turn, in Sterne's novel.[18] This trait can best be observed in the work of Jean-François de Troy (1697-1752), who exhibited frequently at the Paris *Salons* and who catered to the taste of the affluent middle class. Most of his works are marked by a striking element of the hedonistic and several share with *Tristram Shandy* an absolute delight in the erotic. His two paintings, both titled *The Declaration of Love*, are good examples of this. The second version, done in 1731, is the tamer, less suggestive of the two.

It shows a group of seven figures placed casually in the foreground of the picture, against the background of a neoclassical garden and its myth-inspired statuary. Farther off, trees and shrubs recede into the distance. But our attention is held by the elegant ladies and gentlemen arranged along a wooden bench in artfully relaxed attitudes. In the center of the group a young man hands a nosegay to a woman in white brocade who is obviously much older. A second woman looks on with benign interest. To the left, and almost out of our range, a third woman watches with curiosity, apparently a stranger to the party. As this particular "declaration" goes on, two young gentlemen on the right flirt with a girl whose back is completely to us. We are left to assume that the delighted complacency shown in the informal pose of the men and the interest told in their faces is shared by the woman who holds her open fan ready for coquettish employment.

In his painting de Troy has given a piece of life, unplanned and unassuming. In a setting of neoclassical architecture, performing an act inspired perhaps by the gods, the suitor kneels gracefully contorted—his left leg under him, his right thrust forward. The carelessness of the position, the apparent ease with which it is executed, belies any concern for physics or Newton's gravity. Similarly, the gentlemen engaged in flirtation have been captured by de Troy to reveal their total involvement with the young woman. One of them seems literally to hang on to her every word as he leans over the bench, while the other, seated, throws his head back and to the left for a better view. Such a position can only be held for a short time without getting a stiff neck, but de Troy has, like a photographer, frozen the moment, rendering his subjects as much alive today as they were in 1731.

In the earlier version of this work, displayed at the *Salon* of 1725, de Troy treats his *Declaration* with much more frankness, and the result is erotic exuberance not unlike the kind Tristram enjoys with his puns and double entendres pertaining to male and female sexual parts and functions (see illustration). The painting shows a pair of lovers seated on a high-backed couch. Directly above, on a rococo wall panel, a similar pair of "classical" lovers engage in sensual embrace. Of the earthly counterparts, the male vigorously presses his declaration (with its assumed proposal) while the woman languidly considers his words from a half-reclining position. But de Troy, like Tristram, leaves very little to the imagination, for he has bestowed on the woman's dress a brocade pattern that proclaims the sexuality of the situation: a presentational version of her genitalia. Significantly, "classical" architecture, painting, and statuary function in both versions of *The Declaration* as a sanction for and a background against which the humans act out their rite of love. The erotic recurs in these works as a common element of rococo aesthetics that emphasizes passion, and in this antirational attitude the rococo perhaps finds yet another way of resisting the fixity of Newton's universe and the mechanism of Locke's association of ideas.

The impetus for the English rococo was similar but not identical to that in France. For one thing England had no monarch exactly comparable to Louis XIV or the enlightened despots of Europe, though the treatment of Charles I and James II by the English displayed a disillusion with Stuart monarchy similar to that of the French with Louis. Still, Englishmen did not have the same background to the adoption of the rococo that had preceded it on the Continent. For them it represented initially the latest fashion as well as a means for providing grace and elegance to otherwise quotidian items. Then, too, the appeal of the rococo during the first half of the eighteenth century depended a great deal on the concurrent interest in Gothic architecture and ornament and the vogue of *chinoiserie*, since both shared certain characteristics with the French movement. But it is a mistake to assume that the adoption of the rococo by Englishmen reflects merely an interest in ornamentation for its own sake without some deeper kind of rationale. In certain ideological respects the English proponent was not far removed from his French counterpart, whose adoption of the style may be said to have grown out of a general distrust and disillusion with centralized authority.

In England, men found themselves not opposed to a monarch who asserted his power in worn-out modes devoid of substance, but rather caught in a universe even more arbitrary and despotic. When Newton and Locke issued their discoveries it appeared that all men

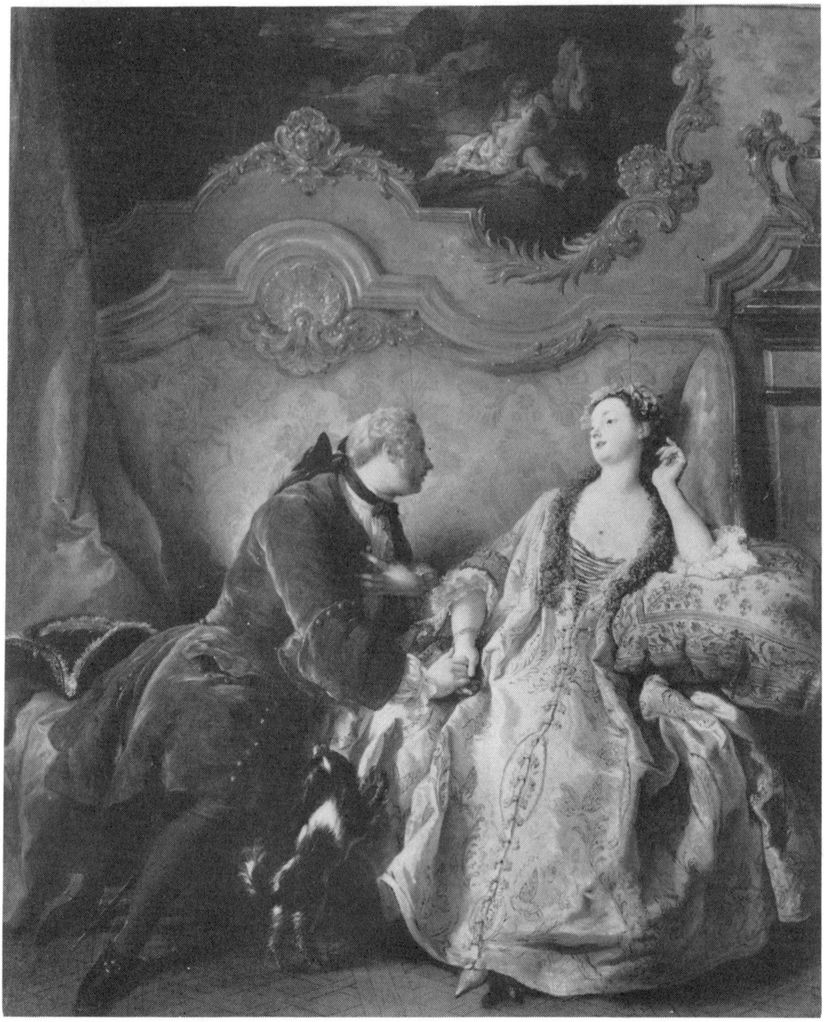

Jean Francois de Troy (1697-1752), *The Declaration of Love* (1725). FROM THE COLLECTION OF MR. AND MRS. CHARLES WRIGHTSMAN, NEW YORK. REPRINTED BY PERMISSION.

were subjects not so much of God's direct will, but of universal laws that controlled the spheres as well as the processes of the human mind. The discovery of a few laws on which nature depended for its operations was both progressive and restrictive. While it proved the power of Baconian induction, it also confronted man with an unquestionable "reality" that had been reached empirically. Newton's observations and theories had fixed with absolute certainty the dimensions of the physical universe in both time and space:

> Absolute, true, and mathematical time, of itself and from its own nature, flows equably without relation to anything external, and by another name is called duration; relative, apparent, and common time is some sensible and external (whether accurate or unequable) measure of duration by the means of motion, which is commonly used instead of true time, such as an hour, a day, a month, a year.
>
> Absolute space, in its own nature, without relation to anything external, remains always similar and immovable. Relative space is some movable dimension or measure of absolute spaces, which our senses determine by our position to bodies and which is commonly taken for movable space. . . .
>
> As the order of the parts of time is immutable, so also is the order of the parts of space.[19]

The desire to find a common explanation and expression for the physical behavior of both earthbound and celestial objects, to regularize the apparently deviant characteristics of observed nature, led Newton and his followers to define the universe in terms of absolute time and space in a way that could be reduced to a series of equations and formulas. As Sypher has pointed out, such a world view debases the notion of God to a mathematical abstraction derived from the phenomena of inertia and gravity. The Deity is no longer anthropomorphic; he is a "force." The desire for simplicity and uniformity was not merely limited to science. As noted previously, towards the end of the seventeenth century architecture was regularized by the assertion of certain laws of proportion that were intended to be standard and universal. Even the production of furniture felt the influence of these rules.[20] More significantly, the last sanctuary from the impact of this mechanistic universe, the mind, was shown by Locke to be something of a machine itself. It is against this conceptual background—a world behaving according to indisputable laws and a perceiving mentality akin—that the rococo style established itself in England.

The reaction to Newton and Locke among the intelligentsia was initially enthusiastic, but by mid-century a countermovement had begun. J. H. Plumb has observed this change in the difference between the reception of Locke's ideas and that of Hume's. "One was immediately acclaimed, the other cold-shouldered. Indeed, there is a remarkable contrast between the period starting roughly from 1680-1720 and from 1760-1800. We find an empiricist attitude sinking down to the lower orders of society, to the *menu peuple*, and a growing distrust of it amongst the governing and socially dominant classes."[21] To the latter one may also add writers and thinkers. Another manifestation of the contrast between the first and second halves of the century is the vogue of sentiment and the cultivation of feeling from about 1760 on. Now, as noted in Hogarth's *Analysis of Beauty* and de Troy's *Declaration of Love*, the sensual element is pronounced, and it is an undeniably important aspect of the rococo "attitude." In fact, the emphasis given by the rococo to emotions and feelings worked two ways: toward sensuality, shown in de Troy's paintings, and also toward sensibility, which made use of passion for moral ends. Even though Locke had explained sensation as merely a physiological reaction to external stimuli, the subsequent history of eighteenth-century aesthetics and morality shows that niceness of feeling, sensibility, came to be held in special esteem. Aesthetic experiences were characterized by the nonrational, "je ne sais quoi," and the rigid moral code of the early decades (a Puritan legacy) found replacement in the notion of sentimental benevolence. Here, of course, there is a direct connection with Uncle Toby and Tristram himself, to say nothing of the novel's sentimental digressions, particularly the famous Le Fevre episode. Moreover, one of the most conventional tags for this novel is "sentimental," which, obviously, rather misses the mark. Both *Tristram* and the rococo have a basic antagonism to rational inquiry and scientific method. Just as rococo decoration develops spontaneously and asymmetrically, so also is it true that the Shandean sentimental cannot be predicted. It is idiosyncratic. Similarly, de Troy's *Declaration* gives the appearance of total naturalness, just as Tristram's "Life and Opinions" poses as an antinovel, continually at the mercy of Tristram's eccentricities.

So several considerations point toward thinking of *Tristram Shandy* as in some way rococo. There is the influence of Hogarth's art and theory on Sterne manifesting itself through the illustrations and other pictorial devices, as well as the fact that both the plastic and verbal mediums share temporal and spatial characteristics. Second, there is the antipathy of the rococo to structure, fixity, reason, and scientific order, an antipathy that surfaces in England during the second half of the century in opposition to new scientific and philosophical attitudes.[22] Finally, there is the sensuality of the rococo, the most common literary expression of which is the sentimental. With this background in mind, an examination of Sterne's novel in terms of rococo attitudes can provide significant information on the meaning of the work. But one must remember that *rococo* used in this way refers to both the artistic style and its rationale, its form and content.

Just how apt to his purpose Sterne found the rococo notions he observed around him or saw in Hogarth can be inferred by measuring the language of criticism for this mode against the technique of his novel. There are several descriptions of the rococo style in art, but Jean Starobinski's list of characteristics is the most inclusive, perhaps because his approach to the problem is the most catholic, since he considers a variety of forms of this mode. Here is his list of descriptive terms for rococo art: effeminate; childlike; cosy intimacy; giddy movement; sinuosity; asymmetry; thin, flexible surfaces; and finally the statement: "The rococo delighted in satirizing its own creations."[23] The first three entries in this list refer either to Tristram himself or to the relationship he tries to establish with his audience. The remainder apply equally well to the style and the content of the novel. To observe this in detail, consider the first chapter of the work:

> I wish either my father or my mother, or indeed both of them, as they were in duty both equally bound to it, had minded what they were about when they begot me; had they duly consider'd how much depended upon what they were then doing;—that not only the production of a rational Being was concern'd in it, but that possibly the happy formation and temperature of his body, perhaps his genius and the very cast of his mind;—and for aught they knew to the contrary, even the fortunes of his whole house might take their turn from the humours and dispositions which were then uppermost:—Had they duly weighed and considered all this, and proceeded accordingly,—I am verily persuaded I should have made a quite different figure in the world, from that, in which the reader is likely to see me.—Believe me, good folks, this is not so inconsiderable a thing as many of you may think it;—you have all, I dare say, heard of the animal spirits, as how they are transfused from father to son, &c. &c.—and a great deal to that purpose:—Well, you may take my word, that nine parts in ten of a man's sense or his nonsense, his successes and miscarriages in this world depend upon their motions and activity, and the different tracks and trains you put them into, so that when they are once set a-going, whether right or wrong, 'tis not a halfpenny matter,—away they go cluttering like hey-go-mad; and by treading the same steps over and over again, they presently make a road of it, as plain and as smooth as a garden-walk, which, when they are once used to, the Devil himself sometimes shall not be able to drive them off it. (Pp. 4-5)

Beside the "cosy intimacy" of its conversational tone we find here "giddy movement" in Tristram's "sinuous" style. From an admonition against procreative carelessness the subject moves rapidly to "animal spirits," and finally concludes with an affirmation of the force of habit. The passage almost literally turns on key words and phrases: *figure* leads to the discussion of animal spirits whose "tracks and trains" in turn lead to the image of horselike animals wearing a path smooth by constant use. Along the way the author pauses to speak directly to us "good folks" and to slip in a double entendre with *uppermost*. Such a style is indeed "flexible" and perhaps also "thin" in its unpretentiousness and loquacity. Regarding Starobinski's reference to the rococo trait of "self-satire," one can find ample evidence of it in the novel. Recall volume 4 where Tristram takes four chapters to get his father and Uncle Toby down the stairs at Shandy Hall. Later in chapter 30 of the same volume Walter, Toby, and Yorick descend another set of stairs after the canonical dinner. Tristram interrupts the description to reassure, "Don't be terrified, madam, this stair-case conversation is not so long as the last" (p. 331). Another more persistent instance of self-mockery can be found in Tristram's pseudoastonishment that the more he writes the further he falls behind in his "Life and Opinions."

Such an application of critical terms from one medium to another and the consequent illumination of Tristram's style indicates a connection between the rococo and this novel that has been slow to form. But the similarities go further. If one pursues this juxtaposition, the novel's meaning is brought into clearer focus. Just as the rococo style reacted initially against the artificial grandeur of the Baroque, and later against the geometrical limitations of the architectural skeleton, and still later, and more importantly in England, against the "clock-work" universe posited by Newton and the mechanistic mind described by Locke, so too does Tristram's "Life" oppose what he perceives to be a rather deterministic existence. Those animal spirits which defy human intervention as they go "cluttering like hey-go-mad" and which so habituate a path that even temptation cannot drive them off, resemble in their actions the motions of the planets as they respond to the laws first discovered by Newton. If the heavenly spheres, once thought to express the essence of God, must conform to an inviolable pattern, what must be man's fate in this life? How impotent must he feel suffering accidents and misfortunes over which he has not the slightest control? "Fortune" as it had been known in the Renaissance is replaced by something equally ruthless and much more impersonal. Toby sustains his wound, his impotence, owing to the physics of trajectory and the algebra of probability. In his attempt to comprehend the accident he first studies maps, fortifications, and manuals on projectiles. Walter, too, seeks first to ward off, and in desperation to compensate for, the hostile vicissitudes of fate by trying to achieve initially a philosophic defense and, failing that, a philosophic equanimity by his devotion to Socrates and other learned authors through the ages. But just as Toby never arrives at the answer to his question of how and why he was injured, neither is Walter's quest for order and harmony in his life answered. And although he regards his rational faculties as his salvation, in many ways thought is his bane. Like Uncle Toby, whose life is spent trying to justify one very significant event, and Walter, whose life is spent combating a reality opposed to rational order, Tristram must endure from conception to consumption an existence comprised almost solely of misfortune. Added to this, moreover, is the further handicap of having a hobbyhorse that continually throws its rider, for unlike Toby's fortifications, Tristram's autobiography cannot be put into a manageable form. Owing to Locke's theory of the association of ideas, the narrative in which he attempts to make sense of his existence shys at every turn. Thus Tristram's body *and* mind suffer inconvenience and discomfort from which there is no release except through Shandean good humor or *vive le bagatelle*. If Tristram cannot master his thoughts and arrange them like any other author, then he will make the best of it and the devil take the hindmost. The tenor of this abandon, contrary to our expectation, is not despair, but salutory skepticism. To describe the resulting attitude we can apply what Sypher says of the rococo: "Rococo begins as a decoration of an abstract system by naturalistic details; but it leads, with its delicate spray and leafage, to a sense of natural piety. God is not only a mathematical mind; He is soon felt to be a spirit, a cosmic breath. Thus the Newtonian system gave rise to a rococo paradox: the geometry of the universe became animated with organic rhythms."[24] With Sterne these organic rhythms assert themselves in Tristram's style—the expression of a controlling mentality through the sinuous play of thought and language. Taken by itself rococo art may seem strikingly devoid of substance. In one sense it is no more than a series of *bagatelles*, trifles. Once its background is juxtaposed, however, the contrast can offer a great deal toward understanding the purpose of this form. At one level it symbolically opposes a deterministic universe. On another the rococo invites its audience to "play" by showing them how to maneuver within the bounds of an abstract "reality." So as Walter Shandy plays the philosopher, and

Uncle Toby the soldier, Tristram plays author, pitting his imagination and animal spirits against the "givens" of his circumstances, finally death itself. But overlying this eschatology, mocking it, is Tristram's liberating form—the rococo.

1. R.F. Brissenden, "Sterne and Painting," in *Of Books and Humankind*, ed. John Butt (London: Routledge & Kegan Paul, 1964), p. 107.

2. The clearest piece of evidence is Sterne's letter to Richard Berenger, sent in March 1760, asking him to solicit Hogarth for an illustration to *Tristram Shandy*: "The loosest sketch in Nature, of Trim's reading the Sermon to my Father &c; would do the Business—& *it would mutually illustrate his [Hogarth's] system & mine*—." *Letters*, ed. L. P. Curtis (Oxford: Oxford University Press, 1935), pp. 99-100. Emphasis added.

3. William Hogarth, *The Analysis of Beauty*, ed. Joseph Burke (Oxford: Clarendon Press, 1955), pp. 55-56.

4. Ibid., p. 45. Emphasis added.

5. Laurence Sterne, *The Life and Opinions of Tristram Shandy, Gentleman*, ed. James A. Work (New York: Odyssey Press, 1940), p. 538. Subsequent references will be to this edition and will appear in parentheses in the text.

6. Hogarth, *Analysis of Beauty*, p. 42. Emphasis added.

7. Ibid., p. li.

8. Jean Starobinski, *The Invention of Liberty: 1700-1789*, trans. Bernard C. Swift (Geneva: Skira, 1964), p. 23.

9. Alan Rose, "The Spatial Form of *The Golden Bowl*," *Modern Fiction Studies* 12, no. 1 (Spring 1966): 112.

10. William V. Holtz, *Image and Immortality: A Study of "Tristram Shandy,"* (Providence, R.I.: Brown University Press, 1970), p. 102.

11. Ibid., pp. 80-89.

12. An authoritative text on the rococo is Fiske Kimball's *Creation of the Rococo* (Philadelphia: Philadelphia Museum of Art, 1943). Kimball refuses to attribute any political or ideological causes to the growth of this style, but subsequent studies such as Starobinski's *Invention of Liberty* and Wylie Sypher's *Rococo to Cubism in Art and Literature* (New York: Vintage Books, 1960) show clearly some of the obvious social influences that molded it.

13. Starobinski, *Invention of Liberty*, p. 14.

14. In England the designs of Thomas Chippendale reflect most clearly the vogue for rococo-inspired decoration.

15. Sypher, *Rococo to Cubism*, p. 27.

16. Ibid., p. 25.

17. Ibid.

18. Concerning this aspect of the novel see Frank Brady, "*Tristram Shandy*: Sexuality, Morality, and Sensibility," *Eighteenth-Century Studies* 4, no. 1 (Fall 1970): 41-56.

19. From Newton's *Principia I*, quoted in Sypher's *Rococo to Cubism*, pp. 13-14.

20. John Gloag, *Georgian Grace: A Social History of Design from 1660-1830* (New York: Macmillan Co., 1956), p. 3.

21. J. H. Plumb, "Reason and Unreason in the Eighteenth Century," *Some Aspects of Eighteenth-Century England* (Los Angeles, Calif.: Clark Memorial Library, 1971), p. 6.

22. Donald Davie in *The Language of Science and the Language of Literature, 1700-1740* (London: Sheed & Ward, 1963) points out that the reaction to scientific and philosophical empiricism was initiated by Augustan satirists, especially Pope and Swift, and that

later Sterne was to take a similar view: "When Sterne adopted Lockean psychology as a structural principle in *Tristram Shandy*, he was exploiting contemporary science in a way not very different from what we have just seen in Pope and Swift" (p. 31).

23. Starobinski, *Invention of Liberty*, p. 39. All these terms appear in the section titled "Order and Variety," pp. 39-41.

24. Sypher, *Rococo to Cubism*, p. 34.

Transcendence through Technique: Whitman's "Crossing Brooklyn Ferry" and Impressionist Painting

Barton L. St. Armand

Brown University

We stand for a robust art founded on the senses.
Camille Pissarro, speaking of the Impressionists

DURING his lifetime, Walt Whitman was conscious of an affinity with certain pictorial artists, most notably Millet and Eakins.[1] Since then, his poems have been compared to an entire gallery of paintings, contemporary as well as modern, ranging from the homely genre scenes of George Caleb Bingham to the avant-garde abstracts of Jackson Pollock.[2] To put into critical action Horace's seductive formula, *ut pictura poesis*—that poetry should resemble painting—is always a tentative and risky business, save when critics have before them the actual visual source of a poem, as in Wordsworth's "Elegaic Stanzas" or Melville's " 'The Coming Storm.' "[3] Yet certain works of literature are so oriented toward the visual and so radical in their point of view that, once we grant as a first premise the interchangeability of media (the equivalency of language with paint and of words with brushstrokes), they can take on a new significance when seen in tandem with equally revolutionary developments in pictorial art.

Iconography aside, technique itself becomes paramount in this kind of comparison: similarity of expression is what matters, for, while specific analogues can oftentimes be revealing, it is the artist's break with a received tradition that startles us most of all. The first major modern school of painting to accomplish this break by discarding subject matter for a primary emphasis on vision alone, on how the eye apprehends, was that of Impressionism. As Kermit Champa writes:

> Impressisonism, more than any prior moment in the history of art, rejects functional analysis out of hand. Its iconology is uninteresting, its sociohistorical role unimportant. The greatness and the depth of impressionist painting lies, so to speak on its surface—a surface which year after year expands its importance as an object of purely visual interest. The history of impressionism traces a process of liberation within which the art of painting achieves for the first time an ideal of sensuous autonomy. Like the art of music, impressionist painting requires the spectator to accept the sensuous importance of the art form itself.[4]

Champa's words are applicable to a Whitman poem that also seems largely concerned with "surfaces" and "object[s] of purely visual interest" and which forces its reader to accept their sensuous importance as an end in itself. This poem is "Crossing Brooklyn Ferry," which originally appeared in the second edition of *Leaves of Grass* (1856) as "Sun-Down Poem," achieving its present title in 1860.[5] "Crossing Brooklyn Ferry" both anticipates and enacts, in its radical technique, the main tenets of Impressionist methods, goals, and themes. For, as Gustave Geffroy defined Impressionism, it is "painting that approaches phenomenalism, the appearance and significance of things in space, and which tries to catch the synthesis of these things in their momentary appearance."[6] From this perspective, even Whitman's change in title is telling: from the static idea of sunset, such as might have been painted by any Hudson River School artist of the time, to an active, kinetic, vigorous study of light and water in motion that we associate with the dazzling seascapes of Monet or the crowded boating parties of Renoir. This shimmering experience of light and vibrant sense of immediacy is far different from the "smooth, mirror-like surface" that characterizes the indigenous American school of painting which Barbara Novak has defined as "Luminism," where "time stops, and the moment is locked in place," though Whitman was quite capable of employing this style as well when it suited his experimental purposes.[7] Whitman's very choice of the gerund *crossing* indicates a delight in the present moment, in the sensuous play of light on flesh, cloth, wave, and metal that so intrigued and animated the Impressionist consciousness, while the entire title indicates the unfinished, sketchlike quality of the experience that the poem attempts to reproduce. The phrase "Crossing Brooklyn Ferry" is as far from "Sun-Down Poem" as "Out of the Cradle Endlessly Rocking" is from another discarded Whitman title, "Out of the Rocked Cradle." In 1874 Claude Monet exhibited a study entitled *Impression: Sunrise* that was singled out for ridicule by the critic Louis Leroy. Through Leroy's derision, the heretofore nameless association of radical artists of which Monet was chief representative became a school overnight, the school of "Impressionism." The title of Monet's epochal painting was actually catalogued as *Impression: Soleil Levant*, the latter half of which might better be translated as "Rising Sun" than "Sunrise." Thus Whitman's instinctive trope toward the active voice in his 1860 revision was uncannily prophetic.[8]

It is even more interesting that Daubigny, whose open-air landscapes were admired by Monet, should actually have painted a storm-tossed ferryboat around the year 1860, while Boudin, Monet's teacher and the man who first introduced him to *plein-air* painting, should have been drawn to brisk scenes of crowded quays, enlivened by bobbing sailboats and steamers trailing long pennants of smoke. This kind of subject, devoid of epic or historical associations, is epitomized by his *Jetty at Trouville* of 1865, and, as if confirming Whitman's intentions in "Crossing Brooklyn Ferry," Boudin wrote to a friend in September of 1868: "The peasants have their painters . . . that is fine, but between ourselves, those middle-class people strolling on the jetty at the hour of sunset, have they no right to be fixed on canvas?"[9] It was of the same kind of slap-dash scenes chosen by Daubigny that Théophile Gautier wrote:

> It is really too bad that this landscape painter who possesses such a true, such a just, and such a natural feeling, is satisfied by an *impression* and neglects details to this extent. His pictures are but rough drafts, and very slightly developed. . . . Each object is indicated by an apparent or real contour, but the landscapes of M. Daubigny offer merely spots of color juxtaposed.[10]

What Daubigny and Boudin were to Monet, Emerson and his fellow Transcendentalists were to Whitman. For it was Emerson who opened the doors of perception for the young poet, the Emerson who wrote in "Experience" (1844) that "life is a train of moods like a string of beads, and as we pass through them they prove to be many-colored lenses which paint the world their own hue, and each shows only what lies in its focus."[11] As Whitman's notebooks reveal, "Crossing Brooklyn Ferry" began as just such a train of moods, yet the result remains a skillfully constructed work of art.[12] In Whitman's own time, like Daubigny's work, the poem must have seemed no more than a rough draft, slightly developed, when compared to more finely finished and varnished poetic specimens. For, from the shaky height of Emerson's Transcendental intuition, Whitman leapt forward to a disintegration of reality dangerously close to those mere "spots of color juxtaposed," which so disturbed Gautier:

> The simple, compact, well-join'd scheme, myself
> disintegrated, every one disintegrated yet part of the scheme,
> The similitudes of the past and those of the future,
> The glories strung like beads on my smallest sights
> and hearings, on the walk in the street and the passage
> over the river . . .

"Crossing Brooklyn Ferry" is a poem that takes the open-air basis of Transcendentalism, paralleled in French painting by the immediacy of the Barbizon school, to an extreme that results in the linguistic equivalent of Impressionism. Even the poem's subject matter anticipates an Impressionist reaction against the high-style history paintings popular with the public and encouraged by the academies, for Whitman focuses on a low-key, offhand scene that tells no story and contains no hints of classic grandeur. The poem is about a casual moment, a fleeting perception, and a common, everyday event that verges on that same "vulgarity" with which Impressionist art was so often charged. Its philosophy, as James Gargano has observed, is one that "any reputable Transcendentalist, in essay, poem or sermon, might have proffered to his audience."[13] Yet this is also a philosophy on which the whole varied and complex mode of Impressionism depended. It is simply that human experience is rooted in sense perceptions and that, in rendering these sense perceptions through the medium of art, the artist allows his viewer (in Whitman's case, his reader) to see precisely as the artist saw, at a particular mood, place, and time. As Albert Aurier defines it, Impressionism's most basic "aim . . . is the translation of the instantaneous sensation with all the distortions of a rapid and subjective synthesis."[14]

In his essay "Circles," Emerson had proclaimed that "the eye is the first circle,"[15] for, in Transcendental theory, ordinary perception was always but the first step toward the higher seeing of Vision. In "Crossing Brooklyn Ferry," Whitman cannot escape this pull toward the numinous, but he lets the other circles of meaning remain implicit by focusing single-mindedly on the sensuous apprehension of a few central things. These central things create a base, a material ensemble, that he never abandons. As Gargano writes of Whitman's strategy, "What dogma 'demonstrates' to the satisfaction of the intellect, the 'soul' must possess by direct perception and feeling."[16] Because human perception is founded upon immutable natural laws, perception itself becomes the bridge between all people who see, who have seen, or who will see. John Sedgwick has written of Impressionist painting that "the real subject of the painting is the light, the real hero the color."[17] Whitman does not go this far because, as a singer of the self, he always remains the true hero of his poems. The "scheme" of his poem is "well-join'd" to Transcendental theory, yet no other Transcendentalist comes as close to Whitman's reliance on the "instantaneous sensation" as a basis of "subjective synthesis."

Whitman's subject in "Crossing Brooklyn Ferry" is neither pure transcendence nor pure technique, but rather transcendence through technique. Like Manet, from whom the Impressionists learned so much, Whitman catches a corner of experience, sees a scene from an oblique, unexpected angle. Also like Manet, who in turn learned from Monet and his group yet stood apart from them, producing such "impressionist" works as *The Departure of the Folkstone Boat* and *On the Banks of the Seine at Argenteuil*, Whitman's flirtation with Impressionism was a relatively brief affair. In "Crossing Brooklyn Ferry" Whitman employs such experimental boldness to catch his reader off guard, first appearing himself as merely a prop in the crowd of objects, people, and sensations that constitute the "subject" of the poem, just as Monet, Renoir, and Bazille often inserted themselves or their friends into a particular canvas. Thus, in the first stanza of his "Crossing," Whitman confronts the river, the sun, the crowd, the reader, and himself (reflected in the "face" of the water) in one all-encompassing glance:

> Flood-tide below me! I see you face to face!
> Clouds of the west—sun there half an hour high—
> I see you also face to face.
>
> Crowds of men and women attired in the usual costumes,
> how curious you are to me!
> On the ferry-boats the hundreds and hundreds that cross,
> returning home, are more curious to me than you suppose,
> And you that shall cross from shore to shore years hence
> are more to me, and more in my meditations, than you
> might suppose.

As in an Impressionist painting, the time is exact and the fall of light is precisely rendered—"sun there half an hour high." But Whitman does something that even the Impressionists could not accomplish, for they could not paint the actual faces and forms of future viewers into their scenes. As Sedgwick comments, these scenes "generally . . . have a holiday or vacation aspect, often though not exclusively summery, and almost always [are perceived] from the point of view of the spectator, the casual observer—the man whose eye looks for nothing in particular but is ready for anything."[18] Whitman, as the casual, insouciant observer depicted in the frontispiece to the 1855 *Leaves of Grass*, is, however, looking for something very particular and definite in the bustling crowd that teems on the ferry. He seeks the actual features of the reader, who, once spotted, will be held by his glittering eye and soon be made a part of its shimmering impressions. Both Whitman and the reader become part of the crowd at the end of this stanza: both are reduced to the status of *l'homme moyen sensuel*, sharing the same basic means and possibilities of human perception.

Only in the most casual and subtle way does the poet's choice of a ferry ride suggest the metaphysical meaning that will become more explicit as the poem progresses, for by the time his "future-reader" peruses this poem, Whitman will long ago have taken his own last ferry ride over a far darker river, steered by a far more ominous boatman. Yet in reading and, more importantly, in responding sensually to this poem, this future-reader will perform an act of necromancy that banishes the threatening images of Styx and Charon and summons Whitman himself back to the ongoing voyage of life. Again, Whitman will be part of the transient crowd of the present. In re-creating and retracing Whitman's impressions, recorded in the poem through sensuous and coloristic descriptions, future-reader permits Whitman to be reborn in his own consciousness. This rebirth, in turn, will be confirmed by the unchanging nature of the phenomena Whitman has catalogued, tallied, and "witnessed."

Whitman's visual images, like those of the Impressionists, are prismatic: "glories strung like beads on my smallest sights and hearings." Yet he, too, is one of these glories, for his ineradicable narcissism allows him to see "the impalpable sustenance of me from all things at all hours of the day." Whitman is his own sun, his own source of light, his own God. In stanza 3 of the poem, he begins an analysis of his "crossing" by concentrating on the phenomena of haze, reflections, and shadows similar to those which so intrigued Monet, Renoir, and Pissarro at places like Sainte Adresse and La Grenouillière. For, as André Pératé writes, the primary endeavor of

Impressionism was "to break up the ray of light, to catch its vibrancy in the air, to follow it as it glides around objects enveloping them with color":[19]

> I too many and many a time cross'd the river of old,
> Watched the Twelfth-month sea-gulls, saw them high in the
> air floating with motionless wings, oscillating
> their bodies,
> Saw how the glistening yellow lit parts of their bodies
> and left the rest in strong shadow,
> Saw the slow-wheeling circles and the gradual edging
> toward the south,
> Saw the reflection of the summer sky in the water,
> Had my eyes dazzled by the shimmering track of beams,
> Look'd at the fine centrifugal spokes of
> light round the shape of my head in the sunlit water,
> Look'd on the haze on the hills southward and south-westward,
> Look'd on the vapor as it flew in fleeces tinged with
> violet . . .

Just as Whitman is being carried on a vessel (the ferryboat itself), so are his impressions of the scene being carried by the words of his poem. Rather than a clinical anatomy of the phenomena around him, what we have is a panoramic view in which no one object emerges as the subject of the poem, but all become integers in the entire equation of vision. As Stanley J. Coffman, Jr., has noted:

> We observe . . . that the images of this catalogue are presented as lists but that the list is not of separate objects, each of which, according to transcendental theory, becomes symbolic of the whole. At least, the catalogue does not depend for its expressive value upon any philosophical assumptions about the nature of the word. Instead, the words become effective as they function in the context of other words, which is to say, they become effective aesthetically: they work through a pattern of motion and light, which is first established, and then altered. Their status as individual symbols disappears in the sense of a single pattern of motion and light.[20]

Whitman's words, then, are similar to brushstrokes in an Impressionist painting: each stroke flows into or modifies another, creating a juxtaposition of colors, nuances, and tones that must be mixed by the eye and comprehended as an ensemble, a total effect, an "impression." Sedgwick writes that "the prime motivation of Impressionist art is what could only be called a religious attitude toward the creative power of sunlight in nature, and its role in fusing all elements of the seen and felt universe in a marvellously alive and momentary, yet complete, recurrent, and therefore timeless unity."[21] In "Crossing Brooklyn Ferry" Whitman himself is the fusing element; it is he who watches, sees, and beholds, and it is in him that the varied phenomena merge and mingle:

> What is more subtle than this which ties me to the woman
> or man that looks in my face?
> Which fuses me into you now, and pours my meaning into
> you?

The cyclical recurrence of these phenomena over time ensures Whitman's rebirth. Again, this is the "philosophy" of the poem, its Transcendental didacticism. As Whitman repeats over and over:

> I am with you, you men and women of a generation, or
> every so many generations hence,
> Just as you feel when you look on the river and sky,
> so I felt . . .

The Impressionists may have evinced a "religious attitude" toward light, but in their single-minded pursuit of technique, of determining the finest nuances of color and tone, they had little thought for the future and even less for the problems of immortality, whether it were artistic or spiritual in nature. Today, however, we can see what they themselves could not fully realize: that each Impressionist has a style, an idiosyncratic approach, that mirrors the personal and the subjective and which confers an enduring individuality on any work of art produced. Whitman always recognized this fact of style, but he sought to balance it against those general laws of seeing and feeling that knit all men and women together, without sacrificing his own individuality.

Therefore, as "Crossing Brooklyn Ferry" develops, Whitman's relationship to his reader becomes even more familiar, almost uncannily personal. I have spoken of the "necromancy" inherent in the poem as future-reader is forced into the role of an unwilling conjuror who summons forth Whitman's ghost. Once this ghost appears, Whitman remains in control, acting as a medium or mind-reader who second-guesses his readers' reactions and implants in them certain shared emotions and perceptions. Whitman's Impressionistic technique is loose and sketchy enough for the reader to evolve a personal response to the images presented, but, at the same time, the "ensemble" is so cunningly composed that it reminds us of just how conscious artists like Monet and Pissarro were of structural relationships within the context of their supposedly random or casually chosen "slices of life." The whole poem is a trap, in a sense, a lure or web spun by Whitman as the noiseless, patient spider who captures through his art those "others who look back on me because I look'd forward to them."

The direction of Whitman's art is twofold: the reader is carried into its crowd, as Whitman himself presses closer, the better to embrace his audience. As in the best Impressionist painting, the viewer is at first startled by the freshness and novelty of a colorful felt-vision of life, then dominated, literally "captivated," by the virtuosity of the style that has dared to render it so boldly. But Whitman does not allow his reader to melt completely into anonymity or languish in static passivity. He anticipates the reader's consciousness in such a way that an exchange of self occurs while both the reader's and Whitman's individualities are still preserved. By addressing the reader directly, not only as the representative of a future generation but as a unique human being, Whitman accomplishes a metempsychosis through sensation:

> Closer yet I approach you,
> What thought you have of me now, I had as much of you—
> I laid in my stores in advance,
> I consider'd long and seriously of you before you were
> born.
>
> Who was to know what should come home to me?
> Who knows but I am enjoying this?
> Who knows, for all the distance, but I am good as
> looking at you now, for all you cannot see me?

At this point (stanza 7), there has been a complete interchange between reader and poet, just as there has been a conjunction of sky and river, and of river and vessel. Yet the river remains paramount because its "bright flow" provides that merger of opposing and seemingly irreconcilable elements which, in turn, leads to the aesthetic synthesis. It will soon—again by implication—become even more than this: the river of time, the endless stream that carries more and more readers to their unsuspected meeting with the ever-waiting poet:

> The current rushing so swiftly and swimming with me
> far away,
> The others that are to follow me, the ties between
> me and them,
> The certainty of others, the life, love, sight, hearing
> of others.

Speaking of the purely physical role of water in Impressionist painting, Sedgwick has characterized it as

> a natural element which promotes the active interplay of tones. Not a smooth glassy surface, certainly not the massive waves of the sea, but the rippled water of streams and ponds. Sailboats, with their ability to catch and cast reflections and the constantly shifting quality of their movement, not to mention the carefree, holiday aspect of their use, and the undirected purity of their movement, are naturals too, and it is not surprising that some of the pictures of the basin at Argenteuil (near Paris) are as beautiful and characteristic pictures as the whole Impressionist movement produced.[22]

Once again, the canvases of Monet—with their dancing water surfaces and vivid motion of flags, gaily dressed vacationers, and creamy sailboats—come to mind when we examine Whitman's Impressionist catalogue of river sights in stanza 3:

> Look'd toward the lower bay to notice the vessels arriving,
> Saw their approach, saw aboard those that were near me,
> Saw the white sails of schooners and sloops, saw the
> ships at anchor,
> The sailors at work in the rigging or out astride the spars,
> The round masts, the swinging motion of the hulls, the
> slender serpentine pennants,
> The large and small steamers in motion, the pilots in
> their pilot-houses,
> The white wake left by the passage, the quick tremulous whirl
> of the wheels,
> The flags of all nations, the falling of them at sunset,
> The scalloped-edged waves in the twilight, the ladled cups,
> the frolicsome crests and glistening . . .

Armand Silvestre, a friend of Claude Monet's, wrote a description of that artist's work in 1873 that seems a gloss on the kinds of images and techniques that Whitman employs here. In what Champa has called "probably the most important (and least known) attempt on the part of a truly contemporary critic to suggest the meaning of both the visual and scientific content of the new art,"[23] Silvestre remarked that Monet "loves to juxtapose on the lightly ruffled surface of the water the multicolored reflections of the setting sun, of gaudy boats, of changing clouds. Metallic tones given off by the smoothness of the waves, which splash over small, even surfaces, are recorded in his works, and the image of the shore is unsettled—the houses are broken down as they are in that children's game where objects are put together from pieces."[24] Like Monet, Whitman seems to be drawn into an increasing abstraction here, as his focus on the "ladled cups" of the "frolicsome crests" produces a metallic, stippled effect.

W. C. Seitz has written that for the Impressionists "reflections became a means of shaking off the world assembled by memory in favour of a world perceived momentarily by the senses. In reflections the artifices so important to workaday life are transformed into abstract elements in a world of pure vision."[25] Yet for Whitman Impressionistic technique is always functional; seeing and feeling are not merely ends in themselves but means toward a greater communication—a communication of the spirit. As the all-inclusive poet who has already outlined his task in "Song of Myself," Whitman cannot entirely lose himself in the shimmering abstraction of reflections, the lure of the "scalloped-edged waves." He must consider the darkness as well as the light.

Thus, in "Crossing Brooklyn Ferry," Whitman also practices what Pierre Courthion has called a "nocturnal impressionism." Courthion observes that some members of the school were "nightwalkers" who chose to work "mostly by gaslight and the illumination in theaters."[26] Whitman, as a former *boulevardier*, was naturally drawn to such scenes, yet his vision remains an open-air exercise that once more goes far beyond simple technique. The Impressionists were fascinated by the coloristic phenomenon of shadows, discovering, as William Gaunt has noted, that blue, "the atmospheric colour *par excellence* of sky and distance" was also "a main component of cast shadow." "The suppression of the earth colours logically followed," Gaunt writes, for "the ochres and browns had no part in the make-up and transmission of light; on the contrary, serviceable though they had always been in other ways, they obscured luminous effect."[27]

Whitman's full immersion in shadow is to occur in stanza 6 of "Crossing Brooklyn Ferry," but this dark night of the soul has already been heralded by the ending of the central Impressionist catalogue of stanza 3, which shades off from the dazzling brightness of a silver haze and violet clouds to an ominous dusk and the artificial pyrotechnics of a threatening industrial landscape. The introduction of violet is a significant touch on Whitman's part, for Courthion notes that "the Impressionists were said to be seized with 'violetomania.' "[28] This charge was leveled in particular at Armand Guillaumin, whose *Sunset at Ivry* (1873) presents a perfect analogue to the lurid closure of stanza 6.[29] Guillaumin's landscape depicts an afterglow blazing like live embers, punctuated by belching factory chimneys and complemented by touches of psychedelic greens, violets, and mauves. The critic Henry Fevre remarked that Guillaumin "is capable of thrusting an insolent sun in front of your eyeballs that makes you lower your lids" while, in his work, "the grass is gilded, the shadows an intense violet." Whitman's confrontation with the shadow is not so extreme as Guillaumin's, yet it remains in many respects as dramatic, melting from the soft gray of a Whistler *Nocturne* to a flare of fierce reds, yellows, and blacks that suggests some fiery urban apocalypse:

> The stretch afar off growing dimmer and dimmer, the
>   gray walls of the granite storehouses by the docks,
> On the river the shadowy group, the big steam-tug closely
>   flank'd on each side by the barges, the hay-boat, the
>   belated lighter,
> On the neighboring shore the fires from the foundry
>   chimneys burning high and glaringly into the night,
> Casting their flicker of black contrasted with wild red
>   and yellow light over the tops of houses, and down into
>   the clefts of streets.

Unlike the shadows in a Monet landscape, which are painterly attempts to render darkness modified by the local color of the light in which it is observed, Whitman's shadows soon acquire a metaphysical meaning. The descent to the "clefts of streets," the contact with the dark, satanic mills of the shore and the hellish landscape of a burgeoning industrial America, inevitably remind Whitman of his own darker self. In stanza 6, the elaboration of this meaning takes us as far from the coloristic effects of stanza 3 as the anguished whorls and black-edged cypresses of Van Gogh are from the sun-dappled figures and foliage of Renoir:

> It is not upon you alone the dark patches fall,
> The dark threw its patches down upon me also,
> The best I had done seem'd to me blank and suspicious,
> My great thoughts as I supposed them, were they not
>   in reality meagre?
> Nor is it you alone who know what it is to be evil,
> I am he who knew what it was to be evil,
> I too knitted the old knot of contrariety,
> Blabb'd, blush'd, resented, lied, stole, grudg'd,
> Had guile, anger, lust, hot wishes I dared not speak,
> Was wayward, vain, greedy, shallow, sly, cowardly, malignant,
> The wolf, the snake, the hog not wanting in me . . .

Cézanne is said to have remarked of Monet that he was "only an eye, but my God what an eye!"[30] In spite of Monet's many personal problems (extreme poverty, bouts with depression, and even an attempt at suicide), his eye continued steadfastly to record what was before it, unburdened by any attempt to inject subjective meaning. His *Unloading Coal, Argenteuil* (1872) might at first glance be taken as some kind of commentary on the doubt, enchainment, and dark side of the human condition similar to that voiced by Walt Whitman in the lines just quoted, but, as Phoebe Pool notes, this work is "uncharacteristic." "The gloomy, dehumanized procession of men carrying coal might almost have been painted by a humanitarian or expressionist working in a spirit of social criticism," Pool comments, "but Monet was probably more concerned with the repeated diagonals of the gangplanks, the atmospheric subtlety of water and light, and the little figures, which may have been suggested to him by Japanese prints he bought in Holland."[31]

In stanza 6 of "Crossing Brooklyn Ferry" Whitman once again demonstrates his Transcendental independence from what was to be pure Impressionist theory. For here he acknowledges that darkness and evil are integral parts of the continuing voyage of life, not simply the catalysts of aesthetic challenges to be overcome by painterly virtuosity. In sharing this belief with his reader and forcing that reader to confess the same doubts to him, Whitman further cements the bond between artist and audience. Whitman is more than Cézanne's mere eye, more even than Emerson's famous "transparent eyeball" through which the currents of universal being pass, for behind Whitman's eye is a very human sensibility. Monet cautioned that the hand must be completely the tool of the eye, yet Whitman always had in view the purposes of any product fashioned by such a tool. In spite of its Impressionist passages, its coloristic highlights, its sense of a special, timeless moment, its choice of a random, "contentless" scene, "Crossing Brooklyn Ferry" is a poem with purposes that transcend pure technique.

Without the over-arching spiritual bond, the "ties" between human soul and human soul, Whitman's art would be, in his own view, only phenomena, only surface, only externality. Objects themselves and the sensations they produce are meaningless unless they become the medium of what Whitman in "Song of the Open Road" calls the "fluid and attaching character." Otherwise, as he writes in "There Was a Child Went Forth," reality would be "all flashes and specks," the measured dabs of color that compose the perfectly rendered but perfectly empty "pure" Impressionist painting, perhaps best represented by the Pointillism of Seurat.

Because Whitman's ultimate intention is to convey a transcendent philosophy through his poetry and not to produce a self-contained, autotelic work of art, he is an Impressionist in technique alone, an Impressionist by accident, just as certain of Turner's paintings or Constable's sketches anticipate many of the concerns, themes, and strategies of the French school that was to follow them. Through his reproduction of the stimuli that allow us to sense what it was like to cross Brooklyn Ferry at a particular moment in the nineteenth century and what it will be like again to do so when the nuances of light and atmospheric effect recreate the conditions of that experience, Whitman has allowed sensation to speak for him.[32] But "Crossing Brooklyn Ferry" is a poem of emotion as well as one of perception, and it is the conjunction of seeing with feeling that finally accomplishes Whitman's silent purposes:

> We understand then do we not?
> What I promis'd without mentioning it, have you not
> accepted?
> What the study could not teach—what the preaching could
> not accomplish is accomplish'd, is it not?

The last stanza of Whitman's poem is an affirmation of and an apostrophe to all those sights that he has already set down for us in stanza 3. It is a supreme testament of acceptance, for in urging the river to "Flow on . . . ! flow with the flood-tide, and ebb with the ebb-tide!" Whitman is committing himself to the changing current of life. He yields himself to a future where he trusts that the coordinates as well as the conditions of his being will be re-created. The reader and Whitman will complete their own "crossing" through the sense-mechanism of the poem, since in the material base of seeing and feeling lie hidden the roots of personal immortality. As Whitman wrote in his notes for the poem, "My body makes my immortal experience." Time, place, and distance avail not, for Whitman, in conquering the individual reader, has also conquered those dimensions and relations that link the self to a specific moment in a specific spot. Whitman sings a hymn of joy to time because the future can only bring more and more readers to fill the vague outlines of the crowd he has sketched. Time must ferry to him more and more disciples who will affirm his own sensations and, through them, his individual being.

Whitman's minute attention to shifting "appearances" are but a recognition of that "necessary film" of phenomenality that will "continue to envelope the soul." The objects of the poet's impressions remain "dumb, beautiful ministers" of spirit and, more importantly, emblems of Whitman's everlasting self. No ferry now crosses the river from Brooklyn to Manhattan, but, precisely because Whitman has allied himself with people as well as with things, this historical fact does not relegate his composition to the status of a period piece. That Monet's sketch entitled *The River* has variously been identified as the Seine at Bennecourt[33] and a view of Argenteuil[34] does not reduce its verve and freshness of handling, either. Yet, while Whitman conceives of his poem as a bridge between reader and artist, Monet's art is a controlled stimulus, the meaning of which remains, as Champa has said, "on the surface." And Phoebe Pool notes that "the boats and human figures seen across the river are scarcely identifiable as such, being represented simply by spots of colour,"[35] while Champa observes that "the figure of Camille is described in a rugged, almost brutally impersonal fashion with broad, heavily loaded brushstrokes that give only the most basic description of position and substance."

In contrast to the placid, impersonal river pictured by Monet, which mirrors (however dazzlingly) the blue sky, white clouds, green hills, and pastel-colored buildings along its shore, Whitman sees his own face haloed as he gazes at the turbulence beneath him: "Diverge, fine spokes of light, from the shape of my head, or any one's head, in the sunlit water!" Whitman is in his poem not merely through the impress of style but through the operation of spirit: "Crossing Brooklyn Ferry" is in fact a living shrine, a repository of his presence. As Gargano writes, "motion, light, shadow, shape, haze, and reflection are infused, as if they were soul or spirit, into the moment which has become a synthesis of past, present, and future."[37] Whitman's water imagery moves inevitably toward the cosmic when he declares: "Suspend here and everywhere, eternal float of solution!" As far apart as Monet and Whitman might be in ultimate intention, it is still interesting to note that Sedgwick uses a phrase of Whitman's ("gangs of cosmo") to describe the effect of one of Monet's late studies of water lilies.[38] "Eternal float of solution" might be an even more relevant description of these splashes of pure color, gliding in pools that reflect sky, foliage, light, and atmosphere in an ensemble that William Gaunt has called "magical," a "final magnificent testimony to the wonder of nature."[39] If there is mysticism in Monet, it is in these last works, which attempt to capture the most ephemeral manifestations of the natural world under the most fleeting conditions of light and shadow, as if the artist himself were determined to say, like Whitman:

> We receive you with free sense at last, and are
>   insatiate henceforward,
> Not you any more shall be able to foil us, or withhold

> yourselves from us,
> We use you, and do not cast you aside—we plant you
> permanently within us,
> We fathom you not—we love you—there is perfection in
> you also,
> You furnish your parts toward eternity,
> Great or small, you furnish your parts toward the soul.

Whether Monet believed in the soul or eternity, as Whitman did,[40] is irrelevant here, for I have not attempted to demonstrate a philosophical similarity between Whitman and the Impressionists, but only a technical and thematic trope. I have extracted what seem to me "Impressionist" passages from "Crossing Brooklyn Ferry" and suggest that the didactic strategy of the poem accomplishes a captivation or possession of the reader that was impossible for the visual artists of the time. Whitman, moving out of his work of art to clasp the reader by a ghostly hand, creates a personal depth that the Impressionists could not achieve through boldness of color, the cunning use of silhouette, or a radically oblique perspective. Monet cannot coax a viewer into one of his canvases in the same way that Whitman can incorporate a reader into his poem, exercising a psychic control based on the phenomena of shared sensation.

But Whitman can and still does stun us with the color, vibrancy, and atmospheric virtuosity of a Monet in stanza 3 of "Crossing Brooklyn Ferry," employing a technique that literally arrests the eye. That he did this in 1856, fourteen years before Renoir and Manet had begun to paint "the shimmering atmosphere of light and water at La Grenouillière, the bathing place of Bougival on the Seine" that Phoebe Pool sees as the real genesis of Impressionism,[41] is an insight only vouchsafed us by the passage of more than a hundred years of critical debate on the worth, place, and revolutionary originality of that school. Yet, as early as 1896, five years after Whitman's death, a writer in *Scribner's* magazine was asking:

> Why do we to-day talk about the poems of Walt Whitman and the landscapes of Claude Monet as lacking in style since none of us denies that they show strong individualities? Is it not because they fail in giving that other style, which Sir Joshua Reynolds called "the grand style," and the meaning of which Buffon suggests in that phrase, "to render properly"?[42]

Now, perhaps it is all too easy to see that, rather than failing to follow a hierarchical grand style, Monet and Whitman rediscovered a mode of vision so simple and so compelling that it reaches out beyond style itself.

1. Max Kozloff, "Walt Whitman and American Art," in *The Artistic Legacy of Walt Whitman: A Tribute to Gay Wilson Allen*, ed. Edwin Haviland Miller (New York: New York University Press, 1970), pp. 32, 34.

2. See, for example, Edwin Haviland Miller, "The Radical Vision of Whitman and Pollock," in *The Artistic Legacy of Walt Whitman*, pp. 55-71, and Henry B. Rule, "Walt Whitman and George Caleb Bingham," *Walt Whitman Review* 15 (1969): 248-53.

3. Wordsworth's poem is subtitled "Suggested by a picture of Peele Castle, in a storm, painted by Sir George Beaumont," and Melville's "A Picture by S. R. Gifford, and owned by E. B. Included in the N. A. Exhibition, April 1865." See *The Poetical Works of Wordsworth*, ed. Thomas Hutchinson, rev. Ernest de Selincourt (London: Oxford University press, 1965), p. 452, and *Selected Poems of Herman Melville*, ed. Hennig Cohen (Garden City, N.Y.: Doubleday and Co., 1964), p. 44.

4. Kermit Champa, *Studies in Early Impressionism* (New Haven, Conn.: Yale University Press, 1973), p. xiv.

5. See Walt Whitman, *Leaves of Grass: Comprehensive Reader's Edition*, ed. Harold W. Blodgett and Sculley Bradley (New York: New York University Press, 1965), p. 158. All quotations from the poem will follow the text in this edition, pp. 159-65.

6. Quoted in Pierre Courthion, *Impressionism*, trans. John Shepley (New York: Abrams, 1977), p. 12.

7. See Barbara Novak, *American Painting of the Nineteenth Century* (New York: Praeger, 1969), p. 97. It is Novak's contention that the American reverence for fact and the Transcendental belief in the "divinity" of light prevented the development of a native Impressionist movement. "The American necessity for the ideal, for 'sentiment,' which needs but a touch of profundity to become 'lyricism,' militated against an objective, analytic dissection of God's world. Sunlight, as a divine attribute, could hardly be broken down into the light of the spectrum" (p. 91). For an example of Whitman's "Luminism," employing that hushed stillness, clarity, gradation of tone, horizontality of plane, precision of detail, and crystalline radiance which Novak identifies as the hallmarks of the style, witness these lines from "There Was a Child Went Forth," which could be compared to any number of harbor scenes or marsh views by Fitz Hugh Lane or Martin Johnson Heade, leading exponents of the school:

> The village on the highland seen from afar at sunset,
> the river between,
> Shadows, aureola and mist, the light falling on roofs
> and gables of white or brown two miles off,
> The schooner near by sleepily dropping down the tide,
> the little boat slack-tow'd astern,
> The hurrying tumbling waves, quick-broken crests,
> slapping,
> The strata of color'd clouds, the long bar of maroon-tint
> away solitary by itself, the spread
> of purity it lies motionless in,
> The horizon's edge, the flying sea-crow, the fragrance
> of salt marsh and shore mud . . .

8. See William Gaunt, *The Impressionists* (London: Thames & Hudson, 1970), p. 90.

9. See John Rewald, *The History of Impressionism* (New York: Museum of Modern Art, 1973), pp. 44, 103, and Gaunt, *The Impressionists*, p. 66, pl. 6.

10. Rewald, *History of Impressionism*, p. 101.

11. Ralph Waldo Emerson, "Experience," in *Emerson: Selected Prose and Poetry*, ed.

Reginald L. Cook (New York: Holt, Rinehart and Winston, 1969), p. 144.

12. See Walt Whitman, *An 1855-56 Notebook toward the Second Edition of "Leaves of Grass,"* intro. and notes by Harold W. Blodgett (Carbondale, Ill.: Southern Illinois University Press, 1959). Here the poem begins as "Poem or passage, / the scenes on the river / as I cross the Fulton ferry" (p. 65).

13. James Gargano, "Technique in 'Crossing Brooklyn Ferry': The Everlasting Moment," *Journal of English and Germanic Philology* 62 (April 1963): 263. Gargano's essay is a masterful demonstration of the role that structure plays in the poem.

14. Quoted in Courthion, *Impressionism*, p. 15.

15. Emerson, "Circles," in *Selected Prose and Poetry*, p. 110.

16. Gargano, "Technique in 'Crossing Brooklyn Ferry,' " p. 264.

17. John P. Sedgwick, *Art Appreciation Made Simple* (Garden City, N. Y.: Doubleday and Co., 1959), p. 136. In spite of its unfortunate title, Sedgwick's book contains a very valuable digest of Impressionist themes and techniques.

18. Ibid., p. 136.

19. Quoted in Courthion, *Impressionism*, p. 12.

20. Stanley J. Coffman, Jr., " 'Crossing Brooklyn Ferry': A Note on the Catalogue Technique in Whitman's Poetry," *Modern Philology* 51 (May 1954): 227.

21. Sedgwick, *Art Appreciation Made Simple*, p. 136.

22. Ibid.

23. Champa, *Studies in Early Impressionism*, p. 97.

24. Ibid., p. 99.

25. Quoted in Phoebe Pool, *Impressionism* (New York: Oxford University Press, 1967), pp. 86-87.

26. Courthion, *Impressionism*, p. 10.

27. Gaunt, *The Impressionists*, p. 19.

28. Courthion, *Impressionism*, p. 102.

29. Reproduced in Ibid., pp. 102-3.

30. Pool, *Impressionism*, p. 61.

31. Ibid., pp. 106-7.

32. Thoreau, who specifically mentioned that he admired Whitman's "Sun-Down Poem," also used the physical sensations prompted by a sunset view to affirm the permanence of shared phenomenality (though his descriptive technique is closer to Luminism than to Impressionism) in a passage from "Walking" (1862):

> We had a remarkable sunset one day last November. I was walking in a meadow, the source of a small brook, when the sun at last, just before setting, after a cold, gray day, reached a clear stratum of the horizon, and the softest, brightest morning sunlight fell on the dry grass and on the stems of the trees in the opposite horizon and on the leaves of the shrub oaks on the hillside, while our shadows stretched long over the meadow eastward, as if we were only motes in its beams. It was such a light as we could not have imagined a moment before, and the air also was so warm and serene that nothing was wanting to make a paradise of that meadow. When we reflected that this was not a solitary phenomenon, never to happen again, but that it would happen forever and ever, an infinite number of evenings, and cheer and reassure the latest child that walked there, it was more glorious still. *Thoreau: The Major Essays*, ed. Jeffrey L. Duncan (New York: E. P. Dutton, 1972), p. 225.

33. Rewald, *History of Impressionism*, p. 228.

34. Pool, *Impressionism*, p. 87.

35. Ibid.

36. Champa, *Studies in Early Impressionism*, p. 25.

37. Gargano, "Technique in 'Crossing Brooklyn Ferry,' " p. 265.

38. Sedgwick, *Art Appreciation Made Simple*, p. 222.

39. Gaunt, *The Impressionists*, p. 160.

40. One of the passages of the embryonic "Crossing Brooklyn Ferry" recorded in Whitman's notebook reads: "I believe whatever happens / I shall not forget / this earth, / I believe I shall walk / and walk among / men and women.— / Wherever I go I believe / I shall often return."

41. Pool, *Impressionism*, pp. 54-55.

42. "Style," in "The Field of Art," *Scribner's* 20 (August 1896): 259.

Gulley Jimson's Painterly Prose

Robert S. Fredrickson

Gettysburg College

DESPITE its enormous popularity as a comic novel, Joyce Cary maintains that *The Horse's Mouth* is a "very heavy piece of metaphysical writing."[1] The metaphysics are existential, but not in any dour, godless, Sartrean sense.

> For good and evil, man is a free creative spirit. This produces the very queer world we live in, a world in continuous creation and therefore continuous change and insecurity. A perpetually new and lively world, but a dangerous one, full of tragedy and injustice. A world in everlasting conflict between the new idea and the old allegiances, new arts and new inventions against the old establishment.[2]

This unending freedom to choose, this unceasing process, gives *The Horse's Mouth* its existential intensity. The novel's success does not rest in any completed form—all forms limit freedom and halt the developing process.[3] Instead, the novel can only succeed by undermining itself as art. Like so much of twentieth-century painting, Cary can only achieve this "free creative spirit" by a radical break with the tyrants of form, society, and tradition. But more than the weight of culture oppresses Cary's artist. All concrete manifestations of inner visions, all words and images, oppose imagination.[4] With everything in the external world in opposition to him, Cary's artist-hero is totally subjective, realizing himself only by alienation. While capable of original vision, he can only express it by altering existing forms, by being, in a sense, destructive. Jimson then is not technically a reliable narrator. If words are necessarily compromising to the moment of vision, all narrators are unreliable. Yet Jimson represents reliably the problem that the artist has in reconciling his aesthetic myth with the reality of modern experience. The material world is unmalleable and thus deadly to the free spirit. The spiritual world is ungraspable and thus unknowable in the material world. Like action painting (which came later and in another country), such artistically unrealizable visions can ultimately solve no problems.[5] Both the artist and the audience are likely to find the product strange. The artist looks upon it as an artifact of a country he once visited; it is alive to the extent that it recalls his ineffable experience within that country. To the audience both the experience and the country are unknown. In this solipsistic predicament, Jimson at times seems like a Dadaist, more interested in rage than in art.[6]

Cary underscores the paradox that underlies all art forms which aim to embody existential content. In doing so he creates an artist whose rightful place is either among the cubists or among post-World War II American painters. Placed in this perspective, it little matters that Jimson, in this work of words, shows us no paintings. Had he not come earlier, Jimson might have represented the culmination of a kind of conceptual art in which material form is inadequate in manifesting ideal content. He is a step beyond Pollock, who represents the ecstasy of the moment of creation with a record of his movement. Jimson only supplies words—the logos; all pictures pale before visions of the spirit.

Jimson, however, distrusts these words ("talk is lies").[7] The book that stands as a substitute for a painting career that can be imagined (only with difficulty) must, by Gulley's definition, fail, since "the only satisfactory form of communication is a good picture. Neither true nor false" (p. 95). Yet with regard to Jimson's life and career, the book in fact gives a better picture than his paintings could. Jimson's paintings can never provide a good picture since they are never completed. Pictures may be a form of communication, but only in the present moment, and then only as a reflection of a present consciousness, one that changes before the paint dries, leaving the picture another relic from the past that must be thrust aside. Jimson may have received recognition as an artist because of a few completed paintings of his Sara Monday period, one of which hangs in the National Gallery, yet he is ambivalent about them. They appear to him to be the work of another man. Only through keeping the process of painting continuous can the value of a work of art be maintained. Jimson, in the confines of this book, never voluntarily quits work on his paintings. He is either forced to abandon them, or they are destroyed. Presumably, he would continue working on one painting indefinitely were he to have the opportunity. To him the value of a work of art is found in the moment of translation, the moment when internal vision becomes paint. As in all translations, much is lost, but at the moment of creation a sort of dynamic reaction takes place: as he recalls it, "the flesh was made word" (p. 59). This then is the moment of art. Tenebrous connections between vision and material are made that a moment later dissolve. Thus Jimson rejects not only his own past in which he participated in each artistic phenomenon from classicism to abstraction, but also all the tradition that came before him. Like Rauschenberg erasing de Kooning for a new work of art, Jimson paints over the past. To him Morlands, Ruffianos, and his own early works are useful only as canvases.

While this intensely visual novel is replete with allusions to art history, and while it includes detailed descriptions of paintings, the book itself proves the opposite of Jimson's contention that talk is lies. It is pictures, static representations of actuality that lie. What Jimson needs is a work of art that is linear in the McLuhan sense, which, like music, flows in time rather than freezes the moment. In response to this need, we are given a prose style that breaks down our illusionistic expectations of a fixed reality by fracturing our usual sense of the actual. This style accomplishes in words something akin to the cubist's overcoming of the time dimension in paint. Just as cubism represents a shimmering, fluctuating reality, its geometric shapes forming patterns that immediately dissolve, Jimson's prose struggles with ephemeral visions. As Ernst Gombrich has suggested in *Art and Illusion*, the ultimate of cubism is a sort of action painting where any suggestion of a static meaning is obscured and we are forced to concentrate on the artist engaged in a Platonic frenzy of creation.[8] In this sense Jimson is like Pollock, but instead of flinging paint, he struggles with words. As a consequence, he is significantly different from Pollock, who in a Freudian vein claims that "the source of my painting is the unconscious," and, therefore, that he does not know what he is doing.[9] Jimson must know consciously his source. He seems to be searching for a means by which he can push this unconscious material into the open. To do so he must have either pictures or words, but each belongs to another realm, a fallen world far removed from the imagination or the id. Jimson takes us a step beyond the dislocations of cubist images to a point where the process is all. For this purpose the stream-of-consciousness novel is perfect, the form itself implying that truth is momentary. We cannot contain an entire novel in a glance. We are always at a particular point. This moment-to-moment struggle to create reality engages the reader because of the sheer expenditure of energy.

The explanation for how the story is being told, that Jimson, deprived of motion on account of a stroke, is dictating his story to a secretary, is not then as artifical as such devices usually appear. That Jimson has been reduced to writing, literally, is symbolic of his quest to find a mode of expression immediate and ephemeral enough for his existential sense of experience. Like Humbert Humbert, he has only words to play with. Yet the book is a tour de force of the possibilities of verbal picture. While by standards of written language this book is jerky and irregular, spoken in fragments with image piled recklessly on image, it has the pulsating energy of oral literature. As with Jimson's paintings, we experience the book while he is working on it.

There remains, however, a sense in which talk is lies. Talk for Jimson is like "shooting peas into a can" (p. 6). It is an activity wherein volatile substances, words, get constrained by logic and syntax. It is conceptualizing, and as such, Cary explains, it necessarily compromises the intuitive vision, the revelation. The moment of vision is a moment of freshness, one that every artist fears will be lost in formulating the art work. Cary tells of Henry James's experience with an ephemeral idea: "For the moment he had translated his intuition into an idea, into words, his excited feeling of discovery began to leak away, and the idea began to seem dull, commonplace, and to supersede the intuitions."[10] Hence Gulley is afraid of talking about his ideas. When struck with a vision, Gulley wishes to go to work immediately because ideas go "soft at the edges" (p. 10). Yet in both talking and painting the problem is not seen until after the moment of action is past. Jimson does not mean to tell lies. It is only that "when you're talking you haven't time to get the words right" (p. 95). The problem begins when you feel you have gone on record. As a painter or speaker Gulley does and says things he later regrets. "Now when I say anything like that, about shooting a man or cutting his tripes out, even in joke, I often get angry with him. And anything like bad temper is bad for me. It spoils my equanimity. It blocks my imagination" (p. 11). Talking is like painting, honest in impulse yet deceitful in retrospect. Anger is dangerous because it is an emotion that builds upon past moments. Any retrospective glance is a conceptualization of the past that precludes living in the present and therefore blocks imagination. Man's existential plight is that each moment requires a response, the response being a means of rebirth, but each moment dies and each response haunts the future. "Words, after speech, reach / Into the silence."[11]

The conflict between our visions and the forms we give them in speech or paint is inevitable according to Cary; "the emotional experience which he [the artist] wants to convey in its original force" is the content, which can only be conveyed by "the manipulation of words, themselves already charged with meaning."[12] Jimson, like Blake, cannot proclaim, as most symbolists do, the inseparability of form and content. While Jimson speaks about "the solid forms of the imagination" (p. 198), a paradox Nosy legitimately questions, his inspiration as a pictorial artist is actually less specified in terms of reality than that of the verbal artist. He tells Nosy about a painting saying: "I see my picture. In fact, I don't sus-see it. I only imagine it, and probably I'm imagining all wrong" (p. 199). Not only are Jimson's internal visions beyond close translation into something one actually sees, even external reality is elusive to the painter. "Took a walk up and down to crack the joints. Sun coming up along a cloud bank like clinkers. All sparks. Couldn't do it in paint. Limits of the art. Limits of everything" (p. 23). Thus, as an effort to re-create an internal or external actuality, a painting is like a poem or a new religion. "They begin as a lot of funny words. Nobody knows whether they're all nonsense or a gift from heaven" (p. 193). Jimson's nonsense is something he admits is no better than a child could do, something that is either a masterpiece of form and color or a "piece of bare-faced pornography that ought to be dealt with by the police" (p. 21). That he can belittle what he has done, that he is so uncertain as to its lasting value, arises from his work's being knowable only in the context of perception. The value of a vision for painter or observer is not fixed, but subject to variables.

As a consequence, there is a dynamic struggle between Jimson's inner vision and his creations. The latter simultaneously are expressions and modifications of the former. The paradoxical "solid forms of the imagination" represent the artist's search for something concrete in the ephemeral vision. Yet the fear is that the concretization will not fulfill but will instead destroy the vision. The tension of this paradox is what is basic to both Gulley Jimson and his mentor William Blake. If form and content somehow are wed, Jimson sees a tyranny in the relationship. Hazard Adams in writing on "Blake and Gulley Jimson" notes that for the modern symbolist the emphasis in the equation of form and content is on form and "with it the growing sense of the artist's being locked within the forms of his own expression."[13] Jimson's experience in painting graphically demonstrates this dilemma. He speaks of painting the "first stroke" as the artist's greatest pleasure. "I have transformed a chunk of wood, canvas, etc., into a spiritual fact." But such pleasure "doesn't last long—usually five minutes" (pp. 192-93). Problems then emerge that show how the artist is imprisoned in his own work. With form, Blakean materiality dominant, the artist finds himself nailed down by his own work. Both "The Mental Traveler" and "The Tyger" are used in *The Horse's Mouth* in part to show how art is a cry of pain and fear in response to the artist's own entrapment. The artist is the "Babe" in "The Mental Traveler" who is caught in a perpetual cycle, beginning and ending with his being nailed to rock. His art is in response to materiality or necessity that torture him and then force his outcries into an artistic form—that is, catch "his shrieks in cups of gold." The cyclical struggle in which the artist is involved is one in which his assertion of freedom binds him into the inevitable. The "bleeding youth" who expresses his creative self when he "plants himself" in "the Virgin bright" becomes then an "aged shadow" to be driven out by a "female babe" and "the Man she loves."[14]

The sections of *The Horse's Mouth* in which we find passages of "The Mental Traveler" are used to amplify Gulley's description of two cyclical struggles in which he is engaged. First he delineates the struggle between the artist and his material, seeing it in terms of the opposition of man and woman. A woman, materiality and necessity, must be reduced to her proper status, that is, spiritual fodder. He sees a girl on a young man's arm and thinks: "Look out, Puggy, that isn't a maiden you see before you, it's a work of imagination. Nail him girlie. Nail him to the contract" (pp. 50-51). A second cyclical struggle is amplified when instead of woman representing the necessary friction for the work of the imagination, it is Gulley's own works, his own art history and that of the nineteenth and twentieth centuries, that provide it. Each development comes in reaction to the past. Just as the artist must work from the brushstrokes already on canvas, he must work in reaction to the tradition that has preceded him. Impressionism is born in him like the little female babe of "The Mental Traveler." His career alternates between pure sensation and formalism, romanticism and classicism. The opposition between attempts to idealize through pure form and efforts to convey the momentary ephemeral sensation is one that Blake develops in "The Tyger." The actions of a God and those of an artist run frighteningly parallel. "What immortal hand or eye / Could frame thy fearful symmetry?" The pure form of a created object, the tyger, is testimony to an artistic impulse, again the action painter's Platonic frenzy of pure creation, which is beyond our conceiving. Rhetorical questions are asked to make us ponder the nature of the artist himself in the act of creation. "What the hand dare seize the fire?" The tyger is to begin with awesome in itself, but even more terrifying is the impulse that brought to reality this form. The tyger is a manifestation of God's power and, as subject matter for art, is symbolic of the intuition of divine power that the artist possesses. For Jimson, as for Blake, no form can hope to frame the real import of an object like the tyger. Hence it is with trepidation he approaches his task. "What immortal hand or eye / *Dare* frame thy fearful symmetry?"[15] Jimson ranges from confident classicist attempts to frame the fearful symmetry to a romantic sense that inspiration and realization are so far apart that the artist engages in an act of great daring when he tries to give form to such awesome content.

Persons who read *The Horse's Mouth* and see it only as picaresque adventures with a rogue-hero miss the fearsome nature of Gulley's experience. As an artist, Gulley's quest is to provide order and meaning in a world that moment by moment denies such. The humor of the book is not in satire, but in a more desperate modern vein where each moment everything is laid on the line. *Carpe diem* as a motif is converted to existential *Angst*. Gulley, constantly harrassed by time's closing in, says, "I'm never really comfortable without a picture and when I've got one on hand life isn't worth living" (p. 22). In this comic dilemma Gulley has the choice of two ways of losing, but to his credit he chooses action over inaction, exposure to the cosmos over enclosed security.

The Blake quotation on the first page of the novel shows the way in which Jimson sees man enclosed:

> Five windows light the caverned man; through one he
> breathes the air;
> Through one hears music of the spheres; through
> one can look
> And see small portions of the eternal world.[16]

It is Jimson's desire to escape the cavern, to live in the open, unprotected from the cosmos. Jimson then is not like the usual man just out of prison who runs for cover. Instead, he says of open space: "I like it. I swam in it" (p. 3).

Gulley feels it takes style to survive in such an exposed state. "You need technique to do a good job at life" (p. 59). Through a sort of cubist verbal style Jimson represents the energy he has to create momentary coherence. The novel's first image sets us up for what is to follow. "Sun in a mist. Like an orange in a fried fish shop" (p. 3). Jimson's aim in using an image like this appears to be the same as that attributed to the cubists by Gombrich—that is, to "make the clues contradict each other and to prevent a coherent image of reality from destroying the pattern in the plane."[17] The image is farfetched enough that we see Jimson is not isolating a moment photographically as the impressionist painters or Stephen Crane might. The perceiver sees the sun and flashes a past moment. The juxtaposition of present and past allows an escape from the peep-show conventions of illusionistic art, providing in Blakean-Jimsonesque terms a means to fly simultaneously through all five windows that light the caverned man. In attempting to blend two sensuous experiences, we fail since we always come across a contradiction that forces us to start afresh. The parallels between the orange and the sun are many. Their color is the same; they exist in an atmosphere that blurs our sight. But no coherent image emerges since the sun is large and luminescent, while the orange is small and without its own light. The hugeness of the cosmos is reduced to the mundane world of the fish shop. A three-dimensional world is so suddenly flattened that we are conscious that all pictures, in words or paint, are artificial reconstructions. Thus the image is painterly, calling attention to the mind that created it.

A problem with such images is one that Jimson recognized well: "Cezanne and the cubists when they chucked up old doddering impressionism, caught their maidens. But the cubists did it too easily. They knocked them down with hammers and tied up the fragments with wire. Most of them died and the rest look more like bird cages than forms of intuition and delight" (p. 66). This problem occurs in his own painting. He looks at Eve in his picture and reevaluates what was supposedly once an inspired color choice. "What a color. Tinned salmon. Why did I do that? What a piece of affectation" (p. 19). Jimson cannot control the meaning of colors or words he has used in new contexts. Eve forces an especially painful retake just after Gulley has been spending time with the real Makay, Sara Monday. "She was a bit too clever, too artistic, too flat, more like a composition in line and color than a real piece of stuff" (p. 41).

Gulley's problem with images in paint or words is most successfully overcome when he uses the device of the epic simile. Here the form, the image, builds by some organic inner logic that may or may not be related to the original impulse, the meaning or content the image was purported to have. Gulley goes along for a ride on the vehicle, losing the tenor. He starts the following image, comparing himself to a worm, to show how lowly he feels when others criticize his paintings. Instead of communicating sorrow, however, the moment is redeemed through fantastic hyperbole:

> As if I had been a happy worm, creeping all soft and oily through the grass, imagining the blades to be great forest trees, and every little pebble a mountain overcome; and taking the glow of self-satisfaction from his own tail for the glory of the Lord shining on his path; when all at once a herd of bullocks comes trampling along, snorting tropical epochs and shitting continents; succeeded by a million hairy gorillas, as big as skyscrapers, beating on their chests with elephant drumsticks and screaming, "Give us meat; give us mates," followed modestly by ten thousand walruses a thousand feet high, wearing battleships for boots, and the Dome of St. Paul's for a codpiece; armed in the one hand with shield-shaped Bibles fortified with brass spikes, and in the other with cross-headed clubs of blood rusty iron, hung with the bleeding hands of infants, artists, etc., with which they beat up what is left of the grass crying, "Come to mother, little worm, and let her pat your dear head and comb your sweet hair for you. (P. 46)

This simile is of a type of epic style that Gulley or the cubists took on in reaction to lyric impressionism. The photographic impression is left behind while the artist engages in a moment-by-moment struggle to create reality out of himself. The decorative simile allows the artist to break out of the form, allows a direct intervention of the muse in order to convey ceremonially the impression of magnitude. The rhetorical pattern justifies the direction the image takes making such contradictions as "snorting tropical epochs" acceptable.

Partly as a consequence of such imagery, a question often brought to bear on this novel is that of Jimson's sanity. For Jimson, the artist is the madman who, in the sense of R. D. Laing, discovers a reservoir of the unconscious self cosmic in size. Cubism is the point where the Blakean romantic and the modern schizophrenic meet. For both the romantic and the schizophrenic the contest is the same: mind versus matter. For the romantic, victory by the mind is both necessary and probable; for the schizophrenic, while victory is overwhelmingly necessary, it is extremely improbable. Material reality constantly denies the schizophrenic a sense of his own existence. Blake's cycles of death and rebirth move at a relatively insouciant pace, while the modern schizophrenic must frenetically be reborn each moment of consciousness. Jimson is more the modern than the romantic. *The Horse's Mouth* is the record of a frenzied effort to stay alive, to keep the heart that dies between beats pulsing. Reality must be restructured every moment, and for the artist it is paramount that each restructuring carry built into its form the possibility of infinite restructuring. Jimson laughs instead of praying, believing them to be the same, because laughter restructures pathos in an instant; it is a way to be born again.

Thus Jimson, like his creator Cary, follows Kierkegaard in believing life to be a series of free choices. Jimson, however, does not make Kierkegaard's distinction between ethical choice and aesthetic choice, the latter being the mere exercise of preference, which cannot lead us beyond the chaos of everyday living.[18] All decisions are qualitatively the same to Jimson, all living like painting.[19] Every action comes in spite of the paralyzing brushstrokes already on the canvas if one is fully awake. Jimson survives because he does not let the past get him down: economic disaster, ruined paintings, a destroyed reputation, failed marriages, jail, and legal difficulties fail to stop him. Like a reborn Christian, he comes up guiltless, even with regard to Sara's murder.

Despite Jimson's "unreliability," he can be identified with Cary in an important sense. Both hold views that allow for further restructuring. Cary in *Art and Reality* elaborates a restructuring of Jimson. Jimson represents a restructuring of the reality of Monday and Whilcher, the narrators of the first two volumes of the trilogy. Cary may be more like Jimson than Sara or Whilcher, but he shares in the energy of all three. Each represents tremendous existential strength, the power to build a cosmos.

While Cary felt confident that he had a coherent world view at the time of his *Paris Review* interview in 1954,[20] *Art and Reality*, written at the end of his life, reveals that he still suffered from Jimson's problem, the "gap between intuition and expression."[21] What gave Cary the energy for his endless restructurings was the faith that an ultimate reality exists from which our individuality of necessity separates us. Each effort at artistic creation is like the launching forth of a filament from Whitman's "Noiseless Patient Spider" toward that ultimate reality. In that poem, completion is secondary; the primary emphasis is on the tireless activity of the spider. It takes "power and fertility," characteristics Cary ascribes to Picasso, to get close to the original intuited childlike vision.[22] It is this type of energy Picasso elicits from us with his paintings that give the trilogy its painterly quality. Our response to cubist painting is not one of repose. We search for order, lose it, search again, and so on, almost infinitely. The three segments of this trilogy build linearly the same response.

1. Joyce Cary, *Writers at Work: The "Paris Review" Interviews*, ed. Malcolm Cowley (New York: Viking, 1958), p. 65.

2. Ibid., p. 55.

3. Northrop Frye in a renowned essay, "Towards Defining an Age of Sensibility," in *Eighteenth-Century English Literature* (New York: Oxford University Press, 1959), pp. 311-18, makes a distinction between literature as product and literature as process. In literature as process "we wonder, not what is coming next, but what the author will think of next" (p. 312).

4. Fred Stockholder, "The Triple Vision in Joyce Cary's First Trilogy," *Modern Fiction Studies* 9 (1963): 276-83. Jimson, says Stockholder, fails because he cannot believe in the " 'world of imagination' until it is expressed" (p. 239).

5. Harold Rosenberg, *The Anxious Object* (New York: New American Library, 1964), p. 37.

6. A. Alvarez, *The Savage God* (New York: Bantam Books, 1972), p. 218, links the suicidal impulse and Dadaism in terms of this type of self-destructive outrage. While Jimson denies his anger, clearly sublimiated rage contributes to his energy, and his work is an expression of this emotional state.

7. Joyce Cary, *The Horse's Mouth* (New York: Harper and Row, 1965). All quotations from the novel are taken from this edition.

8. Ernst Gombrich, *Art and Illusion* (Princeton, N.J.: Princeton University Press, 1960), p. 286.

9. Quoted in Harold Rosenberg, *Artworks and Packages* (New York: Horizon Press, 1969), p. 60.

10. Joyce Cary, *Art and Reality* (Garden City, N.Y.: Doubleday and Co., 1958), p. 112.

11. T. S. Eliot, "Burnt Norton," *The Four Quartets*, ll.139-40, in *Collected Poems: 1909-1935* (New York: Harcourt, Brace and World, 1962), p. 121.

12. Cary, *Art and Reality*, p. 113.

13. "Blake and Gulley Jimson: English Symbolists," *Critique* 3 (Spring-Fall 1959): 11.

14. "The Mental Traveler" is quoted in snippets in chaps. 11-14, sometimes inaccurately. With this and other Blake quotations, I am using the Jimson version.

15. These lines from Blake's "The Tyger" are not quoted in the text of *The Horse's Mouth*, yet they reveal how close to Blake Jimson is in imagination. Emphasis added.

16. Jimson's version of the opening lines of Blake's "Europe."

17. Gombrich, *Art and Illusion*, p. 281.

18. Søren Kierkegaard, *Either/Or*, vol. 2, trans. Walter Lowrie (Princeton, N.J.: Princeton University Press, 1949).

19. Rosenberg observed the following of action painters: "Painting became the means of confronting in daily practice the problematic nature of modern individuality." *The Anxious Object*, p. 38.

20. Cary, *Writers at Work*, p. 55.

21. Cary, *Art and Reality*, p. 41.

22. Ibid., p. 50.

Autonomy and Affinity: Toward a Theory for Comparing the Arts

Laura Rice-Sayre
Henry M. Sayre

Wake Forest University

I

IN his 1912 *Souvenirs sur Paul Cézanne*, the painter Emile Bernard emphasizes the dissimilarity of literature and painting: [les] deux modes étant différents," Bernard asserts, "il s'ensuit l'incompréhension du peintre par l'écrivain." The authority for this assertion is Cézanne himself, whom Bernard quotes: "Le littérateur s'exprime avec des abstractions, tandis que le peintre concrète, au moyen du dessin et de la couleur, ses sensations, ses perceptions."[1] The very awkwardness of Cézanne's utterance—the asymmetrical "abstractions"/"concrète"—seems to underscore the distance between the plastic and the verbal, but by 1912 the inadequacy of his distinction must have been more than apparent to a public that could, at that very moment, witness paintings that by means of their design and color expressed themselves as abstractions, and poems, such as Guillaume Apollinaire's *Calligrammes*, that revealed the word to be concrete material waiting to be shaped.

Since 1912, critics have begun to make inroads into the examination of precisely those dissimilarities noted by Cézanne. In a collection of essays on "Literary and Art History," Jean Laude begins his article in a most Cézannian key: "Absolutely everything distinguishes a literary text from a painting or drawing: its conception, its method of production, its identity as an object irreducible to any other object, and its autonomous functioning."[2] Although both Laude and Cézanne insist on the specificity of the objects created by the literary and the plastic arts, Laude goes on to suggest that the study of these arts may reveal that they share a series of "common structures." Laude points to the paradox that, since the time of Baudelaire, poets and painters have increasingly insisted upon the autonomy of their various productions while at the same time they have increasingly affiliated with one another. This paradox leads Laude to suggest, and rightly we think, that since the time of Cézanne the arts have, in their various ways, been exploring "the production of a new language and the focusing on new readings" (p. 476). In short, Laude suggests that we move away from the subject-oriented level of analysis demonstrated by iconography and iconology and create instead critical tools "capable of specifying levels of comparison registered in the *functioning* of works and not in the alleged psychology of their producers or in their thematic content" (p. 479). Art itself has forced the critic to find new ways to express the interrelations between the plastic and the literary. Collage, for instance, is a method of production that painting and poetry share, and the closeness of this correspondence is especially clear if we compare more radical examples of the collage technique, such as Schwitters's *Merz* and Tzara's Dada poems, the latter being an assortment of words cut individually from a newspaper article, then copied in the order they are drawn from a bag. That the arts have come to assert simultaneously both their affinity (even willful affiliation) and their autonomy is paradoxical, and this paradoxical liaison and denial is even more clearly demonstrated by the example of the collaborative work in which the poet and painter conceive of a work of art together, consider its plastic and verbal elements part of an integral whole in which both text and artwork function simultaneously, and finally demand, at least implicitly, that the production be appreciated as a unit. This kind of collaborative venture has come to be, in this century at least, a major field of endeavor, one that might well owe its popularity—even its possibility—to that radical leveling of distinctions among media which is collage itself. Whatever the case, the sense of the autonomy of the various arts that Cézanne avers and Laude explores (and in Cézanne's case it might well be labeled plastic chauvinism) has been attacked by the arts themselves.

The critics among us who seem to have taken part in this attack also are the semiologists, especially those who are engaged in that branch of semiotics known as poetics (*poétique*). What they have revealed to us is that the plastic and verbal arts are not so much autonomous entities as they are competing sign systems, and that these sign systems, while more or less divergent, may in fact reflect many identical structural principles. Laude indicates a move in this direction when he comes to the conclusion that "painting and poetry constitute a series which, each one taken separately, are linked not to each other but to an identical sequence of a common cultural area" (p. 483). This view of semiological series is first expressed by the Russian Formalists. In his introduction to Serge Doubrovsky's *The New Criticism in France*, Edward Wasiolek says of the Formalists:

> Though the Formalists did not put it in this way, they recognized that the world was one but that there were different ways of conceiving of or forming such facts. The literary series was self-enclosed and self-propelled, but it was not isolated from other series of facts; it had a relationship, but the relationship was not causal or genetic. The series were parallel, and there was an interchange between the various series.[3]

It is this interchange between the semiotic series that constitute the plastic and literary domains that has become central to the study of the interrelations of the arts. In the foreword to his collection of papers from the 1971 and 1972 English Institute, Seymour Chatman has articulated persuasively and briefly the semiotic ground for comparisons between the arts: "Plots [for instance] clearly exist in narratives that are not communicated by means of words—in a mime by Marcel Marceau, a ballet, a cartoon without dialogue bubbles, a Chaplin film. Indeed, it might be said that a central problem for poetics is to distinguish more clearly the nonlinguistic from the linquistic structures in literature and to show how the former are communicated, both at deep and at surface levels."[4] The comparison of the arts is not new, but the insistence upon the interchanges between semiological systems is a new emphasis. We have always recognized—albeit grudgingly—certain connections among the arts. When an art critic speaks of a painter's "vocabulary," he is admitting that painting is a system of signs. When the painter Juan Gris calls the repetition of a circular form in the top of a glass and the sound hole of a guitar "rhyme," and calls three series of lines representing ocean waves, guitar strings, and the lines on a book page "metaphors" for one another, he is not so much searching for a vocabulary, however inadequate, as he is pointing to a structural analogy between the literary and plastic series.[5] And when we ourselves notice the linguistic confusion caused by Cézanne's more or less indifferent usage of the terms *abstract* and *concrete*, we are not confronted so much by the inadequacy of language as by the recognition that these terms are equally applicable to both plastic and verbal arts and that, in using them, we imply certain shared structural principles are at work. In short, what we as critics of the interrelations of the arts have often considered the downfall of critical language—the irksome necessity of one discipline to borrow descriptive vocabularies from another—is perhaps language's greatest gift to the critic: these areas of linguistic overlap may well point to the interrelation of the arts as a dialectic of semiologic series. It is the purpose of this essay to look first, briefly, at the power one semiological system has in influencing another and second, at greater length, to reexamine, in the light of a dialectic interchange of semantic systems, the various sorts of comparisons that have traditionally been made between the arts and to assess the efficacy of these comparisons.

II

Perhaps the clearest example of the autonomy and concomitant affiliation of the arts is the collaborative work of art, a work that joins the plastic and the literary within one binding or frame and demands that we deal with two parallel systems of signification. Intentional collaboration—as opposed to mere illustration or its correlative operation, titling—forces us to realize that each art (that is, each system of signs) influences our perception of the other. But even illustration and titling, at least implicitly, often modify perception. In his book *Philosophy of Art*, Virgil C. Aldrich moves from a discussion of the rabbit/duck drawing that fascinated Wittgenstein

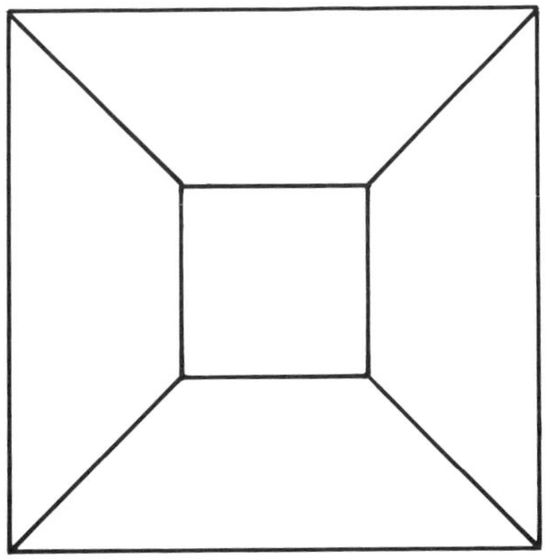

and Gombrich to a demonstration of how strongly the written word can influence our perception of a simple geometric design:[6]

What interests us here is that, as in the rabbit/duck picture, we cannot perceive this design apart from the signification we attach to it. The design cannot signify two things at once. The viewer's perception of the design changes radically as different written titles are given to the design: the tunnel, the suspended square, the truncated pyramid, the bottom of the lampshade, or, simply, abstraction. Our perception of the design is pushed and pulled so emphatically by the signifiers that we feel as if we are experiencing a graphic representation of Henry James's "house of fiction." We can see the tunnel and the suspended square, but never both at the same time. The design must either be a representation or an abstraction.

What is usually less recognized by literary critics, but certainly would seem to be a key to the study of parallel systems of signification, is that we can reverse the lines of influence in this sort of experiment. Our understanding of a poem, for instance, can be changed radically by the plastic illustration we attach to it. Consider Robert Duncan's short poem "Descriptions of imaginary poetries," number 2:

Gaps
Regular straining
Great rips in the febrile
goods
Gapes. A leftover intending.[7]

We can imagine various conflicting illustrations for the poem: Rodin's *The Thinker*, a version of Poussin's *Sabine Women*, Van Eyck's *The Crucifixion*, Picasso's *Guernica*, or Duchamp's urinal entitled *Fountain*. And in each case, the poem's "meaning" is radically altered; its *intention* is filled by a different context.

These two examples provide a useful introduction to the theory of illustration, which is, afterall, the starting point of collaborative ventures between art and literature, and both have far-reaching semiotic significance. The various titles for the geometric design provide us with a clear example of how visual perception—which is to say concrete experience—can be modified by linguistic manifestation. The concrete experience (or sign itself) is a design (the signified, *s*) above which floats what we might call a dance of mutually exclusive titles (signifiers, *S*):

$$\frac{S^1 \ldots S^2 \ldots S^3 \ldots S^4 \ldots S^5 \ldots}{s}$$

On the other hand, the Duncan poem provides us with an example of the opposite phenomenon, for here the poem's reference (the signified) is elusive and the poem itself (the signifier) is fixed:

$$\frac{S}{s^1 \ldots s^2 \ldots s^3 \ldots s^4 \ldots s^5 \ldots}$$

The complexity of the situation outlined here is further heightened when we recognize that, in both cases, we have treated words as signifiers and paintings as signifieds. What is implied is an implicit judgmental bias. For, as we know, the relation of signifier to signified is concomitant with the relation of form to meaning. Whichever of the two media we designate as the signifier in a collaborative venture is, by implication, an empty form waiting to be filled with meaning by its opposite number. And the very notion of treating the arts as if they partook of only one system of signification denies that they are actually separate and competing systems. This is, of course, how we are accustomed to dealing with most illustrated books. Perhaps reflecting their own literary chauvinism, literary critics feel that the text is primary and the illustration secondary, a mere reflection of the text. The artwork is seen as *mere* illustration rather than as collaboration. This bias is especially prevalent when the same artist has not done both. One reason for this bias may be quantitative—there are pages of text and only a few illustrations. A second, more justifiable reason may be that the illustrations are simply pictures of words in the text; the only way in which they add to the text is decoratively. We sense that the text would remain unchanged if the illustrations were torn out. We have, in fact, become accustomed to totally gratuitous illustrations. Ninety percent of the illustrated covers of the paperbacks on grocery store shelves seem pretty much the same: a young girl stands in the foreground; she is terrified; her blouse is ripped exposing one shoulder and part of her breast; a Gothic mansion looms in the background. This sort of illustration seems to have more to do with consumer psychology than it does with any sort of shared aesthetic.[8]

In the case of simple illustration, then, we often feel that the artist's work is secondary, that he is merely giving us a mimetic, visual imitation of a scene in the text, that he reflects rather than interprets or substantially adds to the text. Again, this reaction can be reversed by the context in which we find ourselves operating. We do not often judge a painting by its title, nor, if we are as careful as we ought to be, by a catalog's explication of it: when we operate in the world of painting, it is the painting that is primary and the word that is secondary. In the truly collaborative work, as in the unbiased comparison of the arts, both text and artwork would be seen as semiological series of different orders that must be given related signification or a plurality of related significations by the reader/viewer.

Since the purpose of this discussion is not only to emphasize the extent to which the arts influence one another but also to bring into relief the prejudices we might bring to any comparison and the responsibility of the critic to substantiate, in fact to justify, his bringing together an artist and a writer in one breath, we can best begin by emphasizing that Duncan's poem cannot be dealt with coherently if we arbitrarily insist that it is illustrated by both Duchamp's urinal and Van Eyck's *Crucifixion*. To do so is like trying to see a tunnel and a suspended square at once. Beyond this problem of conflicting perceptions, we face a more basic one: we seem to be taking unjustified liberties if we choose to put the Duncan poem beside either the Duchamp ready-made or the Van Eyck painting. The illustration dictates our perception of the poem and, in fact, changes the meaning of the text Duncan wrote, which stands without illustration in the context of a series of poems about the creation of poetry. In choosing what to compare when discussing the interrelations of the arts, the critic wields a great deal of power and should, it would seem, yield to an equal measure of caution. Not all methods of comparison stand up equally under scrutiny; not all methods respect the autonomy of systems of signification when describing the affiliation of these same systems.

III

In his poem "Description without Place," Wallace Stevens tells us that "Description is revelation. It is not / The thing described, nor false facsimile."[9] "Description" and "The thing described" maintain their autonomy in that they belong to two separate series, each of which operates according to its own structural laws. At the same time, however, an affiliation, an equality of interchange, between these series prevents one from being the "false facsimile" of the other. We begin to see here the "production of a new language" and the "focusing on new readings" that Laude sees in modern art and literature. Magritte's *L'Usage de la parole* 1 (1928-29), in which a carefully painted pipe stands above the words "Ceci n'est pas une pipe," makes something of the same point as Stevens's "Description without Place," save that Magritte would substitute the word *representation* for *description*, in Stevens's formulation.[10] Magritte breaks down three mimetic contracts in this work in order to show these separate but parallel semiologic systems: the painted pipe is not the thing itself; the thing itself is not the word *pipe*; the word *pipe* is not the painted pipe. In breaking down these mimetic contracts (and the implicit acceptance of the "false facsimile"), Magritte focuses on painting and language as systems of signs that operate by their own conventions. They share at least two common characteristics: they are both elements of general human semiology, and, by virtue of this fact, in their very expression they necessarily remake the world. This continual reconstruction is, after all, the point of a poem like Stevens's "Sea Surface Full of Clouds," and it is more radically expressed in Magritte's two *La Clef des songes* (1930 and 1936), in which various mundane images are given new names—a painted egg is labeled acacia (or vice versa, depending upon one's artistic chauvinism).

When artistic collaborations are most successful, it is generally the case that both artists recognize the revelatory power of both their own and the other's media. If they recognize that they can neither represent nor describe the other's work—but only re-create it, "make it new," as Pound would say—the probability that either art will usurp the authority of the other is diminished. Critics who compare the arts are implicated in the same revelatory game, and it is to criticism—and its methods and the contexts it creates to compare the arts—that we should now like to turn the discussion. For as critics of the arts and their interrelations we too often act as if we believe that what we describe *is* the thing described, that our work *is* a kind of false facsimile (just as we too often allow ourselves to treat an image or text as mere representation or description). We forget that we too are "making it new," forging our own myth, as Lévi-Strauss would have it. The following chart traces the ways in which, as critics, we manage to connect the arts. Some of the connections traced here seem to lead to solid ground, to myths we find more or less tenable and hence to the luxury of allowing ourselves to ignore their mythic qualities; others lead to the vast territory of *trompe-l'oeil*, myths we recognize as such and thereby must reject or treat with extreme caution.

If the ideal collaborative work (relation A) is one in which equal status is given to the arts, then it would seem safe to assume that when we are dealing with an interdisciplinary work that is created by one artist who does both the writing and the artwork we have one aesthetic expressed in two modes. These systems of signs remained distinct, although they are joined in the signification of the artist's

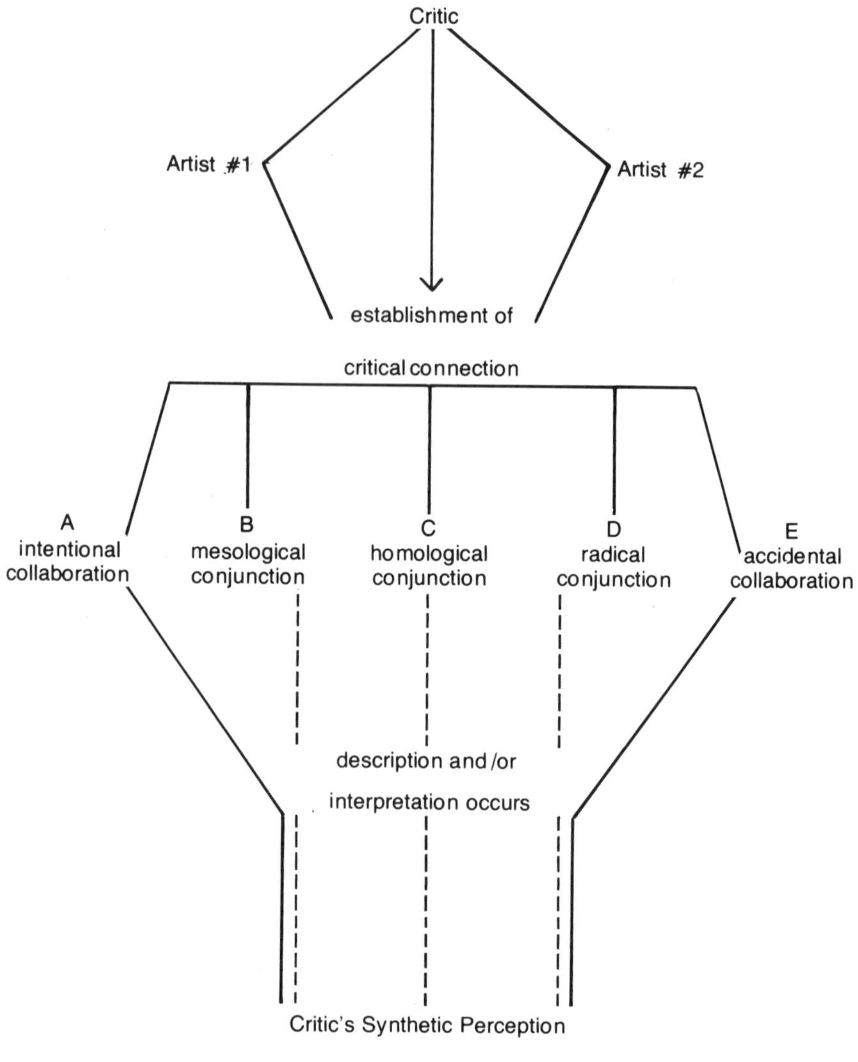
Critic
Artist #1
Artist #2
establishment of
critical connection
A
intentional
collaboration
B
mesological
conjunction
C
homological
conjunction
D
radical
conjunction
E
accidental
collaboration
description and/or
interpretation occurs
Critic's Synthetic Perception

aesthetic. We may, in fact, find the artist adept and inventive in terms of one poetic and inept and derivative in terms of a second. In short, affiliation of the arts allows us to begin to define his aesthetic, while their autonomy allows us to assess his poetics.

Georges Braque's *Illustrated Notebooks 1917-1955* are an example of an interdisciplinary artwork created by one artist. Here the two modes of art seem to complement one another particularly well. Braque writes in his notebook: "Pour moi, il ne s'agit plus de métaphore mais de métamorphose" (For me, it is no longer a question of metaphor, but of metamorphosis).[11] In the center and to one side of the page, we see a vase filled with leaves that combine to form the shape of a flower. An abstract design below the vase suggests either a table or roots sprouting. The vase itself becomes a tree, which is a flower. In the design, the leaves (les feuilles) become a flower, just as on the pages (les feuilles) the designs flower. By means of verbal pun, the design is given depth. At the same time, the verbal message is given a self-referential, plastic quality: across the bottom of the page the word *métaphore* grows and extends itself into the word *métamorphose*. Braque's plastic poetic creates a design that can be read in various ways (leaves/flower: vase/stem: table/roots); his verbal poetic creates both mimetic and self-referential possibilities for the words *métaphor/métamorphose*. In Braque's *Notebooks* text and pen and ink drawings express by means of two different poetics his aesthetic (reality as metamorphic): they are not the aesthetic itself, nor are they false facsimile. Braque's *Notebooks* are, in fact, an example of an almost ideal criticism, for, insofar as they stand as *explications de l'oeuvre* and not the *oeuvre* itself, they allow neither image nor word to usurp the authority of the other. To paraphrase Roland Barthes, they create the "scene" of criticism: a plurality of textual signifiers in which the pluralism of the text is heightened by simultaneously partaking of two discontinuous systems of signs. In short, Braque's *Notebooks* self-consciously render image and word as *a single text*.

But insofar as the *Notebooks* are indeed Braque's *oeuvre* itself, and insofar as we are self-conscious of the distance between that *oeuvre* and our criticism of it, the *Notebooks'* critical ideality is inaccessible. The critic can use them only as a kind of hinge between his word and Braque's work, a hinge that is admittedly useful because it provides the critic with both the authority and the vocabulary by which he can turn from Braque's largely plastic "text" into his own largely verbal one. But like Braque, the critic must recognize that criticism is no longer a question of metaphor but of metamorphosis. The critic must acknowledge that he is remaking the text. Then, and only then, does Braque's ideal criticism begin to become accessible again, for if the critic self-consciously remakes the text, then he is likewise implicated in the text's game.

This is a difficult—but important—point, and we would like to clarify it by briefly remaking a text ourselves, the intentional collaboration of Braque and René Char in the 1963 revised edition of *Lettera amorosa*. The poem itself had been written by Char in 1953, but when it appeared with Braque's illustrations in the revised edition it had been rewritten and augmented. As Thomas Hines notes in his essay on *Lettera amorosa*: "[Braque] himself singled out *Lettera amorosa* as the one poem of Char's that he particularly wanted to rework with the poet."[12] *Lettera amorosa* is structurally a series of poetic fragments interspersed with a series of lithographs. The first thing we notice about the lithographs is that they do not give us visual, mimetic representations of the words in the text. The converse is, of course, also true—the poem never simply describes the lithographs. Rather, the poem and the illustrations work together to create the "letter" (and the semiotic ambiguity here, the leveling of image and word to semiotic equivalence, is certainly intentional).

The "letter" is addressed to a "loved one" who is a woman, artistic inspiration, the occasional rare harmony between being and the cosmos it inhabits, and finally, if we allow ourselves the liberty of assuming that as a text the letter is in part addressed to ourselves, to the ideal harmony between reader and "text." The work as a whole revolves around the idea of the presence or absence of the "loved one" and around the effect this presence or absence has on the artist. Both the poem and the lithos work to show the modulations of the relationship. The work is composed in such a way that we do not always find a fragment of poetry with a litho facing it. Often a lithograph serves as an intermediate connection between the subjective states depicted in two consecutive fragments of poetry, or a fragment of poetry mediates the subjective states depicted in consecutive lithographs. For example, Char writes at the top of the left-hand page: "Qui n'a pas rêvé, en flanant sur le boulevard / des villes, d'un monde qui, au lieu de commencer / avec la parole, débuterait avec les intentions?" (Who has not dreamed, strolling along the boulevards of cities, of a world which, instead of beginning arbitrarily with the word, might start from intentions?).[13] The poet dreams of the immediacy of presence (intention captured whole in the actual) during the period of absence (when the word or signifier does not capture the signified but rather disseminates it as a field of continual substitutions that point to absence rather than presence).[14] At the bottom of the same page, we read: "Quel mouvement hostile t'accapare? Ta / personne se hâte, ton baiser disparaît. L'un / avec les inventions de l'autre, sans départ, / multipliant les sillages" (What hostile movement distracts you? Your person hurries, your kiss—gone. One in complicity with the other, without distinguishing, multiplying their wakes).[15] Here we see not presence but its trace, its "wake." The movement toward absence ("hurries") *is* absence ("gone"). The poet evokes the disappearance of the loved one, the loss that is her absence. On the right-hand page, placed across from the space that separates these poetic fragments, is Braque's mediating lithograph, done in dark pink, pink, and orange. Two birds are in vertical flight toward one another. They are caught at the moment when their beaks meet. The lithograph captures the transiency and the intensity of the moment when lover and beloved are together; the fragments of poetry express desire for presence, but they are written during a period of absence. Char evokes the dream and the memory, Braque the fullness of presence. And the key word here is *evokes*, because it not only implies the longing to "call up" an absence into presence to which Char's poetry testifies here, but also points to the duplicity of Braque's lithograph; that is, Braque's litho is an evocation of presence, not presence itself. Char and Braque are certainly cognizant of this duplicity, for at other moments in their text it is Char who evokes presence and Braque its desire or memory. They share a common aesthetic in that they define reality as that presence which must be continually re-created. The poetic each demonstrates shows the "letter" (whether image or word) as a sign that intends, or is addressed to, that floating signified which can never be captured by either semiological series but is strongly evoked by their interchanges.

Where then, in this modulation between presence and absence, does presence lie if, as it seems, presence is only the evocation of presence (which is to say absence)? The "presence" of *Lettera amorosa* exists only insofar as we have responded (*are* responding) to the "address" of its "letter." *Lettera amorosa* is, in short, a writerly (*scriptible*) text; the plurality of its systems of signifiers (plastic and verbal) achieve the "dream" of presence only in the immediacy of our participation in it.[16] The plastic and verbal modes do not speak to us in the same way, but they do speak to us of the same aesthetic. We partake of these artistic inventions, multiplying the text's plurality by implicating our own text in its wake. Lithograph, poem, criticism—*a single text*.

IV

The critical possibilities we have developed in terms of intentional collaborations become much more problematic in the contexts of the other conjunctions and collaborative ventures that we have suggested in the chart. When a critic is dealing with individual works that never were intended to complement one another, but which have been produced in a common creative milieu, he is making a mesological comparison (relation B)—that is, a comparison that brings an artist and a writer together on the basis of their friendship or mutual participation in a particular artistic movement. Movements like Dadaism and Surrealism were interdisciplinary at their inception and demand that the critic deal with the disparate arts. All too often, however, the desire to give a sense of unity to the disparate results in a series of critical expressions that ignore their own mythic quality and must be exposed as myths. Roger Shattuck's *The Banquet Years*, which is by and large a very useful study, especially in its biographical richness, demonstrates this problem:

> It was a fortunate day for the arts when the rich Spanish genius of Picasso, the steady French logic of Braque, the mystical Jewish intensity of Jacob, and the all-encompassing cosmopolitan lyricism of Apollinaire joined forces in the "central laboratory" of Montmartre. For each of them, this early period of exchange provided a lasting stimulus and a knowledge of the fundamental unity of the arts.[17]

Expressions like "Spanish genius," "French logic," "mystical Jewish intensity," and "cosmopolitan lyricism" are all combined here to "define" something that Shattuck calls "the fundamental unity of the arts." While we would not deny Shattuck's sense that these writers and painters share in a communal effort to translate their era, this kind of "criticism" lacks awareness of its own duplicity. For implicit in Shattuck's internalized generalizations is the belief that Cubist art speaks to all the world, that it is a truly all-encompassing art. This is patent nonsense. It is like Lévi-Strauss universalizing the Oedipal myth, although he had the sense to say his "book on myths is itself a kind of myth."[18] As a system of signs, Cubism (either literary or plastic) speaks only to those who know either its conventions or those conventions that it parodies. Shattuck has attempted here to make a generalized aesthetic (Cubism) into a unified poetic for all the arts; because he believes he is "describing," not "remaking," the Cubist moment, he has lost the ability to recognize his own presence in the dialogue, and he has consequently lost the possibility of identifying his own prejudices within it.

Shattuck's "central laboratory" of Montmartre does, however, represent one kind of mesological study that seems quite valuable: the exploration of the ambiguous network of relationships that evolve within a common creative milieu. This kind of study does allow us to look at the various poetics that were developed in this common milieu, various semiologic structures that translated a common cultural series. Each poetic, though self-enclosed and self-propelled, was created not in isolation from but in relation to other systems of signs. We can define the Cubist aesthetic by examining the interchanges between the poetics. A second kind of mesological study involves the examination of signed manifestos that purport to state a common aesthetic for the different arts, a common ideology for the artists. These two kinds of mesological studies are based on different assumptions, as Laude has shown: "An inquiry into the first is begun not by attending to [any] specific *corpus* with fixed norms nor to any previously defined doctrine but rather to a text which it produces. An inquiry into the second is guided by and contained by principles declared authoritatively and resolutely" (p. 475). If we have outlined the dangers of the first approach, the dangers of the second are greater. A group of signatures attached to a manifesto, for instance, may show revolutionary solidarity rather than a common aesthetic, and the tenets expressed in manifestos are often noisy and ambiguous. Fillipo Marinetti writes in the "Manifesto of Futurism 1909": "The poet must spend himself with ardour, splendour, and generosity, to swell the enthusiastic fervour of the primordial elements."[19] *Primordial* here suggests the same mythic assumptions that we discovered in Shattuck's description of "the unity of the arts," but the dangers of our falling into its trap are greater in that we are tempted to use Marinetti's statement as a hinge between the plastic and the verbal, since it ostensibly applies to both. At any rate, neither Shattuck's anecdotal definition of Cubism nor Marinetti's windy manifesto helps us very much in arriving at any formulation of what significant structures suggest a dialectic of exchange between the plastic and verbal arts in a common milieu.

At times, interdisciplinary criticism brings together an artist and a writer whose affinity is not substantiated by a common work or a common cultural milieu. The homological comparison (relation C) grows out of a critic's subjective perception of a similarity between a plastic and a poetic work. It seems to us that this sort of comparison is the most difficult to substantiate because it is the most subjective and because it may well use the power of one art to influence our reading of a second and in the process misrepresent one or both of the arts. It is the homological comparison in Mario Praz's *Mnemosyne* that Svetlana and Paul Alpers deplore in their article "*Ut Pictura Noesis?* Criticism in Literary Studies and Art History":

> Something is badly wrong when a man as intelligent as Mario Praz compares the cupola, as the crowning feature of a church, with the couplets that conclude the *ottava rima* stanza and the Shakespearean sonnet. In order to make such comparisons, fixed likenesses must be assumed in such elusive and problematic phenomena as form, structure, and harmony. Surely the game is not worth the candle. The arts differ profoundly in their conditions and "languages" (also in their developments and national histories . . .).[20]

The problem here, in simple terms, is that the Alpers see Praz juxtaposing different conventions in ways that allow him to call something "a tunnel" when it could just as well, and with drastically different results, be called "a suspended square." The homological comparison is risky because it allows us to create arbitrary contexts that bring together, for example, Duncan's "Descriptions of imaginary poetries" and Van Eyck's *Crucifixion*. If we had chosen to illustrate the Duncan poem with a Josef Albers painting, something not unlike the geometric design with which we began, we might be able to build a substantial framework for discussion: both took part in the Black Mountain experiment, both may be demonstrating by means of different poetics a shared aesthetic. Without this substantial framework, we might well end up with distortion in the place of explication. We have placed the homological comparison in the middle of the chart because it most clearly demonstrates the presence of a comparison that may well simply mask an absence: the *trompe-l'oeil* of the center.

Relation D on the chart is a context that compares the arts and literature diachronically and has been labeled a radical conjunction, for lack of a better word. In a comparative study of this sort, we find that a writer and an artist use their different media to represent the same, older source. The study is substantiated on the ground of a third element, which both artists explore; that is, the arts are compared to one another insofar as they both illustrate a similar theme. We expect neither a unified poetic nor a dialectic of interchange between poetics here. Rather, this sort of study informs the historical view of a third issue. An example of this sort of conjunction might be a study that included Botticelli's *Birth of Venus* and Pound's description of the birth of beauty in "Canto IV." Botticelli could not have been aware of Pound's work, obviously, but he certainly was aware of his own Christian culture. That Pound is treating the same mythological subject is shown by the detail he gives:

> The silver mirrors catch the bright stones and flare
> Dawn, to our waking, drifts in the green, cool light;
> Dew-haze blurs, in the grass, pale ankles moving,
> Beat, beat, whirr, thud, in the soft turf
> under the apple trees,
> Choros nympharum, goat-foot, with pale foot alternate;
> Crescent of blue-shot waters, green-gold in the shallows,
> A black cock crows in the sea-foam . . .[21]

We find here dawn, or creation; apple trees, sacred to Venus; the crescent, sickle with which Zeus castrated Kronos; sea-foam, the origin of Venus. Pound was, of course, familiar with Botticelli's *Birth of Venus*, but whether he was consciously trying to describe or interpret Botticelli's work is debatable, even beside the point. The solid ground for the critic in this radical context is the essentially diachronic study of the way in which the writer and the artist, each working within his own aesthetic and with his own separate poetic, interprets a third motif. The danger lies in forgetting that this third motif must act as mediator between the arts and that, as critic, the person who makes this radical comparison is "re-inventing" the diachronic history of that third motif.

Finally, we have works in which the two arts are brought together by one of the artists who chooses to re-present or illustrate the work of the other: Picasso has done illustrations of Ovid's *Metamorphoses*; Maillol has illustrated Virgil's *Eclogues* and *Georgics*. This kind of collaboration (relation E) we have labeled accidental, because one of the artists was not consulted about the collaboration. Of such a collaborative venture, Laude says: "The poet may choose his illustrator only from the ranks of living painters. The same does not hold true for the painter" (p. 484). Laude is, we believe, mistaken. Comparatists have studied many accidental collaborations in which the poet has chosen his illustrator from the dead. William Carlos Williams chooses to re-present Brueghel's *Fall of Icarus* in his poem "Landscape with the Fall of Icarus." Auden re-presents this same painting in his poem "Musée des Beaux Arts." Here, the critic finds his interdisciplinary study is substantiated, on a basic level, by the fact that one artist has chosen to align himself with another. The study we are asked to make is diachronic, and often cross-cultural. The problem the Alpers detailed as the plague of homological studies—that the arts differ in their conditions, languages, developments, and national histories—has surfaced on the more substantial ground of accidental collaboration: a context that has become, perhaps, the most important one in recent decades. It is one of the best ways to trace that anxiety known as influence through one generation of artists to the next, as Baudelaire's *Les Fleurs du mal*, for instance, is illustrated first by Rodin, then by Rouault, and finally by Robert Motherwell. This sort of collaboration, which is also conscious re-creation, is prevalent within disciplines as well as between them: Picasso re-creates Velázquez's *Las Meninas*; Borges's Pierre Menard re-writes the *Quixote*; the literature of exhaustion is, at base, parodic. Accidental collaboration is a paradoxical context for the critic, but it is a context that demands he create a new language and a new focus. All the strengths and dangers of the other forms of comparison are brought to bear in our attempts to deal with the accidental collaboration: it underscores the sense of our own implication in the work of art that we feel when we are dealing with intentionally collaborative works and brings to the fore the subjectivity of our own implication as we recognize the almost inevitable parodic nature of our own critique. Most to the point, however, this final sort of collaboration forces us to deal with the arts as autonomous and affiliated. We recognize most fully here the tendency of interdisciplinary studies to confuse aesthetics with poetics. Braque says in his *Notebooks*: "Il n'est en art qu'une chose qui vaille: Celle que l'on ne peut expliquer" (In art there is only one thing that counts: the thing you can't explain).[22] It seems to us that this statement does not close the door on criticism but rather opens it to a new direction, one that would reveal those "common structures" which all arts contain while respecting the difference among the arts and the essential openness of that *single text* (art, literature, criticism) which, continually, is being recreated.

1. Emile Bernard, *Souvenirs sur Paul Cézanne* (Paris: Société des Trente—Albert Messein, 1912), p. 36.

2. Jean Laude, "On the Analysis of Poems and Paintings," *New Literary History* 3 (Spring 1972): 471. Subsequent references to Laude's essay appear in parentheses in the text.

3. Serge Doubrovsky, *The New Criticism in France*, trans. Derek Coltman (Chicago: University of Chicago Press, 1973), p. 23.

4. Seymour Chatman, *Approaches to Poetics* (New York: Columbia University Press, 1973), p. vii.

5. Daniel-Henry Kahnweiler cites Gris's use of these terms in his *Juan Gris: His Life and Work*, 2d rev. ed. (New York: Abrams, 1969), pp. 140-41. See also Christopher Gray, *Cubist*

Aesthetic Theories (Baltimore, Md.: Johns Hopkins University Press, 1953), pp. 98-99.

6. Virgil C. Aldrich, *Philosophy of Art* (Englewood Cliffs, N.J.: Prentice-Hall, 1963), p. 20.

7. Robert Duncan, *Derivations: Selected Poems 1950-1956* (London: Fulcrum Press, 1968), p. 30.

8. As an aside, we might mention that this sort of lurid, gratuitous illustration becomes more interesting—and annoying—when we see it on the American edition of Robbe-Grillet's *Le Voyeur*. Perhaps Robbe-Grillet intentionally arouses the same expectations the consumer generally attaches to novels like those of Harold Robbins or Jacqueline Susann, only to undercut these expectations by the sophistication of his text.

9. *The Collected Poems of Wallace Stevens* (New York: Knopf, 1965), p. 344.

10. There is a full and interesting discussion of Magritte's "Use of Words" in Suzi Gablik, *Magritte* (Boston: New York Graphic Society, 1976), pp. 126-44. Nelson Goodman, in his *Languages of Art: An Approach to a Theory of Symbols* (New York: Bobbs-Merrill, 1968), also argues that representation and description are, by definition, disengaged from mere mimetic reproduction or mirroring (see especially chapter 1, "Reality Remade," pp. 3-43).

11. Georges Braque, *Illustrated Notebooks 1917-1955*, trans. Stanley Appelbaum (New York: Dover, 1971), p. 99.

12. Thomas Hines, "L'Ouvrage de tous les temps admiré," *Bulletin du Bibliophile*, no. 1 (1973), p. 43.

13. René Char, *Lettera amorosa* (Geneva: Edwin Engleberts, 1963), p. 30. English translation by Jackson Matthews, *Hypnos Waking* (New York: Random House, 1956), p. 235.

14. The broadest discussion of this phenomenon is Jacques Derrida's "Structure, Sign and Play in the Discourse of the Human Sciences," *The Structuralist Controversy: The Languages of Criticism and the Sciences of Man*, ed. Richard Macksey and Eugenio Donato (Baltimore, Md.: Johns Hopkins University Press, 1970), pp. 247-72.

15. Char, *Lettera amorosa*, p. 30. Our translation.

16. Roland Barthes develops the distinction between the readerly (*lisible*) and the writerly (*scriptible*) at the beginning of *S/Z*, trans. Richard Miller (New York: Hill and Wang, 1974).

17. Roger Shattuck, *The Banquet Years* (New York: Vintage, 1955), p. 256.

18. Claude Lévi-Strauss, *The Raw and the Cooked: Introduction to a Science of Mythology*, vol. 1, trans. John and Doreen Weightman (New York: Harper Torchbooks, 1969), p. 6.

19. Filippo Marinetti, *Futurist Manifestos*, ed. Umbro Apollonio (New York: Viking, 1973), p. 21.

20. Svetlana and Paul Alpers, "*Ut Pictura Noesis?* Criticism in Literary Studies and Art History," *New Literary History* 3 (Spring 1972): 457-58.

21. *The Cantos of Ezra Pound (1-95)* (New York: New Directions, 1956), p. 13.

22. Braque, *Notebooks*, p. 13.

Literature, Film and Music, Myth

Stumbling on a Smooth Road: Silent Film Comedy and Beckett's *Nouvelles*

Fred M. Robinson

University of Massachusetts

HUGH KENNER has noted that the actions in Samuel Beckett's *nouvelles* owe much to silent film comedy.[1] This is an investigation into the nature of that analogy, in order that we may understand the mechanism of Beckett's narrative strategies, the mechanism of silent film comedy, and how both of these mechanisms are comic. Comedy, then, is our embracing subject, within which this analogy will be elaborated, and the comedy of walking will be the initial focus of that elaboration.

The action of Beckett's stories begins with the protagonist "I" falling down the front steps of what might be his home.[2] What is comical about falling? You are rapidly forced from one context to another, from the logic of habitual procedure (the mechanism of walking) to the state of simply *being there*, all procedures canceled. You have taken part in what Chekhov called the human fate of stumbling on a smooth road.[3] The world, in its being there, is a perfectly natural place; only human beings, in their strange and tilting locomotion, find the world difficult because it fails to conform itself to the logical needs of that locomotion.

Walking is, for Beckett, emblematic of logic: his characters find both to be tedious, if fascinating, tasks and maintain them tenaciously even while giving them up gladly. The protagonist of the *nouvelles* is content to fall, but carries his power of reasoning through the very process of falling:

> Even as I fell I heard the door slam, which brought me a little comfort, in the midst of my fall. For that meant they were not pursuing me down into the street, with a stick, to beat me in full view of the passers-by. For if that had been their intention they would not have shut the door, but left it open, so that the persons assembled in the vestibule might enjoy my chastisement and be edified. So, for once, they had confined themselves to throwing me out and no more about it. I had time, before coming to rest in the gutter, to conclude this piece of reasoning.[4]

The mind reasons, indeed more hectically, even as the body follows its own laws, and so the comedy of the narrative is sustained. There is a world outside into which one may fall, and there is the tenuous world of walking, and these two worlds clash, as if the latter were a harmless foray into the former. This comedy is expressed above in the discrepancy between banal event and elegant language.

The steps, what one falls *from*, occupy Beckett's protagonist at the very outset of the first story, "The Expelled": "There were not many steps. . . . The fall was therefore not serious" (pp. 9-10). There was a given number of steps, but what was the number?

> I have never known whether you should say one with your foot on the sidewalk, two with the following foot on the first step, and so on, or whether the sidewalk shouldn't count. At the top of the steps I fell foul of the same dilemma. In the other direction, I mean from top to bottom, it was the same, the word is not too strong. I did not know where to begin nor where to end, that's the truth of the matter. (P. 9)

Once you have decided whether or not to include the sidewalk, on the way up or on the way down, the logic of counting, the procedure, is easily established. But the "dilemma" is that "a pre-established arbitrary"[5] shadows the procedure. Surrounding the earnestness of purposive behavior is the capriciousness of play. "I arrived therefore at three totally different figures, without ever knowing which of them was right" (p. 9). The "therefore" is important here: if you fail to assume the arbitrary (saying, let's start with *this* step) and pursue logic carefully, you eventually reason to the arbitrary (saying, pick a number, any one of three). To reason this through is to doubt the process of reasoning:

> So you must not think of certain things, of those that are dear to you, or rather you must think of them, for if you don't there is the danger of finding them, in your mind, little by little. That is to say, you must think of them for a while, a good while, every day several times a day, until they sink forever in the mud. That's an order. (P. 9)

"That's an order" is, of course, both imperative and declarative in mood. You are enjoined to reason things through—in Beckett's locomotive vocabulary, to "go on"—by the imperative voice that haunts the ruins of all Beckett's protagonists. You are also simply told that all this reasoning through *is* an order, and order is necessary if we are to proceed—with a life, with a narrative.

For the "steps" are also the steps of a narrative, which has an arbitrary beginning and end. Most narratives conceal the arbitrary nature of this so that the procedure (scene two follows scene one, etc.) can be established as natural. Beckett stresses the arbitrary in order to expose the mechanism of the procedure, the unnatural quality of its ordering. "After all," he begins his second paragraph, "it is not the number of steps that matters" (p. 10). What matters is that something has begun and is going on.

We begin, then, with a fall. So the Christian myth goes: the expulsion from the garden, the Fall from static Paradise into Time—Time conceived, that is, as *Kronos*, a series of points on a line that leads to death. The notions of going on and falling are inextricable aspects of one central comedy; they depend on and define one another. To be born is to fall. We fall into going on, and going on is itself a falling. If you didn't get expelled (from home, from a room, from the womb) you would neither fall nor go on, and there would be no life in time, no narrative, no story.

The Expelled, still fallen, rests his elbow on the sidewalk, settles his ear in the cup of his hand and begins to "reflect" on his situation. It is this quality of "reasoning" that suggests Buster Keaton, the protagonist as logician in an arbitrary world. "So, for once, they had confined themselves to throwing me out and no more about it. I had time, before coming to rest in the gutter, to conclude this piece of reasoning." We can visualize the meditative, seemingly impassive face pursuing its pleasures in the midst of the violent and unforeseeable contingencies of the body, the object in its struggle with other objects. The rest on the sidewalk does not last long. The door slams again, rousing the protagonist to "a whole landscape . . . taking form . . . most dreamlike." He braces himself for flight, like a runner at his mark. His hat sails toward him; they had evidently opened the door to throw it to him. He grabs it midflight and puts it on. Hats are, for Beckett, the signs and talismans of consciousness, or that aspect of consciousness issued to us as an inheritance from the "outer world." The Expelled recalls his father's buying him a hat: "Come, son, we are going to buy your hat, as though it had pre-existed from time immemorial in a pre-established place" (p. 11). It is significant that he now receives his hat while braced for going on; he puts it on and sets off, on everyone's journey for rest. Our motion through time, like the process of reasoning, is circumscribed by the stasis of beginning and end that is another beginning, premise and conclusion that is another premise. His hat, we learn later in "The End," the last of the three *nouvelles*, is a Chaplinesque bowler.

> I set off. What a gait. Stiffness of the lower limbs, as if nature had denied me knees, extraordinary splaying of the feet to right and left of the line of march. The trunk, on the contrary, as if by the effect of a compensatory mechanism, was as flabby as an old ragbag, tossing wildly to the unpredictable jolts of the pelvis. (P. 13)

This is walking as comic mechanism. All great comics have funny walks: Keaton's lean that barely connects pronation, particularly when he is on the trail of something; Chaplin's splay-footed rocking; Beckett's Watt's "funambulistic stagger,"[6] Groucho's barely "compensatory" inclination. What is called to attention is the problem of ambulatory motion itself, as a mechanistic disturbance of rest. Walking is, after all, comprised largely of compensatory mechanisms, and the gait of the Expelled is only a stylization of the procedure. All of this visual comedy serves as an analysis of the problem of setting off, of sustaining an equilibrium to prevent a fall. So it is with the motion of the Expelled as he proceeds through his paces. So it is with the motion of the narrative, the story as something told, through the process of completing itself. Both motions, of character and narrative, are simultaneous in Beckett's use of the first person as narrator/character. The interplay of the two is the life of these texts, and the major source of their comedy.

The source of pleasure in comedy is its boon of harmlessness. Pain and suffering are experienced, but never finally or continuously. Something there is that is indomitable and continuous, that makes pain and suffering an irritable sequence in a larger rhythm.[7] Don Quixote, for example, may suffer terrible mishaps, physical beatings, and humiliations, but his eyes are focused on something more distant (the incorrupt Dulcinea), and that is the source, as even Don Quixote realizes, of his absurd strength—as it is of Chaplin's, though what Charlie's vision is focused on is more mysterious. Beckett's protagonists suffer extraordinarily but speak of their sufferings calmly and reasonably, with the unquenchable rhetoric of ratiocination, as if their somatic life was something apart from their awareness of it. Beckett creates this comic tension by realizing analytically the mechanisms of conventional first-person narration. Such narration assumes the identity of narrator and character: *I* will tell you what happened to *me*, so that you will think it *is* happening to me. Beckett begins "The Expelled" with a discussion of beginnings, endings and steps, designing a metaphor to connect writer/speaker and character. He then typically inserts comments in the narrative that bring us out of the historical past in which the "I" character is making his diurnal rounds, and into the abstract "present" in which dwells the "I" as narrator: "When my father died I could have got rid of his hat, there was nothing more to prevent me, but not I. But how describe it? Some other time, some other time" (p. 11). Or, "I have always greatly admired the door of this house, up on top of its little flight of steps. How describe it?" and "So much for that description" (p. 12). The effect is to make the action seem something remembered from the vantage of whimsical and reasoning detachment, of "recollecting these emotions, with the celebrated advantage of tranquility" (p. 23). These are not unusual strategies for establishing a storytelling retrospection. But Beckett never merely uses conventions, he subjects them to an analytical rigor, here expressing the disjunction of narrator and character as a comic contradiction. Beckett's chimerical "I" is composed of the body of an existing character and the head of a meditator/reflector/narrator that views the exigencies and tribulations of the body with a kind of Keatonesque impassive surprise.

Who, then, is this "I" who can say at the end of "The Expelled,"

> Dawn was just breaking. I did not know where I was. I made towards the rising sun, towards where I thought it would rise, the quicker to come into the light. I would have liked a sea horizon, or a desert one. When I am abroad in the morning, I go to meet the sun, and in the evening, when I am abroad, I follow it, till I am down among the dead. I don't know why I told this story. I could just as well have told another. Perhaps some other time, I'll be able to tell another. Living souls, you will see how alike they are. (P. 25)

The Expelled has just gone through a day and a night and is about to begin another. Here, at the end, he speaks to us from a "present" vantage, as a storyteller, and declares that the same story has occurred again and again, that all his stories are alike, each involving the disruption of stasis into motion, and the tropism of motion toward rest. From what "tranquility" is he recollecting all this?

We turn the page to the second story, "The Calmative," and encounter this opening declaration: "I don't know when I died." This makes more or less conventional narrative sense if we assume that the "I" speaks from an omniscient sphere, is distinct from himself as character, can discuss the character's death. It seems to be an immortal mind reconstructing the steps taken by a body it once occupied. If that's so, then it can narrate these steps, these "stumblings on the distant earth" (p. 27), through to an end. Indeed, it says that "this story . . . aspires to be the last" (p. 35); and later, when hearing steps die away, it says, "How tell what remains. But it's the end" (p. 43). But it's not, the narrative goes on, and in the next story, confidently entitled "The End," the "I" says it "understood then that the end was near, at least fairly near" (p. 47); then later, still confident, says, "I knew it would soon be the end" (p. 69), only to declare, finally, that it "*might* have told" a story, "a story in the likeness of my life, I mean without the courage to end or the strength to go on" (p. 72). As long as the mind exists and can keep on telling stories about itself, then it cannot complete its autobiography. Mind is dependent on body. If the mind only reflected upon itself, what would it say? In order to prove to itself that it exists, it tells stories, conjuring a landscape, a bodily character, a going on.

"I don't know when I died," if it makes any sense, assumes a distinction between the first "I" and the second, between the timeless "I" as narrator and the "I" as a character in time. But if these are identical, if the narrator is telling the story of his life, then the above statement is absurd, because if the "I" can narrate, can *say*, then it exists, must necessarily be one "step" ahead of the progress of the narrative about itself. So the story cannot end, nor the narrator die.

In "The Calmative," the "I" says,

> I'm too frustrated this evening to listen to myself rot, waiting for the great red lapses of the heart. . . . So I'll tell myself a story, I'll try and tell myself another story, to try and calm myself. (P. 27)

If he can tell a story, he can, like Malone in Beckett's trilogy of novels, transport himself from his present condition and imagine himself as an omniscient mind, beyond the "physical fiasco" (a phrase from Beckett's *Murphy*). In this way, the story functions as a "calmative." But how can he calm himself if he *is* the character he conjures in his story?

> once up, propped against the wall, I wondered if I could go on, I mean up, propped against the wall. Impossible to go out and walk. (P. 28)

He is brought to life again, made to proceed, painfully, in a narrative.

> I speak as though it all happened yesterday. Yesterday indeed is recent, but not enough. For what I tell this evening is passing this evening, at this passing hour. (P. 28)

Even though he'll "tell [his] story in the past, none the less, as though it were a myth, or an old fable" (p. 28), it is happening *now*, as something going on. As he says later, having set himself as character into mechanical motion, "For me now the setting forth, the struggle and perhaps the return, for the old man I am this evening, older than my father ever was, older than I shall ever be" (p. 30). It is *now* that the setting forth takes place, the journey once more recalled, the protagonist agelessly old, pulling himself "forward with the help of boughs" (p. 28).

The calm of the narrative, then, is simultaneous with the pain of reliving what one keeps hoping will come to rest. Beckett's later narratives are also dual in nature; his *nouvelles* anticipate and help clarify the voices of the trilogy. Molloy, in the first novel of the trilogy, describes the paradox most clearly:

> My life, my life, now I speak of it as something over, now as of a joke which still goes on, and it is neither, for at the same time it is over and it goes on, and is there any tense for that?[8]

It is over, and so one can calmly recollect it in tranquility. And yet it is *not* over, something is going on, a voice is "only crying out as I have always cried out."[9] None of Beckett's protagonists, from the *nouvelles* on, can cease to live.

With this dual narration, Beckett can elaborate his peculiar silent comedy, in which a voiceless protagonist journeys across an alien landscape while his thoughts are given to us in a kind of detached voice-over. This voice both describes to us the problems encountered in the world—"I longed to be under cover again, in an empty place, close and warm" (p. 52)—and conveys to us the tranquil, reasonable calm that transcends these problems, a calm that in silent film comedy is embodied in the face of Keaton or in the charming grace of the Chaplin tramp. This passage is from "The End" and is precisely Chaplinesque:

> In the days that followed I visited several lodgings, without much success. They usually slammed the door in my face, even when I showed my money and offered to pay a week in advance, or even two. It was in vain I put on my best manners, smiled and spoke distinctly, they

> slammed the door in my face before I could even finish my little speech. It was at this time I perfected a method of doffing my hat at once courteous and discreet, neither servile nor insolent. (P. 52)

The pain of circumstance is transformed by a grace above contingency. What Beckett describes here Chaplin can act out, and it is the silence of the gesture that expresses the grace.

We never, of course, hear Beckett's tramp speak directly. Just as Chaplin and Keaton seem both timeless and innocent, so Beckett's "I" seems to have made his journey many times before, yet reacts to phenomena with an almost childlike surprise. Near the beginning of "The Calmative," the "I" describes his setting forth:

> But little by little I got myself out and started walking with short steps among the trees, oh look, trees! The paths of other days were rank with tangled growth. I leaned against the trunks to get my breath and pulled myself forward with the help of boughs. Of my last passage no trace remained. (P. 28)

Here the sense of encountering the world as if newly hatched (expelled) into it—"Into what nightmare thingness am I fallen?" (p. 36) he says later, and still later: "So I went in the atrocious brightness" (p. 44)—and the sense of doddering through the world as if an old man repeating an endless cycle are simultaneous. The protagonist suffers in the world and suffers the world. The voice is "recollecting these emotions, with the celebrated advantage of tranquility," and so can prefigure the journey pattern, tell an old myth or fable. In this way a comic mechanism and a comic detachment are established.

We seldom experience the character's experiences close up, or through his eyes We watch him go through his paces from a certain distance, from the medium-range vantage at which the silent film comedies characteristically place us. One of the effects peculiar to the silence of Chaplin's and Keaton's classic films is to create a sense of Proustian recovery: *a mind is remembering this: ours*. The protagonists, neither speaking nor miming speech, act out their adventures on a plane distinct from the vocal life of the characters they encounter, whose speech is recorded in titles. The lives of the protagonists seem purely somatic; *we* are their minds. We don't articulate to ourselves what we imagine they are thinking, no; rather, Chaplin and Keaton *express* our thoughts physically. Our profound identification with them, aside from what it is in their characters that makes them attractive to us, is a function of their silence: they walk through an alien and largely hostile landscape like our thoughts embodied but unarticulated. But at a distance. Their bodies endure trials that, in reality, would involve great pain, for themselves and for others. But this pain is not felt (evoked at times, but not felt), because only their bodies are experiencing it. Our minds, their minds, are "immortal" in a Cartesian sense.[10] It is as though we were remembering incidents from our lives, incidents involving, say, hostility or pain or *anomie* or frustration. We move through these as a present memory embodied, and the pain, of whatever kind, is evoked but not experienced. Silent film comedy allows us this privilege of detached identification by allowing us to see ourselves imaged as a protagonist who both functions in and yet exists apart from his environment. That is partially why we laugh when Chaplin eats his shoe in *Gold Rush*: because we can imagine what it's like without being made to feel it. Chaplin can *enjoy* eating it because, in a sense, *he is not really there*, not really in a world in which shoes taste abominable, and others find them to taste so.

This peculiar alienation is expressed in the *nouvelles* by Beckett's analysis of the "I" into its component parts of narrator remembering and character existing.[11] In "The Calmative" the "I," like a creature from another world abroad in a human city, remarks "a number of shapes, male and female, strange shapes," and then tags this with "but not more so than usual" (p. 38), paradoxically indicating his familiarity with this world. Then he says, "It is not my wish to labour . . . antinomies, for we are needless to say in a skull" (p. 38), thereby dissolving the conventional past of retrospective narrations and clarifying the character as a thought set in motion in a mental landscape, by a mind. The cyclist that he sees, "pedalling slowly in the middle of the street, reading a newspaper which he held with both hands spread open before his eyes" (p. 38), is a vision of the "I" as somatic character with narrator head, which Kenner in another work brilliantly analyzes as a "Cartesian centaur."[12] Then,

> suddenly ahead of me a man on the same side of the street and going the same way. . . . The distance between us was considerable, seventy paces at least, and fearing he might escape me I quickened my step with the result I swept forward as if on rollers. This is not me, I said, let us make the most of it. (P. 39)

When he says, "This is not me," he speaks as a character reacting with surprise to the fact of his being propelled by the narrator who remembers him, himself as narrator, the two forming "us." The scene, another one strongly suggesting Chaplin, conveys the element of dreamlike identification and detachment we experience with the great silent film protagonists, and the source of the surprising fluidity of their motion. This is not me. I am not of this landscape, I have been set in motion here. If you attend to me, I will both place you in and take you out of the familiar world, and thus make you experience it with oneiric surprise. When Beckett's "I" reaches the man, we see again Chaplin's alien charm: "I drew a few steps ahead, turned, cringed, touched my hat and said, The right time for mercy's sake! I might as well not have existed" (p. 39). Later, in "The End," he says, "One day I witnessed a strange scene. . . . Strictly speaking I wasn't there" (p. 66).

What Beckett does in the *nouvelles* and in the trilogy is create a voice for his silent protagonists, a disembodied consciousness remembering a life over and over. Yet, like a day or a season, the voice begins anew its cycle, with the innocence of newness ("Of my last passage no trace remained") and the *anomie* as well ("Into what nightmare thingness am I fallen?"). The agency that expels the "I" into this thingness is variously identified in the *nouvelles*. In "The Expelled" the "persons" who toss him out of the house seem close to him, perhaps related. In "The Calmative," he isn't "with anybody," he as narrator sets himself, as character, into motion. In "The End," the more personal "they" of the first story have become institutionalized: men in white dismantle the bed, a man named "Weir" seems in charge of the expulsion. The name suggests a fateful agency, and also perhaps something that diverts the life flow of the protagonists into specific channels for measurement. In any case, "they" are an outer force impinging and imposing on an inner self which, if left to its own resources, would simply *be*, "in an empty place, close and warm." In "The Calmative" this inner self is described as a kind of ancient fetus, "hands twined together . . . head bowed, weak, breathless, calm, free, and older than I'll have ever been" (p. 28). The "I" that describes him is, of course, the outer self as narrator, the man made out of words, the institutionalized self, who sets the inner self into going on. Later in "The End," this Generalized Other becomes the nightmare world itself: "I felt them hard upon me, the icy, tumultuous streets, the terrifying faces, the noises that slash, pierce, claw, bruise" (p. 70).

At the time the protagonist describes this terror, he is in the process of gathering himself into himself, ceasing his journey, coming to an end.

> As for my needs, they had dwindled as it were to my dimensions and become, if I may say so, of so exquisite a quality as to exclude all thought of succour. To know I had a being, however faint and false,

> outside of me, had once had the power to stir my heart. You become unsociable, it's inevitable. It's enough to make you wonder sometimes if you are on the right planet. Even the words desert you, it's as bad as that. (P. 70)

The inextricability of the outer voice and the inner self, however, creates a constant ironic counterpoint. The "outside" being *is* narrating this, addressing an audience ("you"). Words are *not* deserted. And so the "I" as character cannot come to his desired end. An "end," a perfectly arbitrary one, occurs as one of his "visions," a further fiction. Having ensconced himself in an old boat in a shed, he envisions himself "gliding on the waters" in a great "calm" (p. 71). He is chained to the bow and has sprung a leak—indeed, has pried out the plug with his knife.

> I swallowed my calmative. The sea, the sky, the mountains and the islands closed in and crushed me in a mighty systole, then scattered to the uttermost confines of space. The memory came faint and cold of the story I might have told, a story in the likeness of my life, I mean without the courage to end or the strength to go on. (P. 72)

Of course, he who disappears into the water is only a visionary projection of the protagonist "I" still lying grounded in the boat in the shed, who in turn is a visionary projection of the "I" as narrator. The "calmative" he swallows has already been identified, at the beginning of the story of that name, as "a story, I'll try and tell myself another story, to try and calm myself." What is being calmed is his fear of listening to himself "rot"; the stories are shored against his ruins. So any ending is an arbitrary fiction; if the "I" speaks he can't end. Over the calm waters, nobody in sight, comes the memory of still another story, perhaps the real one.

A similar passage ends "The Calmative." The "I" swoons at the end of his day in the city. "Then at last, before I fell, first to my knees, as cattle do, then on my face, I was in a throng. I didn't lose consciousness, when I lose consciousness it [*sic*] will not be able to recover it." No, "reality, too tired to look for the right word, was soon restored, the throng fell away, the light came back and I had no need to raise my head from the ground to know I was back in the same blinding void as before" (p. 45). Any fall is—unfortunately?—only a lapse in the steps of a progress, and those steps only counterbalance a fall. The compensatory nature of this mechanism is most clearly realized, visually, in the forward lean of both Keaton's and Groucho's walk.

How close Chaplin's walk is to a toddler's! A toddler, too, rounds a fast corner hopping on one foot. Beckett's protagonist, too, "turned about and set off in the other direction" by wheeling "round in a wide semi-circle without slowing down, for [he] was afraid if [he] stopped of not being able to start again" (p. 37). The body lives, the mind reasons. It is the interpenetration of these two systems that is the life of Beckett's comedy. The body, the "I" as character, depends on the mind to set him in motion. The mind depends on the body for its matter, about which it reasons. At the end of the three *nouvelles*, while watching the waters rise, the protagonist reasons that "it would take a good half hour, everything included, barring accidents" (p. 72). This is the voice of silent comedy, some timeless voice reasoning the struggles of the body. It should be stressed that Beckett's comedy, like all comedy, is about *human* machines, that what is imposed upon our sense of the machine is the mind, or soul, that thinks about it.[13] On the evidence of the *nouvelles*, in which the borrowing is more obvious than in the trilogy, what Beckett took from silent film comedy were images of the inner and body's self, moving in its divagations to the unarticulated reasoning of a mind. He gave that mind a voice, one so carefully tuned to and yet incommensurable with the body, that the result was not only the giving of voice to silent comedy but the appropriation of a comical silence into literature.

Walking is a quintessentially human enterprise, and comical walking makes this fact resonate: it is like our persistence in sustaining logical procedures in a reality against which these procedures can only seem absurd. Our response to the strange walks of comedians is ambivalent. For a moment we observe with detachment a fundamental motion yet realize how much it is our own, revealed to us now in its marvelous and malfunctioning parts. We are both in and out of place in a generally recumbent world: this is the vision to which both Beckett's "I" and the silent film comics take us.

1. Hugh Kenner, *A Reader's Guide to Samuel Beckett* (New York: Farrar, Straus & Giroux, 1973), pp. 116-17.

2. A fourth story, "Premier Amour," published for the first time in English in the collection *First Love and Other Shorts* (New York: Grove Press, 1974), was not included with "The Expelled," "The Calmative," and "The End." I don't think this was due to what Beckett might have thought to be its inferiority—it is as fine a story—but to the fact that its structure and action differ from those of the other three.

3. Anton Chekhov, *Ward Six and Other Stories*, trans. Ann Dunnigan (New York: New

American Library, 1965), p. 159. The phrase occurs near the end of the comic short novel "The Duel." The character Von Koren says, "You see, one can stumble even on a smooth road, such is our human fate: if one does not err in the main, one errs in the particulars."

4. Samuel Beckett, *Stories and Texts for Nothing* (New York: Grove Press, 1967), p. 10. Subsequent quotations from this work appear in parentheses in the text. The collection was first published as *Nouvelles et textes pour rien* (Paris: Editions de Minuit, 1958).

5. A phrase from Beckett's novel *Watt* (New York: Grove Press, 1959), p. 134.

6. Ibid., p. 31.

7. Soren Kierkegaard, in his *Concluding Unscientific Postscript*, trans. David F. Swenson and Walter Lowrie (Princeton, N.J.: Princeton University Press, 1968), says that the "tragic and the comic are the same, in so far as both are based on contradiction; but *the tragic is the suffering contradiction, the comical, the painless contradiction*," that whatever pain is experienced in comedy is "non-essential" because the "comic apprehension evokes the contradiction or makes it manifest by having in mind the way out" (pp. 459, 462).

8. Samuel Beckett, *Three Novels* (New York: Grove Press, 1965), p. 36.

9. Ibid., p. 25.

10. Descartes, *Discourse on Method* and *The Meditations*, trans. F. E. Sutcliffe (Harmondsworth: Penguin Books, 1972), p. 76: ". . .our soul is of a nature entirely independent of the body, and that, consequently, it is not subject to die with it; then, since one cannot see other causes for its destruction, one is naturally led to judge from this that it is immortal." These are the last words of Discourse V.

11. Beckett's cinematic version of this fictional first person is his *Film*, starring Buster Keaton, in which "the protagonist is sundered into object (O) and eye (E), the former in flight, the latter in pursuit." This is from Beckett's own general notes, in *Film* (New York: Grove Press, 1969), p. 11. O cannot come to rest because E is inescapably conscious of him.

12. Hugh Kenner, *Samuel Beckett: A Critical Study* (New York: Grove Press, 1961), chap. 2.

13. I am borrowing a phrase from Sterne's Walter Shandy, when he speaks of the human machine to his brother Toby. Laurence Sterne, *The Life and Opinions of Tristram Shandy, Gentleman* (New York: Random House, 1950), pp. 288-89.

The Ultimate Music Is Abstract: Charles Ives and Wallace Stevens

John N. Serio
Clarkson College of Technology

ON the manuscript of his String Quartet no. 2, Charles Ives comments: "String Quartet for four men who converse, discuss, argue (politics), fight, shake hands, shut up, then walk up the mountain side to view the firmament."[1] Accordingly, the three movements are entitled "Discussions," "Arguments," and "The Call of the Mountains." In the marginalia, Ives identifies the part of the second violinist with a figure whom he calls Rollo, a symbol for Ives of the literal mind who can only like what he or she has been taught.[2] Rollo's weak phrases and trite melodies, one of which Ives marks *andante emasculata*, are mocked by the contrapuntal dissonances of the other instruments as they each disagree with him. Throughout the manuscript, Ives scribbles derogatory comments about Rollo: "Cut it out, Rollo!" "Too hard to play—so it just can't be good music, Rollo." "Beat time, Rollo!" Then, after a long silence, Rollo joins in with a florid, though easy, melody: "Join in again, Professor, all in the key of C. You can do that nice and pretty."[3]

"All in the key of C." Anyone familiar with the poetry of Wallace Stevens will be reminded of Stevens's own satire on the unimaginative mind in "The Comedian as the Letter C." Like Rollo, Crispin represents for Stevens the failure of the modern imagination to come to terms with the new music of this "still new continent in which to dwell."[4] Educated abroad (Bordeaux) and in nineteenth-century poetics—"That century of wind in a single puff" (*CP*, p. 28)—Crispin finds his mythology of self dissolved by the magnitude of the sea, which becomes "Polyphony beyond his baton's thrust" (*CP*, p. 28). Like Rollo's occasional "tut tuts" in a conversation in which he is out of place, Crispin's feeble music is no match for the sea's: "Against his pipping sounds a trumpet cried / Celestial sneering boisterously" (*CP*, p. 29). Although Crispin alters his point of view when he reaches America (he moves from thinking he is the intelligence of his soil to seeing that his soil is his intelligence), he remains inadequate to the demands of his new surroundings. He slides from being a "realist" who believes "what is is what should be" (*CP*, p. 41—a Rollo?) to an "indulgent fatalist" (*CP*, p. 44) who finds that his environment totally determines his self. Thus, "The Comedian as the Letter C" records Crispin's failure to see the imagination as the saving principle in life. Appropriately, Stevens announces Crispin's figurative death:

> Was he to bray this in profoundest brass
> Arointing his dreams with fugal requiems?
> Was he to company vastest things defunct
> With a blubber of tom-toms harrowing the sky?
> Scrawl a tragedian's testament? Prolong
> His active force in an inactive dirge,
> Which, let the tall musicians call and call,
> Should merely call him dead?
>
> (*CP*, p. 41)

"The music sticks" (*CP*, p. 45), and Crispin, that "lutanist of fleas" (*CP*, p. 28), becomes, like the unappreciative music critics Ives also referred to as "Rollos," "a profitless / Philosopher . . . Concluding fadedly" (*CP*, pp. 45-46).

The similarity between Ives's Rollo and Stevens's Crispin points out in miniature the similarity in artistic expression and aesthetic concern of these two modern American figures who lived, in fact, remarkably parallel lives. Born in 1874 in Danbury, Connecticut (and residing for a time, coincidentally, on Stevens Street), Charles Ives attended Yale from 1894 to 1898, became a successful insurance executive with Mutual Life in New York from 1899 until his retirement in 1930, then spent the rest of his life in West Redding, Connecticut, where he died in 1954. Born in 1879 in Reading, Pennsylvania, Wallace Stevens attended Harvard from 1897 to 1900, studied and practiced law in New York from 1901 to 1916, then became a successful insurance executive with Hartford

Insurance in Hartford, Connecticut, where he died in 1955. Whether they found time for their creative expression by working late into the night after a hard day at the office as Ives often did, or peripatetically on an early morning walk to work as Stevens often did, both wrote out of an inner necessity that could well afford to remain independent of public acceptance.

Although Stevens was just beginning his poetic career as Ives was ending his musical one (in an extraordinary burst of creative energy, Ives composed virtually all his music within a twenty-year span, 1898-1918), the way in which Ives's music slowly gained recognition paralleled the steady growth of Stevens's audience. The first public performance of an Ives work, *Three Places in New England*, for example, took place in 1930, but it was not until 1939 when John Kirkpatrick introduced the Sonata no. 2, *Concord, Mass., 1840-1860* for piano that there was any public response to Ives's musical genius. His Symphony no. 3 was first performed in 1946 and won the Pulitzer Prize the next year, although it had been composed almost forty years earlier. In 1951 Ives turned down an invitation from Leonard Bernstein to attend the premiere of his Symphony no. 2, but it was not until the mid-1960s, a decade after the composer's death, that his first and fourth symphonies made their debut. In a similar way, Stevens, who published poems regularly from 1914 until his death in 1955, first attracted scholarly attention to his poetry in the late 1930s and early 1940s, but it was not until the fifties and the sixties that his true stature as a major poetic force in America was seen.

Both Ives and Stevens strive to bridge the gap between music and poetry. In his *114 Songs*, Ives sets to music poems by Milton, Wordsworth, Byron, Keats, Shelley, Browning, Emerson, Whittier, Whitman, and such contemporaries as Rupert Brooke, Vachel Lindsay, and Louis Untermeyer. Moreover, nearly a third of the song texts are written by Ives himself. In order to convey fully the poetic quality he aims for in his Sonata no. 1 for violin, Ives includes the words from Lowell Mason's "Watchman, Tell Us of the Night" in the musical score itself, presumably for the performers to contemplate while playing. His *Concord* Sonata attempts to render in music the spirit of transcendentalism that he finds in the writings of Emerson, Hawthorne, the Alcotts, and Thoreau. In fact, Ives's book on these figures, *Essays before a Sonata*, must be seen as an integral part of the piano piece itself. As Ives writes: "The music and prefaces were intended to be printed together, but as it was found that this would make a cumbersome volume, they are separate. The *whole* is an attempt to present (one person's) impression of the spirit of transcendentalism that is associated in the minds of many with Concord, Mass., of over a half century ago" (*E*, p. xxv, emphasis added).

Stevens, of course, is one of America's most musical poets. One need only recall a number of titles to see how closely aligned music and poetry are in his work, the title often suggesting the musical structure of the poem itself: "Peter Quince at the Clavier," "To the One of Fictive Music," "Hymn from a Watermelon Pavilion," "Autumn Refrain," "Sad Strains of a Gay Waltz," "Dance of the Macabre Mice," "Asides on the Oboe," "The Man with the Blue Guitar," "Song of Fixed Accord," "Notes [a pun?] toward a Supreme Fiction." Using music as the central analogy, Stevens depicts the imagination as an instrument, usually a guitar, and the poet as a musician or singer. His early, brief lyrics convey feeling through sound and reflect a mellifluous use of language and meter distinctive in the American poetic tradition. His later, extended meditations are sustained, in large measure, by his highly cadenced, almost biblical, blank-verse rhythms. Even his use of cacophony and nonsense syllables, such as "pizzicati of Hosanna" (*CP*, p. 90) and "tink and tank and tunk-a-tunk-tunk" (*CP*, p. 59), are musically precise.[5] The aplomb with which Stevens announces an end to nineteenth-century aesthetics in "Ploughing on Sunday" by instructing his poetic muse to blow his horn, "Tum-ti-tum, / Ti-tum-tum-tum!" (*CP*, p. 20), finds its counterpart in the last chord of Ives's rather traditional Symphony no. 2: it contains every note in the chromatic scale except one.

Although one could pursue in detail the numerous lines of correspondence between Ives and Stevens—their New England temperament, their sense of Americana, their essentially romantic vision—their most distinguishing affinity lies in their attempt to get beyond poetry, beyond music to an abstract sense of the music of poetry and the poetry of music. In a lecture delivered in New Haven, Connecticut, in 1933, T. S. Eliot notes a similar quest in his own work:

> to write poetry which should be essentially poetry, with nothing poetic about it, poetry standing naked in its bare bones, or poetry so transparent that we should not see the poetry, but that which we are meant to see through the poetry so transparent that in reading it we are intent on what the poem *points at*, and not on the poetry, this seems to me the thing to try for. To get *beyond poetry*, as Beethoven, in his later works, strove to get *beyond music*.[6]

Though this comment may very well describe what every serious artist attempts, Stevens and Ives are unmatched in their self-conscious pursuit of this goal. Both have at their center an attempt to get beyond the forms of their making to a higher integration existing beyond form. For Ives, the quest is to express an Emersonian, transcendental ideal, a universal music beyond sound that reaches to a pure or absolute realm. Believing music to be "a transcendental language," Ives feels that "shades of abstraction" may be disclosed through "artistic intuitions" (*E*, p. 71). His music searches for the inexpressible, the unheard music contained in the notes between the notes, the silences.

Like Ives, Stevens believes "Music is feeling, then, not sound" (*CP*, p. 90), as he, too, tries to express the "poem that never reaches words" (*CP*, p. 396). However, the process is much more complex in Stevens, for he denies the possibility of an abstract as he achieves it. As he writes in "Contrary Theses (II)": "He wanted and looked for a final refuge . . . He walked toward / An abstract . . . The abstract was suddenly there and gone again" (*CP*, p. 270). In his extreme self-consciousness, Stevens even sees "disillusion as the last illusion" (*CP*, p. 468); yet the enduring tenor of his poetry is affirmative. He opens the first section, "It Must Be Abstract," of "Notes toward a Supreme Fiction," for instance, with the following paradox:

> Begin, ephebe, by perceiving the idea
> Of this invention, this invented world,
> The inconceivable idea of the sun.
>
> (*CP*, p. 380)

Although perceiving the inconceivable may seem an impossibility, Stevens believes that "The poem refreshes life so that we share, / For a moment, the first idea" (*CP*, p. 382). The ultimate poem, "seen and known in lesser poems," as he says in "A Primitive like an Orb," becomes

> . . . the huge, high harmony that sounds
> A little and a little, suddenly,
> By means of a separate sense. It is and it
> Is not and, therefore, is. . . .
>
> (*CP*, p. 440)

In his essay "The Music of Poetry," Eliot reminds us that "the music of poetry is not something which exists apart from the meaning,"[7] and it is this emphasis on meaning, rather than manner, that informs the musical quality of Stevens's poetry and the poetic quality of Ives's music. In a word, both Ives and Stevens write "difficult" compositions in which the poem or music "resist[s] the intelligence / Almost successfully" (*CP*, p. 350). But it is important to note that the difficulty in Ives lies not so much in his complex technical structures but, as in Stevens, in his ideas. This may seem a somewhat curious thing to say about a composer who is known for his exasperating, if not at times impossible, demands on musicians and conductors alike; yet it is important to see that Ives's musical innovations, such as polytonality, polyharmony, free dissonance, tone clustering, and atonality, are merely the necessary vehicles for his music of idea. In his *Memos* Ives records how one performer could not play his first violin sonata because, as he complained, "there were too many ideas too close together" (*M*, p. 123) in it. Ives believes not only that "substance can be expressed in music" but also "that it is the only valuable thing in it" (*E*, p. 77). Though "practically indescribable" (*E*, p. 75), meaning may be sensed intuitively, Ives says, "process, unknown. Perhaps it is an unexplained consciousness of being nearer God or being nearer the devil—of approaching truth or approaching unreality; [it is] a silent something felt" (*E*, p. 75).

Approaching truth by approaching unreality suggests the manner in which Ives tries to get beyond form, beyond sound to an abstract sense of an ultimate music, "a silent something felt." He does this by breaking down traditional forms and by creating new ones. Ives's eclecticism is at the heart of this process.[8] Snatches of melodies ranging from Beethoven's Fifth Symphony to Brahms's Symphony no. 1, from "Columbia, the Gem of the Ocean" and "Old Black Joe" to "Hello! My Baby" and "Camptown Races," are woven into his musical textures. Yet he never quotes a passage exactly. He may change the key, leave out notes, alter the original measure order, add ornamentation, vary the rhythm, or "resolve" the passage in a shattering discord.[9] His *Concord* Sonata, "called a sonata for want of a more exact name" (*E*, p. xxv), as Ives tells us, is one of the most revolutionary and difficult compositions ever written. It incorporates irregular meters, such as $\frac{4\frac{1}{2}}{4}$, 1024th notes, atonality, and unbarred sections. In addition, it calls for chord clusters to be played with the fist, requires a board exactly 14¾ inches long to be placed on the keys, and even includes a melody for viola and flute. When asked by John Kirkpatrick about how to approach the passages without any metrical markings, Ives replied, "do whatever seems natural or best to you, though not necessarily the same way each time."[10] If Ives's music sometimes jars the ears, that is because he is attempting to stretch "the ear muscles," an activity he believes will also strengthen "the mind muscles and perhaps the Soul muscles too" (*M*, p. 63). Feeling that "initial coherence today may be dullness tomorrow" (*E*, p. 23), Ives appeals to an "auditory imagination" in which the response to his complex sounds and rhythms penetrates "far below the conscious levels of thought and feeling."[11] As Ives himself writes, "Coherence, to a certain extent, must bear some relation to the listener's subconscious perspective" (*E*, p. 98).

A corresponding dialectic informs the works of Ives and Stevens. The very process of the mind, in trying to contain antithetical ideas, renders a higher synthesis. In Ives, the dialectic is often inherent in the musical form he selects, such as a sonata that pits one theme against another, or a quartet or symphony that counters one movement with another. But Ives also manifests a dialectic in the very texture of his music, playing one or more keys against each other (Variations on "America," *New England Holidays*, Symphony no. 4), having two or more pieces of music going at the same time ("Decoration Day"), stereophonically staging various musical clusters (*The Unanswered Question*), juxtaposing lyric melodies with the densest of instrumental backgrounds (Symphony no. 3). For Ives, who tells us that he could "keep five, and even six, rhythms going in [his] mind at once" (*M*, p. 125), music truly becomes a Stevensesque "poem of the act of the mind" (*CP*, p. 240), embodying the fullest of imaginative demands. His *Universe* Symphony, for example, which he insists must remain forever unfinished, epitomizes this ceaseless, dialectical process. Ives says of it:

> I started something that I'd had in mind for some time . . . trying out a parallel way of listening to music, suggested by looking at a view (1) with the eyes toward the sky or tops of the trees, taking in the earth or foreground subjectively—that is, not focusing the eye on it—(2) then looking at the earth and land, and seeing the sky and the top of the foreground subjectively. In other words, giving a musical piece in two parts, but played at the same time. (*M*, p. 106)

This reads almost as if it were a program note to Stevens's "Hermitage at the Center," a late poem that sums up Stevens's major movement. The duality between the earth and the sky in the poem represents the never-ending dialectic between reality and the imagination that characterizes Stevens's poetry as a whole. Both the simultaneity of activity and the unfinished quality that Ives seeks in his *Universe* Symphony are expressed in this poem, for it is actually a poem within a poem, in which the end is merely the beginning:

The leaves on the macadam make a noise—
How soft the grass on which the desired
Reclines in the temperature of heaven—

Like tales that were told the day before yesterday—
Sleek in a natural nakedness,
She attends the tintinnabula—

And the wind sways like a great thing tottering—
Of birds called up by more than sun,
Birds of more wit, that substitute—

Which suddenly is all dissolved and gone—
Their intelligible twittering
For unintelligible thought.

And yet this end and this beginning are one,
And one last look at the ducks is a look
At lucent children round her in a ring.[12]

(*CP*, pp. 505-6)

In his quest for an ultimate music, Ives will not be constrained by the limitations of either performers or instruments. "The instrument!—there is the perennial difficulty," he exclaims, "there is music's limitation. Why must the scarecrow of the keyboard—the tyrant in terms of the mechanism (be it Caruso or a Jew's-harp)—stare into every measure? Is it the composer's fault that man has only ten fingers? Why can't a musical thought be presented as it is born?" (*E*, p. 87). In Ives, it is. Hence, we find him calling for a string quartet to play several measures in a song with piano accompaniment, scoring an ideal celesta that would balance in tone quality with a loud trumpet, requiring a jew's harp to be heard above a full orchestra. The admonition to his copyist found in the margin of his *New England Holidays* manuscript—"Mr. Price: Please don't try to make things nice! All the wrong notes are right"[13] —characterizes Ives's quest to turn "impossibilities into possibilities" (*M*, p. 98). As Henry Cowell, Ives's composer-friend-biographer, writes:

> Some of Ives's Music of the Idea, therefore, was quite frankly written not so much to be sounded (though there is no objection to this if it proves possible) as to be perceived, to be heard in the mind's ear.[14]

This explains how Ives could say, quite matter-of-factly, in his "Postface" to *114 Songs*: "Some of the songs in this book, particularly among the later ones, cannot be sung, and if they could, perhaps might prefer, if they had a say, to remain as they are; that is, 'in the leaf' " (*E*, p. 130). Believing that "a song has a *few* rights," that it should be able "to sing to itself" if it wants to or "to fly where humans cannot fly, to sing what cannot be sung," he concludes his "Postface" with the epigram:

> —In short, must a song
> always be a song!
>
> (*E*, pp. 130-31)

We may now understand how Ives was able to compose virtually all his music without hearing it: "That music must be heard is not essential," he writes, "what it *sounds* like may not be what it *is*" (*E*, p. 84). Or, as he says in perhaps his most famous exclamation: "My God! What has sound got to do with music!" (*E*, p. 84). The ultimate music is abstract.

Just as Ives separates sound from music, Stevens separates words from poetry. The word is a means to poetry, but ultimately its form must be destroyed if one is to perceive the true music of poetry, a perception of the mind that is beyond formulation. As he writes in "Auroras of Autumn," a poem that embodies this quest for "form gulping after formlessness" (*CP*, p. 411):

> This is nothing until in a single man contained,
> Nothing until this named thing nameless is
> And is destroyed. . . .
>
> (*CP*, p. 416)

The ultimate music of Stevens's poetry is an apperception of an independent reality existing outside the mind's conception of it. It is Stevens's attempt to evoke "Not the symbol but that for which the symbol stands" (*CP*, p. 238), "the image at its source, / The abstract" (*CP*, p. 223). Therefore, Stevens, like Ives, strives to get beyond form, beyond the poem to an abstract sense of an absolute reality. As Roy Harvey Pearce observes: "Stevens wants to conceive of confronting and knowing reality directly, not as it might be mediated by the formal elegancies of an ultimate composer of words. Poetic form is made to negate itself and to point to an ultimate vision beyond poems, to poetry as an ultimate and inclusive poem."[15]

Stevens, however, does not share Ives's affirmation of Emersonian idealism, for he does not admit a transcendental reality. As he says in "An Ordinary Evening in New Haven": "We seek / Nothing beyond reality. Within it, / Everything" (*CP*, p. 471). Perhaps more than any other modern American poet, Stevens is aware of the paradox in attempting to get beyond the mind's forms. Any sense of the absolute in him becomes another "fiction of an absolute" (*CP*, p. 404); every formlessness turns into another of the mind's forms. Although he affirms, as he says in the title of one of his poems, that "The Ultimate Poem Is Abstract," he knows that he will never reach it. Though he sees that "It would be enough / If we were ever, just once, at the middle, fixed / In This Beautiful World of Ours" (*CP*, p. 340), he knows, too, that he will always be "Helplessly at the edge" (*CP*, p. 430). What matters in Stevens, then, is not the attainment but the pursuit of the abstract, the act of the mind itself, finding what will suffice. "Sure that the ultimate poem [is] the mind, / Or of the mind" (*CP*, p. 256), Stevens seeks a center that is "a state of mind, / Nothing more" (*OP*, p. 112). This, for him, becomes the "music that lasts long and lives the more" (*OP*, p. 113). This becomes the abstract music of poetry that can transform reality and thus renew the self:

> . . . The freshness of transformation is
>
> The freshness of a world. It is our own.
> It is ourselves, the freshness of ourselves, . . .
>
> (*CP*, pp. 397-98)

The last poem in Stevens's *Collected Poems* illustrates how he resolves this apparent contradiction. "Not Ideas about the Thing but the Thing Itself" is, as its title implies, a poem that attempts to get beyond itself, a poem, to recall Eliot's words, that is "so transparent that in reading it we are intent on what the poem *points at*, and not on the poetry."[16] Though this is an impossible task, the movement of the poem, the meditative act of the mind that it becomes, momentarily succeeds in freeing the thing itself, which exists apart from the mind's idea, or poem, of it. Like Ives, Stevens approaches truth by approaching unreality. That is, he de-creates, he moves from the created, not to nothingness, which would be destruction, but to the uncreated in order to re-create a fresh perception of reality.[17] The attempt to evoke a sense of abstract reality in "Not Ideas about the Thing but the Thing Itself" concerns a bird's cry, "a scrawny cry from outside" that seemed at first "like a sound in his mind" (*CP*, p. 354). But "there is a resistance involved; / And being part is an exertion that declines" (*OP*, p. 96), as Stevens says in another poem; and suddenly, in somewhat of an Ivesian fashion, the scrawny cry becomes "A chorister whose c preceded the choir" (*CP*, p. 534). That is all there is—the note of C escaping before the mind's forms can capture it. It becomes a sound that does not transcend itself, a part of a foreign song beyond human meaning or human feeling. It will remain, forever, beyond human assimilation:

> It was part of the colossal sun,
>
> Surrounded by its choral rings,
> Still far away. . . .
>
> (*CP*, p. 534)

We have come full circle. The note of C, the only key in which Rollo and Crispin could play, has been transformed into an abstract music beyond human conception. It has become part of an ultimate poetry that may be known, but never reached. It has become free, like one of Ives's songs, flying where human beings cannot fly, singing what cannot be sung. It has become not the symbol, but that for which the symbol stands, the image at its source, the abstract. "It was," as Stevens concludes his poem, "like / A new knowledge of reality" (*CP*, p. 534).

1. Quoted in Dr. William B. Ober's program notes for Ives's String Quartet no. 1 (1896) "A Revival Service" and String Quartet no. 2 (1907-13), Turnabout/Vox Records (TV 34157S). Coincidentally, Ober begins his notes with the remark, "What latter-day Plutarch can resist comparing Charles Ives, the composer, with Wallace Stevens, the poet?"

2. John Kirkpatrick explains that "Rollo was a creation of the Rev. Jacob Abbott . . . see *Abbott's "Young Christian,"* memorial edition, 1882. . . . The Rollo Books (1834-58) were only one of his many didactic series, and became a staple in American homes. Rollo is a good little boy with an inquiring nature, and the more he has to have everything explained to him in great detail, the more information could be packed into each Rollo Book. For Ives he became a symbol of the literal mind unable to imagine anything beyond what he'd been taught." In Charles Ives, *Memos*, ed. John Kirkpatrick (New York: W. W. Norton, 1972), pp. 26-27. Subsequent references to *Memos*, designated by the abbreviation *M*, will appear in parentheses in the text. References to Charles Ives, *Essays before a Sonata and Other Writings*, ed. Howard Boatwright (New York: W. W. Norton, 1962), will be cited in the text with the abbreviation *E*.

3. Ober, program notes.

4. *The Collected Poems of Wallace Stevens* (New York: Alfred A. Knopf, 1954), p. 37. Subsequent references to this work, designated by the abbreviation *CP*, will appear in parentheses in the text. References to Wallace Stevens, *Opus Posthumous*, ed. Samuel French Morse (New York: Alfred A. Knopf, 1957) will be cited in the text with the abbreviation *OP*.

5. For a detailed discussion of the musical quality of Stevens's poetry, see Harvey Gross,

Sound and Form in Modern Poetry (Ann Arbor, Mich.: University of Michigan Press, 1964), pp. 215-17, 225-46.

6. Quoted in F. O. Matthiessen, *The Achievement of T. S. Eliot* (New York: Oxford University Press, 1958), p. 90.

7. T. S. Eliot, *On Poetry and Poets* (New York: Noonday Press, 1961), p. 21.

8. Ives uses the term *eclecticism* positively. He writes, for example, that "if a man finds that the cadences of an Apache war-dance come nearest to his soul—provided he has taken pains to know enough other cadences, for eclecticism is part of his duty; . . . let him assimilate whatever he finds highest of the Indian ideal so that he can use it with the cadences, fervently, transcendentally, inevitably, furiously, in his symphonies, in his operas, in his whistlings on the way to work, so that he can paint his house with them, make them a part of his prayer-book—this is all possible and necessary, if he is confident that they have a part in his spiritual consciousness." *Essays before a Sonata*, pp. 79-80.

9. For a fuller discussion of Ives's musical borrowings, see Clayton W. Henderson, "Ives' Use of Quotation," *Music Educators Journal* 61, no. 2 (Octoboer 1974): 24-28. This issue is devoted to Ives.

10. Quoted in John Kirkpatrick's program notes for Ives's Sonata no. 2, *Concord, Mass., 1840-60* (1909-1915), Columbia Records (MS 7192).

11. T. S. Eliot, "Matthew Arnold," in *The Use of Poetry and the Use of Criticism* (London: Faber & Faber, 1933), p. 118.

12. Wallace Stevens, "Hermitage at the Center." Copyright 1923 and renewed 1951 by Wallace Stevens. Reprinted from *The Collected Poems of Wallace Stevens* by permission of Alfred A. Knopf, Inc.

13. Quoted in Paul C. Echols, "The Music for Orchestra," *Music Educators Journal* 61, no. 2 (October 1974): 38.

14. Henry and Sidney Cowell, *Charles Ives and His Music* (New York: Oxford University Press, 1955), p. 179. Stevens, in a letter to Henry Church, writes: "I like words to sound wrong."

15. Roy Harvey Pearce, *The Continuity of American Poetry* (Princeton, N.J.: Princeton University Press, 1961), p. 382.

16. Matthiessen, *Achievement of T. S. Eliot*, p. 90.

17. See Stevens's discussion of modern reality as "a reality of decreation" in "The Relations between Poetry and Painting," in Wallace Stevens, *The Necessary Angel: Essays on Reality and the Imagination* (New York: Vintage Books, 1951), pp. 174-76.

Myth and the Mystery of Evil

Lee W. Gibbs

Cleveland State University

THE mass media have recently been saturated with a deluge of material reflecting a revival of interest in satanism, witchcraft, and the occult. Newspapers, popular magazines, academic periodicals, religious journals, paperback books, television, movies, records, hard-rock musical groups and their songs—all manifest a contemporary obsession and fascination with the black arts.

In casting a ray of light upon some causes and implications of this revival of the demonic and the occult, this paper should partially illuminate a dark page of contemporary history.

I

A few years ago, it would have been inconceivable to talk seriously about widespread belief in and practice of devil worship and witchcraft in an enlightened, computerized era dominated by science and technology that have put man on the moon and brought him back and that have so diminished the limits of time and space that the world has been transformed into an interdependent global tribe or village.[1] Yet various contemporary writers are plausibly affirming that satanism and witchcraft are more prevalent today than at any time since the Middle Ages.[2] Any attempt to comprehend the meaning of this renascence of satanism and witchcraft must take into account the following intimately related but distinguishable factors: (1) satanism and witchcraft reemerge in times of cultural crisis and transition; (2) the current revival of satanism and witchcraft is a rejection of traditional Judeo-Christian beliefs, values, and institutions; and (3) contemporary satanism and witchcraft are part of a romantic, antiintellectual reaction against a society and culture dominated by a scientific rationalism and an emphasis upon technological control.

CULTURAL CRISIS AND TRANSITION

Contrary to a common view held at both popular and academic levels, it was not the Middle Ages but the Renaissance that was the golden age of the occult. Historians have observed that the sudden revival of witchcraft and witch-hunting in western Europe began in the fifteenth century, reached its apex during the age of the Reformation, and continued into the mid-eighteenth century. Although building upon traditions of the Middle Ages, to be sure,the Renaissance was not a period of demythologization but one of remythologization. The more exotic side of humanism credulously rehabilitated the occult traditions of antiquity.

There is a striking analogy to be drawn between the Renaissance and the contemporary historical era, where similarities are more compelling than differences. First and most important, the Renaissance was an age of historical transition between medieval and modern world views. The patterns of the modern world view are now in process of disintegration, and this age of transition—comparable to the Renaissance—has been variously designated as "post-modern," "post-industrial," "post-Christian," "sociotechnic," "technocratic," "technetronic," and so on. In both the Renaissance and the contemporary period, there is a decisive break with the immediate past and a sense of discontinuity: the Renaissance humanist rejects his benighted medieval past and compensates by idealizing antiquity; the contemporary humanist rejects his bourgeois and modern past and idealizes the folk and the primitive.

Social and personal identity crises are inevitable concomitants of an age of rapid transition because of the erosion of established cultural institutions and of the value system that undergirds it. The anxieties endemic to such eras manifest themselves in many ways: an irreconcilable chasm appears between the obvious and the impossible, between the universalism of learning and the ubiquity of the absurd; the debate sharpens between proponents of the active life and of the contemplative life, between responsible involvement and dropping out; there is a revolution in education, with the rejection of much traditional learning as irrelevant, often in favor of the ancient or the primitive and esoteric; terrestrial disorders lead men to seek order in the stars; love philosophies rule when the old rationalist assumptions fall into disrepute; the coarsest hedonism and the most ethereal mysticism are found side by side, occasionally even together; a golden age of mysticism is accompanied by a great witch craze. The revival of satanism, witchcraft, and the occult, therefore, should be properly regarded as a part of the larger correspondence between the Renaissance and the contemporary age.

Rejection of Traditional Judeo-Christian Beliefs, Values, and Institutions

The contemporary revivification of interest in the black arts should also be regarded as part of the larger movement in Western civilization away from traditional Jewish and Christian beliefs, values, and institutions and toward nontraditional forms of religion. In an age of major cultural crisis and transition, the first attack of sensitive social critics is directed toward the religious and philosophical presuppositions that have sanctioned the whole nexus of social institutions. The modern scientific industrial civilization of Europe and America was demonstrably grounded in and sanctioned by the Judeo-Christian tradition. As a new culture is in process of emerging with new questions and new problems that the old religious forms do not raise and could not have raised or answered, the old religious symbols, rituals, and values become meaningless and irrelevant to the new social situation. The quest for new religious forms becomes peremptory.

The present era of transition is not areligious or antireligious but antitraditional and antiinstitutional regarding religion. The forms and expressions of the contemporary religious quest are personal, inward, eclectic, and confusing in their multiplicity. Psychotherapy, sensitivity-training groups, the human potential movement, body cults, the exploitation of psychedelic drugs and other chemical agents, magic, astrology, spiritualism, Eastern mysticism and transcendental meditation, the Jesus movement, Black Islam and sporadic appropriations of African religion—all these forms of nontraditional religion are unified in constituting a common protest against the complex of the religiophilosophical presuppositions and values that have provided the metaphysical foundation and sanction for the modern society molded by science and technology.

Reaction against Scientific Rationalism and Technological Control

The impact of science in both its theoretical and applied senses upon modern culture has led modern man to accept a narrowly empirical understanding of knowledge and truth; knowledge and truth are defined as that which can either be demonstrated (as in mathematics) or shown inductively to be reasonably certain through the application of scientific method (as in the empirical sciences). Moreover, the ever-increasing secularization of life encouraged by the accomplishments of science and technology has made modern man feel more and more at home in this world, which has become for him the exclusive locus of meaning and value. Secularized man understands himself, his natural and social environment, and all events solely in terms of the nexus of finite physical and historical causes that are accessible to scientific and historical inquiry.

Modern man's application of his scientific knowledge has now been extended from the domination, manipulation, and control of the natural environment to the social environment as well—that is, to economics, politics, art, education, and science itself. Theodore Roszak has pointed out the close interrelationship of science, technology, and social engineering in today's technocratic culture:

> the roots of the technocracy reach deep into our cultural past and are ultimately entangled in the scientific world-view of the Western tradition. But for our purpose here it will be enough to define the technocracy as that society in which those who govern justify themselves by appeal to technical experts who, in turn, justify themselves by appeal to scientific forms of knowledge. And beyond the authority of science, there is no appeal.[3]

The prevailing intellectual atmosphere of such a scientifically and technologically oriented culture has rendered modern man incapable of experiencing any of the nonrational dimensions of existence. The absurd, the inspiring, the uncanny, the awesome, the terrifying, the ecstatic, the transcendent, the mysterious—none of these fits into a production- and efficiency-oriented society. The current appeal of devil worship, witchcraft, and the occult must be seen as a desperate attempt of certain people to put some fun and mystery and magic and enchantment back into their otherwise colorless and humdrum lives,[4] to recall and experience again those things in this world that cannot be analytically explained by the most rational inquiry or the most informed skepticism.

II

One of the clearest examples of the crisis faced by modern man and his secularized civilization appears in the general impotence of men to deal with the demonic realities of the twentieth century. World wars, Nazi extermination camps, worldwide economic depressions, poverty and starvation in the midst of plenty and affluence, assassinations, urban riots, the incessant threat of thermonuclear destruction—all are manifestations of "senseless acts." Apocalyptic visions of a dark invasion of satanic forces pass momentarily through the mind of modern man, and emotions that he dreads to feel make him shudder with confusion. But, predisposed against belief in the devil and prejudiced against the power of mythical-symbolic language, he goes on making his rational explanations of the senseless and irrational. The presence of evil in the world has been and remains the greatest challenge to religion, the great atheistic fact, the chief evidence against belief in an all-good and all-sovereign Creator God.

Yet the prevailing rationalism and secularism of the modern temper have led to the reduction of this most awful of mysteries to an intellectual puzzle or problem to be solved rather than to the recognition of evil as the primary threat to any ultimate meaning or purpose in human life.[5] The classical modern intellectual formulation of evil as a problem or dilemma to be solved by philosophical theism has been set forth by David Hume: "Is [God] willing to prevent evil, but not able? then is he impotent. Is he able, but not willing? then is he malevolent. Is he both able and willing? whence then is evil?"[6] Archibald MacLeish has more recently compressed the dilemma into a catchy jingle:

> If God is God He is not good
> If God is good He is not God.[7]

John Hick has outlined the more specifically theological formulation of the problem in terms of the conflict between an ultimate monotheism and an ultimate dualism.[8] Absolute monotheism entails an ultimate monism. If God is God, and if God is good, there cannot be any coequal contrary reality; and therefore evil must in the end be subject to God's sovereignty and must exist by a permissive will proceeding from his purpose for creation. But this emphasis upon the divine sovereignty obscures the fact that evil is genuinely evil and utterly inimical to God's will and purpose. Yet the emphasis upon evil as God's enemy and the life of faith as a constant warfare with the forces of evil tends to give evil an independent status in relation to God the Creator, thereby challenging the absolute power and freedom of God.

There have been innumerable attempts to solve these philosophical and theological problems in modern theodicies, that is, in justifications of the ways of God with man. These theodicies have tried to mitigate, if not obliterate, the negative, nonsensical, and irrational implications of the presence of evil in the world. Philosophically, distinctions have been made between metaphysical, natural, and moral evil. Evil has been explained in terms of the principle of plenitude; the aesthetic view of the perfection of the universe; the theory of the ontological priority of good that denies ultimate reality to evil; the reality and consequences of free will in an orderly world; the building of moral and spiritual character through danger, conflict, and suffering; the wastefulness of creative evolution; the neurological and emotional sensitivity of the human organism and spirit; and the givenness of human solidarity that calls forth the virtues of human sympathy and self-sacrifice. Theologically, distinctions have been made between God's direct ordaining will and his indirect, accidental, or permissive will. The theological emphasis has been upon the goodness and reality of the world created and governed by a good and loving God; upon pain and suffering as a just divine retribution for human sin (both original and actual); the setting of evil in the context of redemption (the *O felix culpa* motif); and the final dichotomy between heaven, where good will be eternally rewarded, and hell, where evil will be eternally punished.

Nevertheless, in the final analysis the mystery of evil is not a problem to be solved but a reality to be experienced. All the rational and quasi-rational explanations and solutions to the problem of evil pale into insignificance when genuine tragedy and innocent suffering are suddenly encountered or experienced firsthand. Detached meditation on the general problem of evil very quickly gives way to concrete personal participation. Abstract, objective, rational explanations of the senseless and irrational are then existentially perceived to be intellectually, morally, and aesthetically unworkable and repugnant. The various philosophical and theological theodicies, both individually and collectively, are seen to be mutually destructive. Even at the logical level, the final result of the attempt at theodicy is hopeless contradiction and radical incoherence. Morally and aesthetically such simplistic rational explanations are judged to be despicable insults—ludicrous, outrageous expressions of optimism in the face of that which is inexplicable, unjust, and absurd. The affliction of pain and suffering, often beyond the limits of human endurance, dehumanizes persons and submerges them into the horrors of loneliness, emptiness, despair, and cynicism.

The symbolic images that are intuited by the poet and incorporated by myth and poetry are the proper means of communication for expressing the immediate experience of such a profound, nonrational, transcendent mystery.[9] If myth is confused with literal, scientific, descriptive truth or knowledge, it is open to insuperable logical and moral objections. But properly understood in its own categories, it is incomparable and irreplaceable in its capacity for presenting—and also for suggesting a possible resolution of—the profound mystery of evil. For only the drama of poetic imagery and myth can express and evoke the intuitive feeling-perceptions experienced at the unconscious and semiconscious levels of the human psyche.

Since time has run out on easy rational explanations of the senseless and irrational, and on moralistic exhortations for impotent men to engage in social action programs, I would suggest that time will be far more profitably spent reflecting upon the multivalent mythical-symbolic representation of evil than rehashing the tired and worn-out rational arguments that are, in the long run, inadequate to the painful reality of evil in the world. The dark figure of the Evil One has been much neglected in recent times because belief in him has been dismissed as either a psychological aberration or the survival of an outmoded superstition. But we may not take God seriously and explain away the devil with psychological and sociological explanations. If there is no devil, there is no God. Furthermore, even though the devil appears at first sight repulsive, closer inquiry reveals that he is really a very interesting and fascinating personality: grotesque, romantic, humorous, pathetic, grand, noble, and tragic.

III

The symbolic imagery and cycle of legends that constitute the mythical narrative about the devil and all his works have been and remain one of the most fascinating and promising attempts on the part of man to come to grips with the mystery of evil. The devil and his demonic entourage are the legacy of the widespread human tendency to attribute (rightly, I would argue) the ultimately mysterious and incomprehensible origin and presence of evil in the world to nonhuman, transcendent, supranatural powers. In order to construct some kind of framework within which a proper (that is, a mythical-symbolic) interpretation of the mystery of evil may be undertaken, the concluding part of this paper will set forth a tentative historical-evolutionary typology that sketches the original undifferentiated unity of the divine and the demonic in man's primordial religious experience of the numinous; the later dualistic differentiation and segmenting of the demonic from the divine; and the ultimate reintegration of the divine and the demonic in a religious perspective that is "beyond good and evil."[10]

THE UNDIFFERENTIATED UNITY OF THE DIVINE AND THE DEMONIC

Rudolf Otto has persuasively shown in his phenomenological description of the primordial religious experience that the *mysterium tremendum et fascinans* embraces diverse and contradictory elements, which for a later stage of religious consciousness are mutually exclusive. Early man experiences this paradoxical simultaneity of positive and negative, rational and irrational, daunting and fascinating, friendly and terrible, good and evil, in the deity as an original and natural unity. One essential emotional constituent of the experience of religious awe before the "Wholly Other" is demonic dread, which first begins to stir in the feeling of something "uncanny," "eerie," or "weird." This feeling forms the starting point for the development of religious consciousness in history; both "gods" and "demons" spring from this root feeling-experience.[11]

But the element of daunting awefulness is only one aspect of primordial religious experience; the numinous has at the same time another aspect in which it shows itself as something uniquely attractive and fascinating:

> These two qualities, the daunting and the fascinating, now combine in a strange harmony of contrasts, and the resultant dual character of the numinous consciousness, to which the entire religious development bears witness, at any rate from the level of the "daemonic dread" onwards, is at once the strangest and most noteworthy phenomenon in the whole history of religion. The daemonic-divine object may appear to the mind an object of horror and dread, but at the same time it is no less something that allures with a potent charm, and the creature, who trembles before it, utterly cowed and cast down, has always at the same time the impulse to turn to it, nay even to make it somehow his own. The "mystery" is for him not merely something to be wondered at but something that entrances him; and beside that in it which bewilders and confounds, he feels a something that captivates and transports him with a strange ravishment, rising often enough to the pitch of dizzy intoxication; it is the Dionysiac-element in the numen.[12]

The depiction of Yahweh in early Judaism clearly manifests the ambivalence of his divine-demonic character. There are many passages in the Old Testament that bring into relief the apparently arbitrary and incalculable "wrath or anger of Yahweh," a numinous quality that, like a hidden force of stored-up electricity, discharges itself indiscriminately against anyone who comes too near. Furthermore, there are numerous other passages that set forth the conviction that Yahweh is the source of evil as well as good, thereby squarely locating the origin of evil in God himself.[13]

THE DUALISTIC DIFFERENTIATION AND SEGMENTING OF THE DEMONIC FROM THE DIVINE

As religious consciousness develops, the original unity of diverse and contradictory elements in the primordial experience of the numinous split apart and order themselves antithetically according to the principle of opposites. God is identified with principles of reason and morality; he is exclusively identified with the qualities of absolute Light, absolute Truth, absolute Beauty, and absolute Goodness. Even his love is tempered with order and justice, for it is willed love rather than felt love, the masculine Logos rather than the feminine Eros.

But since light is recognized only in contrast to darkness, truth to falsehood, beauty to ugliness, goodness to evil, such a rationalized and moralistic image of God must of necessity be accompanied by a devil whom he does not consciously will to create. To segmentalize and moralize the image of God by eliminating those aspects which represent wrath and evil does not, in itself, eliminate the negative elements from experience of the numinous. Therefore, alongside the image of God appears a second image of deity—the image that represents only the negative side of God. That deity is the devil. The diabolical is nothing other than the underside of the divine, the counterface of God.[14] The consequent dualism insists that good and evil, God and the devil, are utterly and irreconcilably opposed to each other and that their duality can be overcome only by one ultimately destroying the other. As the figure of Satan becomes clearer and more distinct, his powers are magnified until he is almost an independent and autonomous god. The Prince of Evil threatens to break loose entirely from God's sovereign control.

It is indeed a remarkable development of religious consciousness whereby Satan, the angelic servant of God entrusted to the unpopular but necessary maintenance of the divine justice, becomes the devil, the deadly archenemy of God and man.[15] Historically, the origin of religious dualism leads back to the teachings of the Persian Zoroaster (ca. 7th century B.C.). Zoroastrianism teaches an omnipresent dualism, a universal antagonism between good and evil that is conceived metaphysically as well as ethically. A positive and a negative force, a creative and a destructive impulse, confront one another from the very beginning of all things. Sometimes they are referred to as "Twins" who derive from an original Father. These Twins are associated with light and darkness: the Prince of Light is Ahura Mazda or Ormazd; the Prince of Darkness is the evil spirit Angra Mainyu or Ahriman. Although Zoroaster insists that Ahura Mazda cannot be the author of evil (thereby leaving the question about the origin of evil veiled in mystery), he insists that the good and wise Power will ultimately prevail in the Last Days against the Antagonist.

The influence of this Persian dualism upon later Jewish thought is undeniable, and early Christianity emerged in the milieu of late Jewish apocalypticism. By the end of the first century A.D., all of the major threads were drawn together into the rich tapestry of the Christian picture of the devil.[16] For the devil of medieval and modern Christianity is a mythical synthesis of many diverse and originally independent traditions. These various traditions include the following: "the satan" who zealously accuses men before God; the war in heaven with the forces of God led by the archangel Michael; the expulsion of Lucifer from heaven; the fallen angels who were his followers (that is, the Watchers of Genesis 6 and 1 Enoch); the monstrous primeval dragon or serpent Leviathan; and the deceiving serpent of the Garden of Eden.

A persistent tradition of Christian dualism can be traced from the beliefs of early Gnostics to the medieval Paulicians, Bogomils, Patarenes, and Cathars.[17] Although a sharp religious dualism does not necessarily lead to devil worship, it often creates a favorable background for its emergence and for orthodox suspicion. There is more incentive to enlist in the devil's ranks if he is on more or less equal terms with God than if he is subordinate to God and acts only on God's sufferance, as in orthodox belief. It is no mere historical accident that the Gnostic sects were accused of satanism by orthodox Christians, or that the full flowering of Gnostic ideas and beliefs in French Catharism of the thirteenth century was attacked by the Inquisition with the same accusations later used against witches.

The early development of full-blown satanist theory was greatly influenced by the heretical beliefs of the medieval dualists.[18] There is a very pronounced ambivalence of attitude toward both God and the devil in the theory of satanism, and this ambivalence is manifest in the two main branches or divisions of devil worship. The first of these, to which the name satanism is more strictly applicable, is a worship of Satan, the adversary of God and of Christianity. Satan is regarded as an evil being, a malicious and perverse rebel against God, a lost archangel. The worshipers of the devil knowingly and willingly enter into a damning alliance with God's adversary and practice forbidden rites that are a defiance of and sacrilege to the true God. A second group, sometimes referred to as Luciferians or Palladists, adore Lucifer, the equal and foe of Adonai, or Yahweh. In their view, the supernatural being who is the enemy of the Christian God is a good and benevolent god, while the Christian God the Father, the God of the Old Testament, is and remains an evil god, hostile and treacherous to man and the enemy of morality and truth. Lucifer is identified as the god of Light, the good principle, while Adonai is the god of Darkness, the evil principle. God and the devil have reversed roles! Quite often, Jesus Christ is also condemned as an evil being, since he is the Son of God the Father. If God the Father and God the Son, the creators of Jewish and Christian law and ethics, are thought to be evil, the necessary result is a denial of the whole Judeo-Christian moral code and the conventional rules based upon it.

Herein lies one of the most important and fascinating characteristics of satanism, namely, the complete transvaluation or reversal of Christian values.[19] In the words of William Shakespeare's witches in *Macbeth*, "Fair is foul, and foul is fair"; or in the words of John Milton's Satan in *Paradise Lost*, "Evil, be thou my good." Christian piety, with its virtues of otherworldliness, self-denial, suffering vicarious love, humility, chastity of heart and mind and body, are condemned by the devil worshipers as corrupt, colorless, unnatural, and deadening. Devil worshipers believe that Satan rules this world and that the immediate rewards of his service are pleasure and power. They are intensely preoccupied with sensual pleasure and worldly achievement. They admire pride, strength, and force; they revel in self-assertion, domination over others, lust, dirt and filth, violence, cruelty, and all passionate sensations.

The same ambivalence of attitude toward God and the devil manifested in the worship and theory of satanism is also expressed in the symbolic imagery used to depict the nature and character of the devil. In the complex picture of Christian myth, Lucifer has two distinct and seemingly contradictory roles to play. On the one hand, he is depicted as horrific, repulsive, and loathsome with his horns, cloven feet, and tail (borrowed either from the satyrlike Pan and/or the ancient goatgod of pagan fertility rites). In this guise, the "anal characteristics" of the devil persistently recur in the descriptions of him. His color is black, which is associated both with the place of his abode in the darkness and with filth; he emits sulphurous smells and leaves behind horrible stenches; the kiss of shame, which ritually symbolizes the absolute obeisance of his followers, consists in kissing the devil's posterior; the devil is well known in both narrative accounts and pictorially for dropping his pants and showing off his posterior; the central ceremony of the Black Mass desecrates the consecrated host by kneading it on the buttocks of a nude woman serving as an altar; the host is mixed with menstrual blood, urine, and feces; Dante in the *Divine Comedy* makes the still point of the turning world, around which he passes toward purgatory, Satan's anus; Bosch, in his painting of this world as hell, enthrones Satan on a privy, from which the souls that have passed out of his anus drop into the black pit of hell.

On the other hand, he is depicted as the greatest, most powerful, and most resplendent of the archangels; and he remains an archangel of dark beauty and deceptive glory—a supernatural, spiritual entity who plots against man's welfare and God's purpose with a subtlety and cleverness far beyond the range of the most intricate human intellect. Satan in this guise always has the seductive outward aspect of an angel of light; and only an expert in holiness can discern him, for his supreme craft lies in deception and confusion of the truth. In the ultimate lie, the most deceptive of all the masks of the Father of all Lies, is the figure of the absolutely righteous and moral God. As the characters of God and the devil are more fully elaborated, they sometimes change roles in such a way that the image of God becomes diabolical and the image of the devil divine. For as the image of God is composed of goodness piled on goodness, virtue piled on virtue, power piled on power, he becomes unbelievable, unapproachable, insufferable, and monstrous. But in conceiving the image of the devil, the creative imagination of man empties all of its repressed and sensuous contents. The result has been the romantic tendency to see the devil as a titanic, tragic figure, as he is in Milton's *Paradise Lost*—the archrebel against authority, fearless, determined, defiant in the face of superior force, unhumbled in defeat. "Better to reign in Hell than serve in Heaven." Such an image evokes a willing (or unwilling) admiration; it strikes a deep chord of sympathetic response in man because man can see so much of himself in it. With such an emphasis on the magnificence and nobility of the devil's pride and power, it is not surprising that some have attempted to enter his service, or that Satan and satanism retain their alluring fascination.

The Ultimate Reintegration of the Divine and the Demonic

Although the dualistic representation of the conflict between God and the devil is a necessary stage in the development of religious consciousness and, in many ways, a very attractive and powerful interpretation of the mystery of evil, this position is not viable for the strict monotheist. Absolute monotheism entails an absolute monism. Every monotheism that consistently maintains the perfect goodness of God is bound either to let go the absolute divine power and freedom, or else to hold that evil exists ultimately within God's nature and/or purpose. To deny God's absolute power and freedom is to take the first step toward cosmic dualism by compromising the divine sovereignty; to admit the existence of evil in the divine nature and/or purpose is to make God the author of evil. A careful investigation of the mythical-symbolic representation of the mystery of evil suggests that the final oppressive responsibility for the origin and existence of evil rests upon God himself, who is alone sufficiently able to bear such an awesome burden. There are two quite distinct—but perhaps ultimately complementary—ways in which this final reabsorption of evil into the divine has been depicted: mystically and eschatologically.

The Mystical Resolution

Both Western and Eastern mysticism stress the higher unity or reconciliation of opposites in the divine without, however, doing away with the dialectical tension that remains in the polarity. The mythical accounts of the dualistic conflict between God and the devil contain a number of strong hints of the ultimate identity of God and Satan (for example, the tendency of God and the devil to create each other, to change roles with each other, and so on). The mystical intuition of the mutual interdependence or correlativity of opposites also suggests the inner identity of the divine and the demonic. At this deeply intuitive level of awareness, the mystic sees how inseparable (but not irreconcilable) good and evil are. God and the devil are relative terms, and God would cease to be if there were no devil. God is the union of opposites par excellence; he is absolutely paradoxical in that he represents in every respect thesis and antithesis, and at the same time synthesis. Lucifer in this context becomes the symbol not of deliberate malice and rebellion but of the necessary "dark side" of God, of shadow revealing light by contrast, of darkness as "the light-bearer" (*luci-fer*). He corresponds to an essential polarity in God, which the Chinese call yin as distinct from yang, or to what the Hindu Shaivites call Shakti as distinct from Shiva—namely, the dark, negative, and feminine aspect of God in complementary opposition to the light, positive, and masculine.

The interdependence and inner unity of the shadow and the light in the divine is clearly illustrated in the hidden identity of the "wrath" and the "love" of God. This love is far from being sentimental or doting, for it is inseparable from the awe-inspiring quality of holiness.

> In mysticism, too, this element of "energy" is a very living and vigorous factor, at any rate in the "voluntaristic" mysticism of love where it is very forcibly seen in that "consuming fire" of love whose burning strength the mystic can hardly bear, but begs that the heat that has scorched him may be mitigated, lest he himself be destroyed by it. And in this urgency and pressure the mystic's "love" claims a perceptible kinship with the *orge* itself, the same "energy," only differently directed. "Love," says one of the mystics, "is nothing else than quenched wrath."[20]

In the mystical vision, then, God is not to be exclusively identified with good alone or with evil alone; but, nevertheless, he is in the good and in the evil. God is in growth and in decay; he reveals himself in life and in death. Even evil, temptation, wickedness, and sin elicit the good. Mystically speaking, even the existence and work of the devil are filled with the presence of God.

The Eschatological Resolution

There is a second way of resolving the conflict of opposites that is more in line with the mainstream traditions of Zoroastrianism, Judaism, and Christianity than is mysticism. Neither Judaism nor Christianity can be separated from the messianic hope that some day, *in spite of* all the past and present rational and empirical evidence, the Kingdom of God will be made visible. In the eschatological redemption of evil, a present interim dualism is affirmed within the ultimate setting of an unqualifiedly monotheistic faith. Eschatological hope does not try to put on blinders to the stubborn reality and incomprehensibility of the ambiguous mingling in human experience of good and evil, virtue and vice, pain and pleasure, despair and joy. If there is to be any eventual resolution of the interplay between good and evil, or any decisive bringing of good out of evil, it must lie beyond this present life and beyond the enigma of death. The mystery of evil cannot be resolved by looking to the past, seeking there an explanation of its origins, or by looking at the present. The only possibility is to turn toward the future, hoping that God will bring some future good out of past and present evil. Such expectation of a triumphant future resolution of the mystery of evil brings both the origin and the continuing presence of evil within the all-encompassing will and purpose of God.

In the eschatological vision, the sufferings of men will, in the light of the infinite future good, be rendered justifiable; all of the pain, travail, and wickedness that have been experienced will be seen not to have been merely evil, for they will have been used in the creation of infinite good. The good eschaton will be an unending and therefore unlimited good that will render worthwhile *any* finite suffering endured in the course of attaining it.

Man's intellectual and imaginative resources are utterly inadequate to even suggest what the divine power and wisdom of God hold for the future. The divine creation and especially the divine nature are virtually infinite in range and complexity, in glories and wonders. The only possible way that the nature of this eschatological fulfillment can be dealt with at present is in terms of the rich, concrete, picturesque, symbolic imagery of myth. The Kingdom of God has been depicted as a state of exultant and blissful happiness, symbolized as a joyous banquet where all rejoice together. The Kingdom of God has been depicted as a time of universal peace and justice and prosperity, when the lion and the lamb lie down together, and when all tears of sorrow will be wiped away. The eschatological vision ultimately calls for a new heaven and a new earth.

The traditionally orthodox form of the eschatological vision also affirms the ultimate doom and destruction of the devil. But there has been a continuous countertradition that has argued for the ultimate redemption of Lucifer and of all his followers (cf. the *apocatastasis* of Origen in the third century A.D.). This countertradition was denounced as a heresy in the fifth century A.D.; nevertheless, it persists. Both ancient and modern traditions entertain the possibility of the eventual remorse of the spirit of Evil and his reconciliation with God.

In virtue of this wider context of eschatological vision, there can be a partial, although most significant, transformation of the present encounter with evil. Faith, which is hope in things not seen, will hold that ultimately all evil serves a good purpose. Even during the dark night of trial and suffering—when affliction eclipses the presence of God and the demons of horror, emptiness, and loneliness possess the whole self—the man of hope will paradoxically remain faithful in the midst of his misery. The challenge of incomprehensible and overwhelming forces of evil will lead him to even greater faith and hope—and yes, even love for the absent God. He will accept the ambiguity of his human existence and drink his cup of anguish to the full—all the while hoping against hope and in the teeth of mocking absurdity that "in everything God works for good with those who love him" (Rom. 8:38-39).

1. Eric Maple, in *The Dark World of Witches* (New York: A. S. Barnes, 1962), p. 199, reaches the following optimistic conclusion: "The power of an idea which has dominated the human mind for countless ages cannot be dissolved in a few years by the mere waving of the scientists' wand, but it is possible now that the legends are fading from the memories of the country people that witch-belief in its traditional form has gone for ever." Another study on the devil concludes that "it would seem best to act as though evil spirits did not exist, until such time as their existence is forced upon us." See Henry A. Kelly, *The Devil, Demonology and Witchcraft* (Garden City, N.Y.: Doubleday, 1968), p. 131. Kelly apparently believed that "that time" had already arrived when he wrote a later essay entitled "Death of the Devil?" published in *Commonweal*, November 6, 1970, pp. 146-49.

2. See C. H. Wallace, *Witchcraft in the World Today* (New York: Award Books, 1967), pp. 12, 29; and Susy Smith, *Today's Witches* (Englewood Cliffs, N.J.: Prentice-Hall, 1970), pp. 107, 127-28.

3. Theodore Roszak, *The Making of a Counter Culture* (Garden City, N.Y.: Doubleday and Co., 1969), pp. 7-8.

4. The reactionary character of contemporary devil worship and witchcraft has been captured in David St. John's *Diabolus* (New York: Weybright and Talley, 1971) in the following dialogue between Valerie Theirs and protagonist Peter Ward:

> She pressed his hand, then said, "Peter, how much of this devil-worship do you suppose is going on? And why?"
>
> He sipped from his glass and set it down. "In the British Isles there are said to be fifty thousand devil cultists, and in America at least half a million. I think it's probably symptomatic of revolt against science and our dehumanized urban lives; against impersonal machines like computers that plan and program our lives without recourse to personal appeal. And if witchcraft is anything at all, it's a personal thing. So the spread of cults and Satanist marriages. Stores can't keep Tarot cards in stock, and astrologers are more popular than astronauts. To a lot of people, I suppose, witchcraft seems to offer one final hope of getting hold of their lives, putting it all together."
>
> "Then that would explain Luci's interest in the occult. She's always been spoiled, pampered, and directionless. The sensual aspects would have a particularly strong appeal for her." (Pp. 69-70)

5. During the process of secularization, the very idea of mystery was radically altered in the vigorous attempt to do away with all obscurantism and superstition. Mystery is originally the experience of the nonhuman dimension of reality that is known in primordial religious rite and ritual; mystery in this sense is not to be conceptually understood or manipulated but revered in a sense of wonder. With the appearance of scientific skepticism and liberal optimism, however, the mysterious came to be regarded either as a tricky intellectual problem to be solved or a guilty secret to be exposed. In either case, the mystery was understood to be an intolerable barrier to reason and/or justice.

Gabriel Marcel is responsible for making the critical distinction between dealing with evil as a problem and as a mystery. Marcel describes a problem as that which arises in the context of mere functions where every part is clearly perceived by a detached subject and a "thing" or an "object" in relation to other things; a problem, therefore, is in principle able to be solved by using the proper rational technique or procedure. Evil regarded as a problem is reflected upon in a detached way—that is, without personal involvement or participation—and hence is viewed from the outside as a technical disorder. This way of regarding the matter presupposes that reason can discover the causes and the hidden ends or aims of the phenomenon of evil. But, Marcel goes on to say, evil that is only described or observed is no longer evil that is suffered; in fact, it ceases to be evil. The evil that is truly evil is that which is experienced through personal involvement, through participation in a larger whole that reason cannot get outside of so that it may look upon it calmly and objectively like a spectator. This is evil as a metaproblematical mystery. Marcel defines a mystery as "a problem which encroaches upon its own data, invading them, as it were, and thereby transcending itself as a simple problem." As a mystery the presence of evil in the world is no longer merely a problem, because it can no longer be solved by rational and technical means. It can only be responded to with hope and/or despair, faith and/or cynicism, love and/or hate. See Marcel's essay "On the Ontological Mystery" in *The Philosophy of Existence* (New York: Philosophical Library, 1949), pp. 8-12; see also *Being and Having* (Boston: Beacon Press, 1951), pp. 171-72.

6. David Hume, *Dialogues Concerning Natural Religion* (New York: Hafner, 1953), p. 66. Hume is "quoting" the ancient Greek philosopher Epicurus (342?-270 B.C.), whose words are transmitted through the writing of the Christian Lactantius (ca. A.D. 260-340); see chap. 13 of "On the Anger of God" in *The Writings of the Ante-Nicene Fathers*, vol. 7 (Grand Rapids, Mich.: Wm. B. Eerdmans, 1970), p. 271.

7. Archibald MacLeish, *J.B.* (Boston: Houghton Mifflin, 1958), p. 11.

8. John Hick, *Evil and the God of Love* (New York: Harper & Row, 1966), pp. 21-22.

9. Symbolic images are specific, pictorial psychic images that are imaginatively intuited and "bring together" or join rational and irrational, positive and negative, conscious and unconscious elements—elements from both inner and outer worlds. Symbolic images are "multivalent" or "polysemous" because the diverse and contradictory elements united in them are so great and multifarious. A myth is an imaginative, numinous story or narrative that utilizes multivalent symbolic images to relate an act or series of events of ultimate cosmic significance. A "complete myth" is a complex unity of mythic stories that sets forth a drama of universal significance in which the individual person may participate, thereby giving meaning, purpose, and structure to all human existence.

10. Like all typological schemes, the division into stages is somewhat artifical and oversimplified. However, the reader should keep in mind three important points. First, the evolutionary scheme being developed here is not meant to be a straightforward narration of what happened in history; rather, it is meant to be a framework in terms of which the correlation of many historical facts may be discerned and interpreted. Only after such correlations of facts have been discerned can what actually happened in history be understood and narrated. Second, the evolution of religious consciousness that is being typologized is not an irreversible linear process; that is, it is not a process in which the movement to stage three means leaving stages one and two completely behind. The evolution of religious consciousness is *a complexifying process*, the adding of new layers of awareness. As a new level is added, it may become primary and predominant over the others, but it never totally eradicates the earlier stages; it is always possible to regress into earlier levels of religious awareness. Third, the ontogenetic development of the individual religious consciousness has to pass through the same stages as the phylogenetic development of the religious consciousness of the human race. The evolution of religious consciousness that has taken place during the thousands of years of human history must be reenacted, or otherwise reappropriated, in the psychological and spiritual development of each person.

11. See Rudolf Otto, *The Idea of the Holy*, trans. John W. Harvey, 2d ed. (New York: Oxford University Press, 1958), pp. 14-16.

12. Ibid., p. 31.

13. There is the picture of Satan as a functionary in the divine court (Job 1:6-12). There are the words of Second Isaiah: "I form the light, and create darkness: I make peace, and create evil; I the Lord do all these things" (Isa. 45:7). The prophet Amos asks rhetorically, "Does evil befall a city, unless the Lord has done it?" (Amos 3:6), as does also the Wisdom writer, "Is it not from the mouth of the Most High that good and evil come?" (Lam. 3:38). The author of Ecclesiasticus says, "Good things and bad, life and death, poverty and wealth come from the Lord" (Eccles. 11:14). Again, in the prophetic interpretation of Old Testament history God employs the cruelties of the heathen Chaldeans and Assyrians to discipline and punish his chosen people (e.g., Jer. 1:15; 7:14; 50:25; and Isa. 10:5 ff.; 28:21). In other contexts, too, God is depicted as using suffering for the moral and spiritual training of his children (e.g., Deut. 8:25; Prov. 3:11-12; Ps. 94:12).

14. Alan Watts has picturesquely expressed this insight in the following words: "For even God's universe has spawned the Devil, who arises not so much from his own independent malice as from God's 'arrogance' in assuming omnipotent kingship and identifying himself with unalloyed goodness. The Devil is God's unconsciously produced shadow." See *Nature, Man and Woman* (New York: Random House, 1970), p. 89.

15. The name Satan comes from the Hebrew name meaning "adversary" or "opponent." In postexilic Judaism, "the satan" was translated into Greek as *diabolos*, meaning "an accuser," with the implication of "a false accuser," and therefore "a slanderer"; this is the Greek word from which the English "devil" is derived. An excellent and concise account of the historical transition of "the satan" into the malicious devil is found in Richard Cavendish, *The Black Arts* (New York: G. P. Putnam's Sons, 1967), pp. 281-99.

16. Carl Jung has suggestively pointed out that religious dualism reaches its apex only after the rise of Christianity. "The Antichrist," he says, "is nothing less than the counterstroke of the devil, provoked by God's Incarnation; for the devil attains his true stature as the adversary of Christ, and hence of God, only after the rise of Christianity, while as late as the Book of Job he was still one of God's sons and on familiar terms with Yahweh. Psychologically the case is clear, since the dramatic figure of Christ is so sublime and spotless that everything else turns dark beside it. It is, in fact, so one-sidedly perfect that it demands a psychic complement to restore the balance. This inevitable opposition led very early to the doctrine of the two sons of God, of whom the elder was called Satanaël. . . . In reality every intensified differentiation of the Christ-image brings about a corresponding accentuation of its unconscious complement." *Aion*, trans. R. F. C. Hull (Princeton, N.J.: Princeton University Press, 1959), pp. 42-43. Elsewhere Jung says that "the opposition between light and good on the one hand and darkness and evil on the other is left in a state of open conflict, since Christ simply represents good, and his counterpart, the devil, evil. This opposition is the real world problem, which at present is still unsolved." *Psychology and Alchemy*, trans. R. F. C. Hull (Princeton, N.J.: Princeton University press, 1968), p. 19.

17. This "heretical" dualistic tradition is traced with great erudition by Steven Runciman, *The Medieval Manichee* (Cambridge: Cambridge University Press, 1960).

18. Historically speaking, many sects and groups have been accused of devil worship, but genuine satanists have probably always been rare, as they are today. The accused sects cloak themselves in secrecy, to avoid persecution, and it is often impossible to tell whether they are consciously devoted to adoration of the devil. When I refer to the "theory of satanism," I am referring to beliefs and practices that have been attributed to satanists both by their orthodox accusers and by those who call themselves satanists. I am "bracketing" the moot question about whether or not satanist theory is the product of the fantasies of witch-hunters who procured confessions from persons who were psychologically demented because of torture or of persons who were consciously and willingly committed to the worship and service of the

devil.

19. This satanic transvaluation of Jewish and Christian values should be compared with that of Friedrich Nietzsche, who has been called—among many other things—a "proto-witch." See *The Genealogy of Morals*, trans. Horace B. Samuel (New York: Modern Library, 1954), esp. pp. 640-54.

20. Otto, *Idea of the Holy*, p. 24. Cf. the following statement of Alan Watts: "Thus the love of God inspires a fear, which, if one does not flee from it, becomes a rapture enabling the mind to perceive it as light and splendour. But if this fear becomes panic, if one runs from it, the same radiance becomes the fire which is never quenched and the worm that dieth not, so that the damned who writhe in Hell are burned by the same fire which delights the angels in Heaven." *Myth and Ritual in Christianity* (Boston: Beacon Press, 1968), pp. 34-35.

Sculpture and Architecture

Sculpture, Painting, and the Human Body

F. David Martin

Bucknell University

> One need only shut oneself in a closet and begin to think of the fact of one's being there, of one's queer bodily shape in the darkness (a thing to make children scream at, as Stevenson says), of one's fantastic character and all, to have the wonder steal over the detail as much as over the general fact of being, and to see that it is only familiarity that blunts it. Not only that anything should be, but that *this* very thing should be, is mysterious.
>
> —William James

OUR awareness is incarnated. As Husserl succinctly puts it, "In every experience of spatial objects the body, as the perceptual organ of the experiencing subject, is co-perceived."[1] Thus, no other thing—that is no three-dimensional or material object, as distinguished from such "nonthings" as ideas or values—is as important to us as the human body, for it is the thing that makes possible the showing forth of all other things. The human body, moreover, is supremely interesting aesthetically, not only possessing fascinating textures but manifesting the most complex of all three-dimensional shapes, the subtle transitions of muscular movement producing inexhaustible three-dimensional configurations. Those configurations, in turn, take on added interest because they often are expressions of a personality. Furthermore, although there may be other things in the world as sensuously attractive—the full glory of autumnal leaves, for example—the human body also possesses a sexuality that incomparably enhances its sensuousness. No wonder, then, that we prize the human body, especially when it is beautiful. Goethe even claims that " no evil can touch him who looks on human beauty; he feels himself at one with himself and with the world."

It is not surprising, therefore, that the human body—clothed or unclothed, beautiful or even ugly—has been and still is a favorite subject matter of painting. Often it has been the favorite, as with many of the paintings of Titian, Rubens, Ingres, Renoir, Matisse, and Picasso. Yet it is somewhat surprising, perhaps, that the human body has been an even more favored subject matter of sculpture. In the West—except for the period between the fifth and fourteenth centuries,[2] and until works such as Boccioni's *Develoment of a Bottle in Space*" (1912) and Picasso's *Musical Instrument* (1914)—the human body, especially nude, has been considered to be the noblest and almost exclusive subject matter of sculpture.[3] Dewitt Parker claims, for example: "The sculptor has this advantage over all other artists, that his chief subject matter is the most beautiful thing in the world—the human body."[4] Moreover, as Camus maintains, sculpture captures the fleeting expressions of the body:

> The greatest and most ambitious of all the arts, sculpture, is bent on capturing, in three dimensions, the fugitive figure of man, and on restoring the unity of great style to the general disorder of gestures. . . . Its purpose is not to imitate, but to stylize and to imprison in one significant expression the fleeting ecstasy of the infinite variety of human attitudes.[5]

And Henry Moore insists:

> For me sculpture is based on and remains close to the human figure. That works both ways. We make the kind of sculpture we make because we are the shape we are, because we have the proportions we have. All those things make us respond to form and shape in certain ways. If we had the shape of cows, and went about on four legs, the whole basis of sculpture would be different.[6]

Even abstract sculpture, according to Reg Butler, is aesthetically appealing "because it contains within it certain references [to the human body] which are acceptable, and these are based not only in my culture but in my biology. So that if dogs made sculpture they would make sculpture with different plastic values from ours."[7] Barbara Hepworth, usually an abstractionist, remarks: "I love working on a large scale so that the whole body of the spectator becomes involved."[8] Every sculpture is, unlike a painting, significantly similar to our bodies because it occupies a significantly noticeable area of three-dimensional space. Yet, as Herbert Read notes, it still is remarkable that "at least nine-tenths of all sculpture ever carved is devoted to one subject—the human body."[9] Why do sculptors devote themselves more to the human body than do painters?

Read's explanation is based on the Narcissus myth: "A youth falls in love with his own image as reflected in a clear spring, and being unable to endow that image with corporeality, pines away and dies."[10] There is an element of truth in this myth: the insatiable desire we have to arrive at a satisfactory three-dimensional image of our bodily selves, a material counterpoint for the mental images of our bodies. Mirror images help, of course, but they are always seen as far behind the mirror as we are in front. We cannot rub against or even touch our image, for what is "in" the mirror is not there at all. The image has no being of its own, entirely dependent upon what it reflects. Like the image of a painting, a mirror image has no physical tangibility. And as with a painting, the mirror image can only present the surface of our bodies, the mass being represented by cues of perspective. Such images, with their unreal quality, are not very satisfactory material counterpoints of our mental images of ourselves. "Hold it up sternly! See this it sends back! (Who is it? Is it you?)" (Walt Whitman, "A Hand-Mirror.") Nonreflected sight of ourselves helps, but we can see only a part of ourselves. Touch of ourselves and other people also helps, but usually such perceptions of mass are blurred with irrelevancies, such as embarrassment or concealing clothes. Sculpture often strips away these irrelevancies.

Through its forms sculpture can bring out three-dimensionality directly, making possible clarifying embodiments of both the exterior and the interior of the human body. Two-dimensional images are usually not very revealing of our bodies as occupying a place that resists invasion by other things, our ability to advance to and occupy other places, our sense of haptic volume bounded, however vaguely, by tactile sensations, and our kinesthetic sensations. (The terms *tactual, tactile* and *haptic* are often used rather loosely. Under the tactual I include both tactile sensations—that is, feelings of things external to the skin—and haptic sensations—that is, muscular, visceral feelings within the skin. Kinesthetic sensations are the awareness of the movements associated with tactual sensations.) Two-dimensional images are outlines of ourselves in these respects because they cannot disclose mass and volume directly. This is not to suggest that paintings are necessarily inferior to sculptures in revealing the human body, for paintings often can reveal many aspects of the human body far more richly and subtly than sculpture—for example, as in Rembrandt's portraits, the color, warmth, and softness of flesh, the luminosity of the eyes, and the character complexities of the face and hands. However, paintings generally cannot reveal the mass and volume of the human body as richly and subtly as sculpture because paintings can only directly depict surfaces. Paintings are configurations of two-dimensional shapes that can only suggest the three-dimensional. This indirect depiction necessarily lacks the depth that is so helpful in clarifying that strange "thickness" so basic to our awareness of our bodies.

Paintings, furthermore, because they lack an 'impacting between', cannot reveal as forcefully as sculptures our awareness of our bodies as three-dimensional centers thrusting out into our surrounding environment. By an impacting between, I mean that space around a sculpture which, although not a part of its material body, is still an essential part of the perceptible structure of that sculpture.[11] And the perceptual forces in that surrounding space impact on our bodies, changing that space from an empty or transparent between, as with a painting, to a thick or translucent between charged with dynamic tensions. With a painting the space between us and the canvas is, ideally, an intangible bridge to the painting, which, for the most part, does not explicitly enter into our awareness of the painting. Tactile sensation is not completely absent, for there is, of course, the stimulation of the painting on our eyeballs, but there is no impacting force to this tactility, and, in turn, the haptic resonance, the echoing within the body, is minimal. For example, because of the compression of its imaginary space, the denizens of Picasso's *Les Demoiselles d'Avignon* in the Museum of Modern Art powerfully project toward us visually. Yet even in such an extraordinary example, we do not perceive that encroachment as going so far as to enter the real space of the museum room. We are not clientele in the same room. We necessarily remain at arm's length from these painted prostitutes. There is no physical invasion, for these girls are imaginary rather than space-displacing presences. However charged the space within the picture, the space without remains uncharged. We take no notice of the outside or real space, for that would distract us from the space within, the imaginary space of the painting. The encroachment of the girls is psychological, derivative from our mental associations with real three-dimensional females, rather than physical, for the space outside the canvas remains empty of significant forces. All perception of an external thing, as Merleau-Ponty convincingly demonstrates in *The Phenomenology of Perception*, involves a resounding within our bodies of that thing physically forcing itself on our bodies, either directly, as when some thing rubs against us, or indirectly, as when the pressures from a thing flow into the space between the thing and us. The greater the volume and the mass, generally, the greater the pressures. Since the canvas of a painting—that solid rectangle to be hung on a wall—is usually thin and light, it does not exert much physical force in one's perception. But, much more importantly, when one stands back from the wall and perceives the canvas and its pigments *as a painting*, then the painting creates an imaginary space that conceals the actual three-dimensionality of the canvas. A painting, as Susanne Langer observes:

> is made by deploying pigments on a piece of canvas, but the picture is not a pigment-and-canvas structure. The picture that emerges from the process is a structure of space, and the space itself is an emergent whole of shapes, visible colored volumes. Neither the space nor the things in it were in the room before. Pigments and canvas are not in the pictorial space; they are in the space of the room, as they were before, though we no longer find them there by sight without a great effort of attention. For touch they are still there. But for touch there is no pictorial space. The picture, in short, is an apparition . . . the whole picture is a piece of purely visual space. It is nothing but a vision.[12]

Thus, the impacting forces of a painting into the between are minimal in our awareness. The between appears transparent. We seem to perceive straight through the between, as if it were irrelevant, as if it contained no forces.

A sculpture, on the other hand, does not create an imaginary space but transforms real space. There is no concealing, as with a painting, of actual three-dimensionality. Whereas a painting excludes its material body (the canvas) when it is perceived as a painting, a sculpture includes its material body when it is perceived as a sculpture. Thus with a sculpture, even when we do not actually touch the material body, we can sense its power penetrating the surrounding space and pressing into our bodies. The shadows, the reflecting surfaces, the bulges and hollows, the textures, and the attraction or repulsion of the material itself—all these pull our bodies in and out. Unlike a painting, which is usually "all there" and can be seen from one "fixed-focused" position, the hidden aspects of a sculpture—especially with sculptures in the round—lure our bodies around. Kinesthetic sensations reinforce our tactual sensations: the encroachment of a sculpture is not only psychological, as with some paintings, such as *Les Demoiselles d'Avignon*, but physical. Whereas the forces of a painting are confined within its edges or frame—which help anchor the imaginary space of the painting to a place, however tenuous, in real space[13]—the forces of a sculpture, since they are generated by three-dimensional material that is not concealed, activate the surrounding space, making us explicitly aware of the impacting surrounding space as part of the perceptible structure of the sculpture. It is the impacting between, as I have argued elsewhere,[14] that accounts for the distinctiveness of sculpture.

Gaston Bachelard remarks: "Immensity is within ourselves. It is attached to a sort of expansion of being which life curbs and caution arrests, but which starts again when we are alone. As soon as we become motionless, we are elsewhere; we are dreaming in a world that is immense. Indeed, immensity is the movement of a motionless man."[15] Gaston Lachaise's *Floating Figure* in the Sculpture Garden of the Museum of Modern Art, with its ballooning buoyancy emerging with lonely but powerful internal animation from a graceful ellipse, is exceptionally revealing of this need for expansion, this instinctual longing of our bodies to be united with something beyond. More than any other art, sculpture, because of its expansiveness—its three-dimensional impact into the between—enables each man to reunite the two-dimensional image of himself he finds when he looks at reflecting surfaces with his tactual and kinesthetic sensations of himself. The mirror image is only a ghost of our bodies. If only Narcissus had had a sculpture of himself, presumably he would have been saved.[16] Sculpture vivifies and clarifies our bodies in their fullness. The sculptor shapes sculpture, and sculpture shapes us.

The sexual instincts, according to Read, are also involved in the perception of sculpture of the human body. "Not only do we tend to idealize the object we love and desire, but also we transfer to an ideal representation of the human body those desires that we cannot satisfy in reality."[17] Pygmalion falls in love with the marble mimic of the ideal girl he sculpted and asks Aphrodite to give the marble life. His desire is granted, the marble being transformed into flesh, and Pgymalion marries his beautiful creation and names her Galatea.[18] For those of us who neither sculpt nor have influence with Aphrodite, the beautiful statue may also provoke sexual desires. Unlike Pygmalion, however, we can receive only psychological satisfaction; on the other hand, sculptural beauties, such as the *Aphrodite of Cyrene* in the Museo Nazionale delle Terme in Rome, are available to all. Even without head and arms, this *Aphrodite* in a sense is more essentially a woman than a real woman because the female shape, texture, grace, sensuality, sexuality, and beauty are interpreted by an artistic form and thus vivified and clarified. With all those enhanced feminine qualities, the seductive forces of *Aphrodite* impact into the between more vividly than those of most real females, and we are bound to be drawn close and circle her. If the guards are not looking—for she is watched over by some of the most zealous puritans of Italy—we touch and caress her. Even the most perfect real woman—at least from a male-chauvinist viewpoint—is always moving away, or talking too much, or covering up, or in bad light, or sick, or getting old. The sculptor can make her stand still, shut her up, strip her, give her good light, and keep her healthy and young. Then "the frustrated lover of love," as Camus remarks, "can finally gaze at the Greek caryatides and grasp what it is that triumphs, in the body and face of the woman, over every degradation."[19] And the sculptor can do the same for males, of course, as Michelangelo did with his *David*.[20] The painter can do many of these things too, of course, and with respect to the sensuousness of the flesh he can far surpass the sculptor, as Giorgione, Titian, Rubens, Renoir, and Modigliani, among many others, have proved. Yet the painter, unlike the sculptor, has to sacrifice the direct presentation of three-dimensionality, and in doing that he loses much of the seductive force. Beauty is more than skin deep. Painters are not Pygmalions. Thus statues even more than paintings teach us how to idealize our actual lovers, training us to perceive what we want to perceive. But conversely, as Read points out, the human body can also be used by the sculptor to reveal sadism or masochism or nihilism, seeking "to destroy the body image as an object of desire,"[21] as, for example, almost any sculpture by Giacometti does. And, of course, the painter can also do this, as, for example, the "women paintings" by De Kooning.

The extensive use of the human body as a subject matter of sculpture helps confirm our withness with things, for it is our bodies as three-dimensional things that are with things as three-dimensional. Even when a human body is only very vaguely portrayed, if at all, the sculpture is usually and easily anthropomorphized. For example, Lipchitz's *Song of the Vowels* in the Musée National d'Art Moderne in Paris, which seems to float through space despite its great weight, at first appears as completely lacking any reference to the human body, the harp to be played by the wind. But then we notice fingers and they suggest a hand that leads to an arm, and then we inevitably perceive a player holding a harp. Lipchitz recalls:

> I hired a mason to help me with the base, an Italian who spoke very little French. While we were working, the mason suddenly said, "I am very proud to work on this." And I said, perhaps a little rudely, "Why are you proud? Do you like it?" He said, apologetically, "Of course, some people like those unknown soldiers more." (Because in every town in France there are those awful monuments to unknown soldiers.) "But I prefer this." So I said, "Why do you prefer it?" and the mason said "Perche parla!" "Because it speaks!").[22]

This kind of remark often occurs. When discussing with students Arp's *Growth* in the Philadelphia Museum of Art, a statue that is only remotely suggestive of the human body, I have noticed that they usually describe the animations of the statue in terms of a human vitality, not a vegetable or animal power, or some power immanent in all things. Such anthropomorphic description is in part a consequence of the impacting between of sculpture, which involves our bodies in a spatial withness more directly than does painting, and so we tend to perceive sculpture more than painting in bodily terms. Except perhaps for the dance, no other art is as conducive to empathy—"to feeling into"—as sculpture, for most sculpture is a compelling invitation to bodily identification.

Piaget observes that "space is . . . the product of an interaction between the organism and the environment in which it is impossible to dissociate the organization of the universe perceived from that of the activity itself."[23] However, the awareness of this inseparable unity occurs only in the aesthetic experience, when we are "thinking from" some thing rather than "thinking at" it. Then, we lose explicit self-consciousness, our awareness of a subject/object dichotomy. Even in the aesthetic experience, nonetheless, there usually is some awareness of "here" and "there." In viewing a film, for example, we are at least implicitly aware that the space created by the film is imaginary, discontinuous with our space in the theater. We know that we cannot get up from our seats and traverse an intermediate space into the film space. In the case of the dance—the most "bodily" art of all in the sense that the body is always involved in its performance[24]—we can, unless an usher or someone stops us, get into the dance space, but except in some rare avant-garde dance this destroys the dance. A sculpture and our bodies, however, are at different ends of the same space, and that sculpture energizes the space between. No other art, except architecture sometimes, has the concentrated impact of the between of sculpture.[25] Sculpture "bangs" into our bodies with convergent forces, and this heightens our body awareness. We feel *physically with* sculpture, more than with painting. That is why even basically abstract masses, such as Lipchitz's *Song of the Vowels*, sometimes seem to "speak."

The contents of the Salle Camondo, the first room to the left of the entrance in the Jeu de Paume in Paris, provide excellent examples of the basic differences between the ways painting and sculpture involve the awareness of our bodies, for the room is filled with some of the finest works of Degas: nine paintings of dancing scenes and fourteen bronze sculptures of dancers (thirteen small and one large). Whereas the colors of the paintings are a feast for our eyes, the colors of the sculpture are not particularly vivid. Whereas the paintings "stand up" and "stand back," the sculptures bend toward us, some of them like clenched fists opening up to greet friends. Whereas the spaces of the paintings are discontinuous with the space of the Salle Camondo, the spaces of the sculptures are continuous. The sculptures stretch out, despite their imprisonment in glass cages, into the between and sweep our bodies into explicit continuity with them. Both the paintings and sculptures are rhythmic gestures, diagrams of the dance. But whereas in the sculptures the real three-dimensional structures of the dancers, however transformed, are preserved, in the paintings the three-dimensional structures are abstracted from, and we must recreate those structures from the cues of perspective. The paintings give us disembodied images of the lines, colors, lights, and textures of dancing scenes. The paintings sing the qualities of the dance abstracted from real volume, shape, and weight. They illuminate scenes hermetically sealed off, which are therefore clearly distinct from the actual scene of the Salle Camondo. The sculptures, on the other hand, sing the qualities of the dance in harmony with real volume, shape, and weight. The sculptures pulsate. Hence not only the lines of sculptures but also their masses are perceived with reference to our hands imaginatively or actually traversing their surfaces (as is also the case imaginatively with the lines of the paintings). The colors of the sculptures and the lights and shadows glancing off the dark bronze, unlike the colors, lights, and shadows of the paintings, have impacting force. They push out into the between, propelled by three-dimensional material. They insinuate themselves into the actual space of the Salle Camondo, and we feel our bodies as very tightly unified with the impacting between and the material bodies of these dancers. Our tactile feelings and, in turn, our haptic and kinesthetic feelings are much more strongly stimulated than with the paintings, although the poses of the sculptured and painted dancers are quite similar. We stretch and strain, push and pull, tense and relax with the sculptured dancers, the rough, "unfinished" surfaces helping to make their movements a continually outgoing process. The sculptures, unlike the paintings, are verbs before they are nouns. The life rhythms of the sculptured dancers set in motion in the depths of our beings some secret chord that was waiting to be struck. We join their dance, whereas we remain apart from the painted dancers.

In relation to the painted dancers, haptic and kinesthetic feelings are much less intense because of the lack of significant tactile stimulation and the immobility of our bodies. Awareness of our bodies as part of our experience is not very evident with the paintings because there is no impacting between, and the marvelous revel of colors, lines, shapes, lights, shadows, and textures as they reveal the dancing scenes are best taken in by a quiet settling down in a fixed position. We stand back or sit down and look. Furthermore, compared with the sculptured dancers, the painted dancers seem more set in their positions, and this tends to lessen empathetic identification. We do not strain with them as much as with the sculptured dancers. The sculptures force us to move not only because their movements appear so incomplete that they seem to request our aid but also because they are in the round. We perceive their unfolding unto fullness only by moving around them, and their impacting betweens strongly activate our tactile and, in turn, our haptic feelings. Tactual and kinesthetic feelings strongly reinforce each other. That balance on one leg seems so delicate we feel ourselves automatically compensating in our own balance; that slanting shadow hides a part we want to perceive; that glancing light pulls us around; that concavity draws us in; that convexity pushes us back; that stretch of the leg pulls us to the right; that thrust of the arm swings us to the left; that impacting between strikes our skins and reverberates through our bodies. Whereas the painted dancers are still, the sculptured dancers seem to tremble. Whereas the air in front of the paintings appears to have no temperature or movement, the air around the sculptures appears hot and moving, like the air sizzling above a highway on a torrid day. The betweens of Degas's sculptures are charged, like electric fields. The betweens of Degas's paintings are an empty field. For anyone perceiving them sensitively, the sculptures make one move, but the paintings make one halt. In turn, there is some visual disorientation in perceiving the sculptures. With the paintings, however, our vision is very clearly oriented. Degas's sculptures increase tactual feelings and their flow, whereas his paintings decrease them. Degas's sculptures vibrate throughout our bodies, whereas his paintings—because they are abstractions from the solidity of things—vibrate mainly in our eyes. We feel the skin of the painted dancers; we feel the flesh and bones of the sculptured dancers.

Our bodies are pressed on by sculpture, whereas with paintings our bodies are relatively unpressed. We are physically included in the space of a sculpture, whereas we delude ourselves if we try to physically include ourselves in the space of a painting. Being more than skin deep—that is, more than a two-dimensional representation—the mass of a sculpture, even if we do not actually touch the sculpture, throws out forces that penetrate our skins and reverberate within our bodies. We are physically jarred into an awareness of a sculpture. As the sculptor Richard Stankiewicz remarks:

> Things may be objectively present without having the affective power that we call "presence." The extraordinary object, the one with presence, is one which is subjectively and tyrannically there: it can no more be ignored than being stared at can. It seems to me that this charged quality of things is what a work must have to be sculpture.[26]

A painting "presences" also, of course, but much more weakly physically because what is represented in a painting, because of the limitations of the medium, can only suggest or re-present but not present mass.

With sculpture our vision is both more kinetic and "weighted" than with painting, for with sculpture we feel the moving mass of our bodies along with our sight. Our "travels" with sculpture are much longer and heavier than our "travels" with painting. If, for example, one aesthetically perceives the vast and magnificent collection of the ripe and robust sculptures of Henri Laurens in the Musée National d'Art Moderne in Paris, a heightened awareness of the volume and mass of one's body is inevitable, as well as withness with these works—comforting for the skinny, not so comfortable for the fat, and stimulating and illuminating for everybody. If, on the other hand, one aesthetically perceives the radiant collection of Monets in the underground gallery of the Marmottan Museum in Paris, there will be as one emerges a heightened awareness of the colors, lights, and textures of the world, but for a while our bodies and our withness with three-dimensional things are likely to be ignored. Then, as Santayana puts it: "The soul is glad, as it were, to forget its connections with the body. . . . This illusion of disembodiment is very exhilarating."[27] Indeed, we are likely to feel much more tired after perceiving Laurens's sculptures than after perceiving Monet's paintings. Yet for those with overflowing nervous energies, catharsis of nervousness is much more likely to follow the perception of Laurens's sculptures.

The gesture, as R. P. Blackmur points out, is much more fundamental to sculpture than to painting:

> The great part of our knowledge of life and nature—perhaps all our knowledge of their play and interplay—comes to us as gesture. . . .Let us say that good sculpture has a heaviness or lightness which has nothing to do with stone or wood or the carver's trade [surely an overstatement], but has everything to do with the gesture which illumines the medium.[28]

Unlike painting, sculpture involves the ever-changing posture of three-dimensional encounters.[29] The gesture of a sculpture tends to attract our attention more than a gesture of a painting and even, sometimes, draws forth a reciprocating gesture. In the Musée National d'Art Moderne I recently witnessed an amusing example of these phenomena. A group of chattering boys were ignoring with adolescent bliss a blazing display of Vuillard and Bonnard paintings, some with female nudity with a variety of gestures. But as they approached a standing Maillol nude, they became quiet and their pace slackened. They began to circle, more and more slowly, and then one boy placed a coin in her outstretched hand.

When confronting other people, the between is impacted by their presence. "To be," in Sartre's words, "is to be *for* someone." The liveliness of others would seem, therefore, to insure more impact, despite all the distractions, than even the most powerful sculptures can exert. Yet except when we experience another human being aesthetically (that is, at moments when our consciousness is so penetrated and permeated by the "other" that our consciousness has no energy left for explicit self-consciousness), distractions usually siphon away much of the impact. The most powerful of these distractions is undoubtedly "the look." When the "other" looks—except when it is a "loving look" in an appropriate context—the space between us is divided into the "other's" space and our space. In turn, impact into the between is usually decreased. There is neither the centripetal "drawing in," as there is with most of Henry Moore's sculptures, nor the centrifugal "pushing out," as there is with most of Giacometti's. Instead, the impact into the between is more or less neutralized, the power flowing into the between being short-circuited to the degree that "the look" intensifies our self-consciousness. When "the look" of others upon us is in a socially respectable context, as when as teachers we are conscious of being observed by students, the impact into the between of these students may only be weakened. When, however, "the look" of others upon us is not in a socially respectable context, as when we are caught as voyeurs, the impact into the between may be annihilated. Perhaps more than any other emotion, shame evokes vivid self-consciousness, which, in turn, sharply separates our world into the subject/object dichotomy. And when we distance ourselves as subjects from objects, we also distance ourselves from the impacting forces in the between.

Marcel Duchamp's mysterious last creation that he worked on secretly from 1946 until his death in 1966—*Étant Données: 1. La Chute d'eau 2. Le Gaz d'éclairage (Given: 1. The Waterfall 2. The Illuminating Gas)*—is a fascinating example of how self-consciousness can destroy our sense of the impacting between. As I approach the permanent installation of this work in the Philadelphia Museum of Art, I come to an open doorway that leads into a small room whose roughly stuccoed left wall contains an arched brick doorway that frames an old Spanish door. There are no knobs or handles, and I realize that the door cannot be opened. I notice, mainly because of the stains around them, two small oblique holes at eye level. The door both bars me from what is beyond it and yet allows me to see through it. I bring my eyes to these holes. There is the tactile feel of the weathered wood—like sculpture—but my view is locked into a fixed position, more so than with any painting I have perceived, for not even the slightest shifting of the head is possible. A shocking scene bathed in strange, brilliant light thrusts itself toward me. I see in the foreground a battered brick wall apparently a few feet in from the door—distances seem strangely unreal and difficult to judge, for I can see only with fixed eyes—with a jagged hole beyond which, on a bed of what appears to be real leaves and twigs, lies a nude young woman, realistically molded and erotically spread-eagled on her back. Her face is farthest from my view and almost completely hidden by seemingly real blond hair. Her vagina is curiously deformed. Her legs extend toward the door but her feet are hidden by the brick wall. Her left arm stretches to the left, and her left hand holds a faintly glowing gas lamp. In the distance behind the lamp is a romantic lake with a hilly, wooded landscape and above a blue sky filled with soft white clouds, in the style of French academic painting of the nineteenth century. In the depth of this landscape is an artificial waterfall effect produced by a moving light, the only moving element. The impact into the between, despite the obstructing door, is powerful. Again I survey the nude. I hear someone behind me—my "look" is being "looked on"—I am aware of my voyeurism—my self-consciousness overwhelms me—the impact of the between, which had been peculiarly concentrated on the skin around my eyes, drains way. I step back from the peepholes and "look" at my "looker."

This short-circuiting of the impacting between is the primary reason why this work is misdescribed as sculpture. Even the tactile sensations of the peepholes on one's face are dissipated by the

"Peeping Tom" phenomenon, and one's vision cannot be complemented here by touch. The freezing of the eyes to the peepholes, moreover, immobilizes our bodies. There is no kinesthetic reinforcement of tactual sensations. Furthermore, even if no one is with us or enters the room, we are aware of the possibility that our ludicrous position may be observed. We cannot escape the self-consciousness that insulates us from the impacting between. In his strangely ironic and humorous way, Duchamp shows what sculpture is by showing what sculpture is not.

Sculpture is a vivification of our withness with things by means of the impacting between. The bodies of "others" are the things we are most noticeably with, except that "the look" tends to separate us from that withness. As Giacometti observed, "One doesn't walk around a man like a tree." The frontal confrontation—as in the handshake—is basic to relationships with others. But we can and do walk around a *sculpture* of a man in somewhat the same way as we do a tree. Scultpure—even with those intense gazes of Giacometti's figures—takes away the actual look, and in doing so sculpture can animate our withness with the sculptural likeness of the human body rarely achieved in interpersonal relationships. By returning us to a closer unity with likenesses of the human body, sculpture may even teach us how to overcome "the look" and the self-consciousness that alienates us from others. The look becomes beautiful. The handshake becomes a "giving-receiving" unity, a "carnal intersubjectivity" (Merleau-Ponty). "Two hands fold into one"—Heidegger poeticizes—"a gesture meant to carry man into the great oneness."[30] Especially on the death bed there is the need to hold hands.

Unlike painting, sculpture presents the human body without reducing its three-dimensionality to two dimensions. Furthermore, because of its impacting between, sculpture portrays more forcefully than painting our awareness of our bodies as three-dimensional centers thrusting out into surrounding space. For these two basic reasons, sculpture generally can reveal more vividly than painting the seductive power, the gesture, the encounter, the fullness, and the *physical withness* of the human body with things. That is why the human body has been an even more favored subject matter of sculpture than of painting.

1. Edmund Husserl, *Ideas: General Introduction to Pure Phenomenology*, trans. W. R. Boyce-Gibson (The Hague: Martinus Nijhoff, 1952), 2;144. For a discussion of this point, see my "The Autonomy of Sculpture," *The Journal of Aesthetics and Art Criticism* 34 (Spring 1976): 278 ff.

2. From the fifth to the tenth centuries there are few sculpted nudes in Christendom. In the eleventh century generally only the sinful are nude—Adam and Eve or one of the damned in the Last Judgment. The proscription of the nude led the medieval sculptors to intricate investigations of faces, hands, and drapery. By the twelfth and thirteenth centuries the body begins, at last, to become unconcealed *beneath* the dress, as in the *Eve* of Reims. In the fourteenth century, Giotto's relief design representing sculpture on the Campanile of the Cathedral of Florence—the sculptor is shown sculpting a nude man—is one of the earliest indications of the return of the nude.

3. A fascinating exception to this exaltation of, and concentration upon, the human body before the twentieth century is the work of the nineteenth-century sculptor Antoine Barye. Whereas his nudes seem to have succumbed to rigor mortis, his animals are usually exceptionally lively.

4. Dewitt Parker, *The Principles of Aesthetics* (New York: Appleton-Century-Crofts, 1947), p. 227. Horatio Greenough, one of the first American sculptors, went into more grandiloquent detail: "the human frame, the most beautiful organization of earth, the exponent and minister of the highest being we immediately know. This stupendous form, towering as a lighthouse, commanding by its posture a wide horizon, standing in relation to the brutes where the spire stands in relation to the lowly colonnades of Greece and Egypt, touching earth with only one-half the soles of its feet—it tells of majesty and dominion by that upreared spine, of duty by those unencumbered hands. Where is the ornament of this frame? It is all beauty, its motion is grace, no combination of harmony ever equaled, for expression and variety, its poised and stately gait; its voice is music, no cunning mixture of wood and metal ever did more than feebly imitate its tone of command or its warble of love. The savage who envies or admires the special attributes of beasts maims unconsciously his own perfection to assume their tints, their feathers, or their laws; we turn from him with horror, and gaze with joy on the naked Apollo." In Melvin Rader, *A Modern Book of Aesthetics*, 3d ed. (New York: Holt, Rinehart and Winston, 1960), pp. 2350 ff. In the final years of the last century Hermann Obrist was one of the first sculptors in practice and theory (*New Possibilities in Art: Critical Essays, 1896-1900*) to oppose what might be called the "Greek prejudice," the glorification of the human body: "The fatal delusion that the human figure is the alpha and omega of sculpture has been a stumbling-block for generations. True, the human figure contains wonderful potentialities for the sculptor. But look at the Tortoise Fountain in Rome. Its basins are a riot of sculptured forms, perhaps the most luxuriant in the world, but what has the shape of their contours to do with the human nude?" Quoted by Carola Giedion-Welcher, *Contemporary Sculpture* (New York: George Wittenborn, 1960), p. 164.

5. Albert Camus, *The Rebel*, trans. Anthony Bower (New York: Random House, 1956), p. 256.

6. *Henry Moore on Sculpture*, ed. Philip James (London: MacDonald, 1966), p. 115.

7. Quoted by Paul Waldo Schwartz, *The Hand and the Eye of the Sculptor* (New York: Praeger, 1969), p. 19. Xenophanes made the same point about painting long ago. "But if cattle and horses or lions had hands, or were able to draw with their hands and do the works that men can do, horses would draw the forms of the gods like horses, and cattle like cattle, and they would make their bodies such as they each had themselves." In *The Pre-Socratic Philosophers*, ed. G. S. Kirk and J. E. Raven (Cambridge: Cambridge University Press, 1966), p. 169.

8. *Barbara Hepworth: A Pictorial Autobiography* (New York: Praeger, 1970), p. 41. Anthony Caro claims that "all sculpture in some way has to do with the body. For instance, my [abstract] sculptures . . . are partly dependent upon the spectator's height from the floor when he is standing up: on his vertical stance, his consciousness of flat ground. Sculptors . . . are necessarily conscious of the body." Quoted by Richard Whelan, *Anthony Caro* (New York: E. P. Dutton, 1975), p. 115.

9. Sir Herbert Read, *The Art of Sculpture* (New York: Panthenon Books, 1956), p. 25.

10. Ibid., p. 29.

11. For an analysis of the 'impacting between', see my" 'The Between': Brancusi, Moore, and Giacometti," *Dialectics and Humanism* 2 (Spring 1975): 23-43.

12. Susanne Langer, *Problems of Art* (New York: Charles Scribner's Sons, 1957), p. 28.

13. For how painting and sculpture differ in "placing" themselves in real space, see my "Sculpture and Place," *Dialectics and Humanism* 3 (Spring 1976): 45-55.

14. F. David Martin, "The Autonomy of Sculpture."

15. Gaston Bachelard, *Poetics of Space*, trans. Maria Jolas (New York: Orion Press 1963), p. 184.

16. Sculptors have always found in self-portraiture a fascinating subject matter. See Albert E. Elsen, *Origins of Modern Sculpture* (New York: George Braziller, 1974), p. 39.

17. Read, *The Art of Sculpture*, p. 32.

18. Compare Pliny's notorious account of Praxiteles' "Cnidian Venus," placed in a shrine with entrances fore and aft. "Its shrine is completely open, so that it is possible to observe the image of the goddess from every side; she herself, it is believed, favored its being made that way. Nor is one's admiration of the statue less from any side. They say that a certain man was once overcome with love for the statue, and, after he had hidden himself (in the shrine) during the nightime, embraced the statue and that there is a stain on it as an indication of his lust." In J. J. Pollitt, *The Art of Greece, 1400-31 B.C.* (Englewood Cliffs, N.J.: Prentice-Hall, 1965), p. 128.

19. Camus, *The Rebel*, p. 256.

20. Indeed, it may be the case generally that the sculptor finds the male body an even better subject matter than the female—certainly this was the case with Donatello and Michelangelo—because the male body lends itself more to the aggressiveness that helps energize the space surrounding the material body of a sculpture. Maybe Donatello and Michelangelo were not homosexuals after all—just sculptors. On the other hand, Brancusi had a much higher regard for the female body. His *Leda* might be perceived as Jupiter transforming himself into the swan of the Leda myth. But Brancusi said that "it is Leda, not Jupiter, changing into a swan. A man is ugly as a frog; a swan has exquisite curves, like those of a woman's body." Quoted by Herbert Christian Merillat, *Modern Sculpture* (New York: Dodd, Mead, 1974), p. 28.

21. Read, *The Art of Sculpture*, p. 33.

22. Jacques Lipchitz, *My Life in Sculpture* (New York: Viking Press, 1972), p. 124.

23. Jean Piaget, *The Construction of Reality in the Child*, trans. Margaret Cook (New York: Basic Books, 1954), p. 217.

24. A good dancer is a mobilized statue, and many statues reveal the mobility of the dance, as with Degas's sculptured dancers. Thus the common concern for the moving body brings many sculptors and dancers, despite all the differences of their arts, into close interrelationships. Rodin, for example, drew inspiration from the movements of Cambodian dancers. Isadora Duncan's dancing is reflected in Bourdelle's reliefs for the Théâtre des Champs Élysées in Paris. Diaghilev recruited Pevsner and Gabo for his ballet "La Chatte" in 1926. Calder worked for Martha Graham's Company in 1935, and in 1939 he received a commission for a water ballet for the New York World's Fair. Zorach relates that Martha Graham studied sculpture for expressive gestures and that he studied dance for the same reason. William Zorach, *Art Is My Life* (Cleveland, Ohio: World Publishing Co., 1967), p. 131. Maurice Béjart used one of Nicholas Schöffer's Spatio-dynamic sculptures as the source of the human rhythmic movement in one of his ballets of 1956, and the sculpture of Marta Pan has served as starting points for some of his choreography.

25. See my "The Arts and the 'Between', " *The British Journal of Aesthetics* 17 (Winter 1977): 22-36.

26. Richard Stankiewicz, *Sixteen Americans*, ed. Dorothy C. Miller (New York: Museum of Modern Art, 1959), p. 70.

27. George Santayana, *The Sense of Beauty* (New York: Charles Scribner's Sons, 1936), p. 29.

28. Quoted by Hilton Kramer, *The Age of the Avant Garde* (New York: Farrar, Straus,and Giroux, 1973), p. 449.

29. This flexibility of the relationship of our bodies to sculpture accounts for the more variable placements of sculpture compared to painting. Thus, recumbent sculpture, as on medieval tombs, is not nearly as odd as recumbent painting. With painting, a vertical placement in relation to the floor or ground, unlike many sculptures, is usually obligatory, for only then can painting be perceived optimally as a two-dimensional image creating an imaginary space. With sculpture, on the other hand, variations from the vertical are more natural and aesthetically feasible. Thus the famous slant of the ramp of Frank Lloyd Wright's Guggenheim Museum is more disadvantageous to the paintings than to the sculptures.

30. Martin Heidegger, *What Is Called Thinking?* trans. J. Glenn Gray and F. Wieck (New York: Harper, 1972), p. 16.

The Arcology of Paolo Soleri: Technology as Cosmology

Joseph Grange

University of Southern Maine

"My name is Ozymandias, king of kings:
Look on my works, ye Mighty, and despair!"
Nothing beside remains. Round the decay
Of that colossal wreck, boundless and bare
The lone and level sands stretch far away.
—Percy Bysshe Shelley

RECENT years have witnessed a notable growth of interest in the work of the architect Paolo Soleri. *Futurist, visionary, mystical,* and *prophetic* are but a few of the terms used to describe his effort to create a new image of urban dwelling.[1] Soleri's architecture is, however, not merely an adventure in novel urban design. He surrounds his work with philosophical concepts and thereby presents his architectural thinking as the embodiment of a world view. It is this Weltanschauung that is of significance, for it provides a new understanding of the meaning of being human—a redefinition of humankind that can serve as the intellectual basis of a culture that has allowed technology to triumph.

The aim of this essay is to analyze the fundamental principles of Soleri's arcology and point out its merit and price. What is gained is a rational and systematic understanding of the kinds of changes required to render our cities more efficient and functional. What is lost is the primacy of lived human experience together with its primordial attunement to nature as an unfathomable source of meaning.

The gains derived from Soleri's world view are the outcome of cosmological thinking. Its losses spring from a neglect of the cosmogonic dimension of human existence. Though ancient in their origins, cosmology and cosmogony find their modern counterparts in scientific rationalism and existential phenomenology. Cosmology thinks rationally, transforming concrete experience into abstract, representational concepts. Cosmogony thinks phenomenologically, preserving the realm of lived experience as a viable medium of disclosure.[2] The interplay and opposition between these schools of thought provide the backdrop for this essay.

Soleri's arcological vision allows us to inquire into the origins and destiny of technological man. To be sure, the question of technology and its impact on human beings has been debated many times. What justifies another effort is the peculiar light that Soleri's thought throws upon the issue. Within its glow the foundational dimensions of the question loom forth, and the stark silhouette of technological man emerges. And this is so because the arcology of Paolo Soleri offers nothing less than a *cosmology for technology*.

Arcology as Cosmology

Arcology is the term Soleri coined to label his systematic approach to the problem of human dwelling on earth. A blending of two words—*architecture* and *ecology*—arcology is the "thought-construct" into which the problems of urban existence are poured and that, in turn, resolves them. What establishes arcology as a cosmology is this stress upon thought. But it is thought of a very special stripe: cosmological thinking insists upon rational analysis as the only acceptable form of thought. Plato in the *Timaeus*, Descartes in *The Meditations*, and Whitehead in *Process and Reality* exemplify this tradition. In the long view provided by the history of Western philosophy, there is nothing radically new or previously unattempted in Soleri's thinking. What is novel in arcological thought is, as we shall see, its single-minded reliance on technology as the means to achieve its end.

The defining characteristics of cosmological thinking require attention. As its name implies, cosmology always looks for the reasons behind experiences, seeking to locate the underlying rational structure that is then taken to be more real than the experientially felt reality. It aims for explanations rather than meaning since its guiding purpose is control of the future rather than involvement in existential meaning. Cosmology achieves its methodology of control by reducing all experiences to a single level of analysis. For example, the Cartesian world view was gained through the reduction of all experience into the physical and the mental. From this vantage point the sinuosities of experience and its polyphonic dimensions can be traced back to more fundamental levels. Thus cosmology embraces a kind of thinking that seeks the lowest common denominator—an explanatory floor—that can then be used to reconstruct experience in a more intellectually satisfying manner.

It is this passion for the uniform and the predictable that sets apart true cosmological thinking. Order (*Cosmos*) and Plan (*Logos*) are the animating principles of cosmology. Reacting to *Chaos*, the formless void that engulfs reason and threatens mankind, cosmological thinking resembles salvational religion, for it seeks a saving grace. The salvific act is the conversion of the world into categories susceptible to rational analysis. At bottom, then, cosmological thought retains a theological thrust, for its efforts are directed toward securing the future through a plan.

Despite its religious undertones, cosmology maintains an anti-fideist posture toward the world. Its primary mood-state is fear, an attunement that translates itself into a defensive-aggressive attitude. Fear of chaos breeds a lack of trust in the original power of man and nature to collaborate. Thus withdrawal from nature by way of the use of logical categories of thought is a hallmark of cosmology's comportment toward the world. Its language shows this, for impersonality, dispassionate expression, and objective prose are among its major characteristics. For example, deeply felt human experiences are called positive and negative reinforcement, dysfunction, and operant conditioning.[3] Born out of fear, cosmology insists on the ordered, the planned, and the systematic, for that is the only way in which it can make sense out of human existence.

In contrast to such reductive thought, cosmogony situates itself on the level of felt human experience. It regards lived human experience as sufficient for understanding the authentic dimensions of the cosmic drama. Like cosmology, it endorses a world order but its effort is directed toward understanding the meaning of that order. And it does not feel a need to abstract from human involvement in the world in order to gain a handhold on the future. Remaining satisfied with a concrete description of the things in themselves, cosmogony tells a story (*mythos*) and invites human participation. As in Hesiod's *Theogony*, foundational human experiences such as justice (*Dike*), destiny (*Moira*), fate (*Ananke*), and the inevitability of World Strife (*Polemos*) are used to describe the meaning of the interaction between man and nature. Explanation is avoided and human being is seen as capable of achieving the meaning of these experiences.

Cosmogony aims at the disclosure of meaning rather than abstract conceptualizations. Human being is viewed as a region of disclosure, as the open, within which elemental forces find their realization. Obsession with the future is relaxed in favor of an implicit trust in the mystery of being human and its intimacy with the world order. As a result, human freedom is preserved as coequal with the mysteries of cosmic experience. Cosmogony refuses reductionism and keeps intact the plane of lived experience: it lays forth human consciousness as a zone to be safeguarded, for within it the mysteries of existence are enacted.

In this letting-lie-forth, cosmogony adopts the attitude of phenomenology, which lets being show itself in exactly the way in which it shows itself from itself.[4] Rather than seeking a salvific future, cosmogony calls attention to the profound depths of lived human experience. It lays bare the *Ur-experience* in all its ineffability. Chaos remains the void but is viewed as an unfathomable source of meaning. Cosmogonic wonder and understanding replace the rational intellect, which cannot endure the long night of the unknown. Cosmogonic thinking is therefore more a process of uncovering meaning than discovering facts. It is—as we shall see in more detail—a thinking that is a re-calling, an act of remembrance.

Awe rather than fear is the mood-state of cosmogony, and its language reflects this attitude. Personalizing the human/world drama, cosmogony speaks of pain, hubris, astonishment, the tragic and the ecstatic, but always as modes of disclosure. Such language gives the world a face and defines the process of being human as an intimate dialogue with the cosmic. The medium of disclosure whereby human beings gain insight into their world is not the rational intellect but rather the *Agon* itself, the moment of participation in the creation of meaning. Here struggle is seen as revealment, not competition. The process of revealment is carried out by human beings in their being—in other words being human *is* disclosure. Cosmogony has no need to reduce being human to another more explanatory level. It trusts being human as sufficient to its own end. As the disclosure of meaning and the effective presence of dialogue, being human achieves its highest dignity: it lights up the world.

What ultimately distinguishes cosmogony from cosmology is its act of remembrance. Cosmogony re-calls being human back to itself so that it can participate fully and concretely in the world drama. Re-collecting itself from its scattering by the abstract intellect, being human is enabled to stand forth as whole and speak with the world. For cosmology, on the other hand, the move from *Logos* to logic is both very short and very far. It is short because all that is required is an act of forgetting. It is far because eventually cosmology turns into a world view that shapes history and creates and destroys whole cultures. What cosmology throws into oblivion is the originary experience of participative struggle with the world order—the primordial *Agon* preserved in the heart of cosmogony. Once that is forgotten, the way is opened for man to dwell in anthropocentric arrogance. Imbued with fear, yet retaining its defensive-aggressive posture, cosmology is freed to manipulate the world. The arrogance of such gestures is not felt, for everything is regarded as "rational, planned, and systematic." Ever more massive efforts to control the environment ensue, and suddenly manipulative thought has become a way of being-in-the-world.

In sum, then, cosmology envisions a world machine and human being is reduced to the status of mechanic-in-attendance. Cosmogony calls upon man to become a region for the disclosure of meaning by remaining faithful to lived experience.

What are the basic components of Soleri's cosmology? Three concepts form the backbone of his attempt to transform thinking about urban existence: miniaturization, complexification, and implosion. These three principles are, in turn, based upon a world understanding that expresses itself solely in physicalist language. Let us look closely at the three principles:[5]

> *Miniaturization*: For Soleri the clue to understanding nature as an evolutionary process is the fact that its successful entities demonstrate an ability to compact their forms into ever more involuted systems of energic intake and displacement. For example, the butterfly's form is precisely adapted to its function: flying by use of air currents.
>
> *Complexification*: The other side of miniaturization is not simplification through elimination but complexification through the compression of forms into unitary yet diversified structures. Here the model of the human brain is paramount, for its infoliated lobes dramatically express complex functions through miniaturized form.
>
> *Implosion*: The device whereby nature achieves these effects is not the extension of matter (explosion) but its intensification by way of indrawing energy supplies (implosion). Thus the infoliation of plant seeds acts as a retention of potentiality that unfolds through the explosive power of solar heat and lights.

These three principles drawn from a microscopic analysis of nature are employed on the macroscopic plane to structure Soleri's cities of the future. These vast structures—termed *arcologies*—miniaturize, complexify, and implode urban dwelling. Thus, in place of the present urban sprawl, Soleri would build cities upward, drawing urban life inward and compressing its energies into a single frame. In this way, land use is minimized and energy, both natural and human, maximized through its implosion and complexification. Instead of a city without visible limits stretching endlessly from a central core of decayed urban existence to an unending repetition of suburban sameness, Soleri's cities in-gather the population into a single, complex building that has diversified functionality by reason of its imploded complexification. Urban separatism symbolized by discrete structures—be they commercial, domestic, or industrial—is transformed into an organic and holistic system that conserves, preserves, retains, and recycles energy in a self-sufficient urban complex.

Soleri's transformation of urban existence is not to be understood as a narrow instance of urbanology, the analysis of design and function in city planning. Arcology sits on a broader understanding of the world: it is, in fact, only an exemplification of a world view. The Weltanschauung of arcology is a monistic and thoroughgoing physicalism that envisions all reality as configurations of energy. Urban planning is an outcome of this

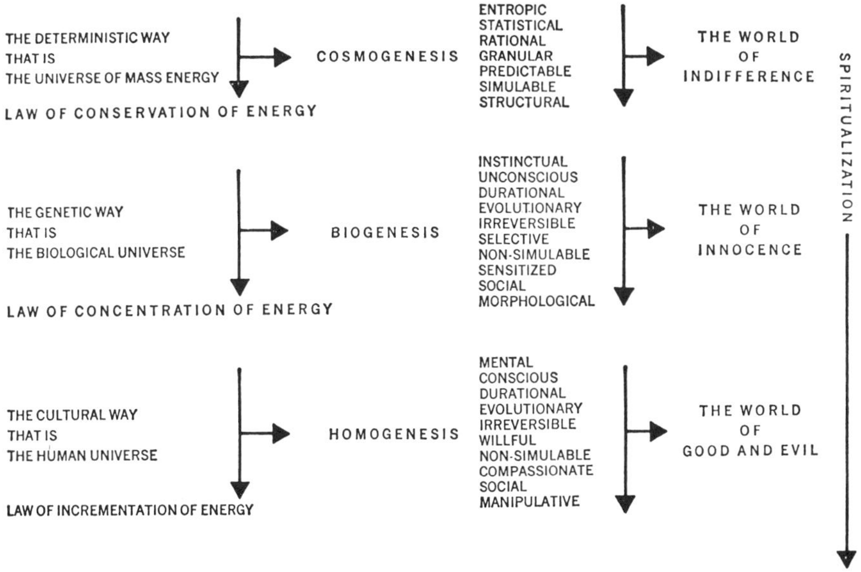

metaphysics, and to understand the full dimension of Soleri's cosmology, we must inquire into this theory of reality. Despite the fact that much of Soleri's writing has a scattered and episodic focus and is expressed in an all but impenetrable latinate style, he does provide in one essay a diagrammatic sketch of his metaphysics.[6]

What is noteworthy in this diagram of reality is its single vision of the really real: energy. All history, natural and human, is the outcome of varying rhythms of energy. The three ways of nature—cosmogenesis, biogenesis, and homogenesis—reflect only modes of energy, and their qualitative differences remain ultimately reducible to energy. Energy and its expression are sufficient for understanding the drama of human being and nature. This reduction of experience comports exactly with the fundamental thrust of cosmological thinking: an explanatory level of analysis is required before the meaning of experience is articulated. Obviously, this cosmic diagram is a method of control, for it points toward the future and suggests that humankind, equipped with such a map, can begin the long journey toward another stage of evolution.

And the destiny of this journey is also hinted: it lies along the line of spiritualization. Thus the full face of cosmological thinking shows itself. Energy moves from "indifference" through "innocence" to "good and evil." Normative thought, morality, and ethics appear as the outcome of the world rationally explained. As befits the age of science, fact and value converge into a unified system of energy.

The city, therefore, is but an exemplar of the future of human being. It is concrete, self-manifesting, and monumental, but only as a moment in the monistic development of energy. The circle of cosmology closes upon itself and reveals all the intricacies of human experience—joy, terror, anxiety, peace, empathy, sympathy, compassion, guilt—as but variable manifestations of energy.

These features of Soleri's thought—scientific rationalism, ethical overtones, and evolutionary prophetics—become the handwriting for an endorsement of technology as evolution. Having grounded his cosmology in an unreflective acceptance of the scientific scenario of evolution, Soleri is in a position to canonize technology as the ultimate instrument of human spiritualization. This is carried out by way of a wholesale borrowing from the thought of Teilhard de Chardin, though, significantly, little direct recognition of this thinker is to be found in Soleri's writings. Arcology as a specific instance of cosmology finds its place on the much broader plane of evolutionary thinking. Evolution is the central fact and meaning of the history of energy. In modern times energy has become conscious of itself through technology. Heretofore, energy was without an heir; now its offspring has been born and is growing up. Technology, as the child of energy, is now the means of evolution. And as we shall see, technology is no neutral instrument: it is in fact and reality the destiny of energy and, *a fortiori*, the fate of human being.

TECHNOLOGY AS EVOLUTION

To realize what is at stake in the question of technology,[7] we should see that technological thought is itself a cosmology. It possesses a world view that envisions nature as displaying a fundamental character. This character is the basic level of meaning to be found through rational analysis. Technological thinking consistently thinks of nature as a stock, a reserve that is to be ready-to-hand at the moment of human demand.

To think reality as the multifarious display of energy is to think technologically. This type of thinking is representative thought. It re-presents the world through its objectifications; and once the world is re-pictured, man is freed toward the project of making use of that picture. This type of thinking is in fact a form of provocation. It pro-vokes a response by addressing the world in a manner that demands a single and certain response: the deliverance of a stock.

From this perspective, time takes on a singular meaning. The modes of past and present fade before the insistent call of the future. But future's call is empty since it cannot foretell the uses of stock. This complex of re-presentational thought, pro-voking world understanding and the vacuous call of time, conjoined to an evolutionary philosophy, is the signature of all cosmological technology. It customarily cloaks itself in the language of duty, perspiring optimism and human destiny, but at bottom cosmological technology is a monistic physicalism that denies the primacy of lived human experience.

Of course, Soleri's published writings seem to contradict such an interpretation. They speak often and eloquently of compassion, the evil of greed, and the needs of man. As noted above, much of this dimension of Soleri's thought owes its direction to the inspiration of Teilhard de Chardin.[8] A brief look at Teilhard's system will serve to indicate the source of Soleri's humanism.

Teilhard saw all matter as containing the germ of divinity. Divine germination, however, awaited human cooperation, for the emergence of human consciousness signaled the turn of the evolutionary spiral from the cycles of geosphere, biosphere, and zoosphere to our age, the moment of the noosphere. At this moment evolution has become conscious of itself and man, as its arrowhead, can move universal being in the direction of divine reality. This *Divine Milieu* is characterized by love, union, and the loss of individual personality in a larger cosmic self. Omega point is the divine/human destiny and its coming-to-be depends upon human cooperation in the cosmic drama.

Teilhard's position is, of course, more complex than the above summary, but such a sketch serves to point out its main lines of understanding. What is significant is the fact that Teilhard required a focus for the history of matter and achieved it through defining the divine as the immanence of the profane. Soleri's writings suggest a similar effort, although to date he has stopped short of creating a theology. So far he has settled for semireligious language, employing phrases such as *Civitate Dei*, "man-Christ," and "the magnet (which stands as God)" to intimate the potential sacrality of his world view.[9] The lever that enables Soleri to turn technology into a semidivine cosmology is his concept of "esthetogenesis."

Though nowhere defined, *esthetogenesis* for Soleri is fairly easy to grasp. Recalling his cosmic diagram, we note that the future remained unnamed: it awaits a label. After cosmogenesis, biogenesis, and homogenesis, the next phase must be esthetogenesis. Here the artist takes over and deploys technology to give birth to the future—the birth of beauty as the redemption of the personal and social world. It is this marriage of value and technology that justifies the assertion that evolution is now technology and that technology is now cosmology.

At this point the significance of the city in Soleri's cosmology shows itself. It is to act as a kind of node drawing all human energies into a single complex focus that will—in its turn and à la Teilhardian evolutionism—hurl humankind into the next stage of development. Evolution is divine self-becoming and technology is the new sacrament that *ex opere operato* lavishes the grace of esthetogenesis on man. The City is not meant merely to enable human beings to become more human; it is also destined to draw out of man the divine seed that will germinate and become the Future of Man.

It is this understanding of the relationship between art, technology, and urbanology that informs Soleri's cosmology. We can see how technology, once a tool, has now become an evolutionary expression. More than that, technology is so intimately married to cosmology that it is now evolution itself. What saves Soleri's thought from being identified with so many other secular "futurist" visions is the fact that he hints at the world's as yet unrealized sacrality. For some time now, the modern age has awaited a synthesis of its self-understanding, a philosophy that would do justice to all its achievements and not neglect its need to retain ancient experiences such as the sacred, the divine, and human destiny. All cosmological thought sooner or later must try to incorporate the cosmogenic. Soleri does this through his ability to combine religious, artistic, scientific, and cultural experiences within a single vision. Arcology sacralizes technology and thereby becomes the first real and likely candidate for the throne of Comte's "positive" science of man.

It is this potential of Soleri's thought that deserves recognition and examination. Arcology is neither a secular approach to human development nor a dogmatic religious creed: it spans both dimensions and in a remarkable way offers itself as the future religion of technological man. The price to be paid for such a religious vision is what is of real interest. As we shall see, arcological cosmology demands a great deal—the relegation of nature to the ontological status of an abstraction. From the arcological point of view, nature disappears as an experiential dimension of human existence and is replaced by an image of man as the arrowhead of evolutionary energy.

TECHNOLOGICAL RELIGION AND THE ELIMINATION OF NATURE

Cosmogony stands in fundamental opposition to cosmology. And yet Soleri's arcology has been able to retain certain cosmogonic motifs and thereby establish its religious credentials. What is seemingly preserved in Soleri's synthesis is the cosmogonic theme of mystery as the real presence of the unknown. But mystery is not the same thing for cosmogony as it is for cosmology. Cosmological thought agrees that the future is unkonwn, but it suggests its fundamental meaning. Energy will be the ultimate base of the future. To be sure, its face will be changed, but its primordial explanation will still be there. Call it divine, sacred, mysterious, esthetogenetic, or the very grip of the creative future—the arcological cosmologist already knows its message: energy has donned another guise.

What is the mystery in cosmogony? Because cosmogony refuses reductionism, the mystery is always nature itself. Nature is *Phusis*:[10] the emerging, abiding presence of being itself. It is never to be reduced to something else, such as divinity, energy, the one or the many. The "withdrawing" is the meaning of cosmogonic mystery. Being as the withdrawn demands that human being dwell with it even as it withdraws. There is no command that it be captured through representational thought and abstracted into something that man can command. It is the simple shining forth of the manifold richness of the presence of being as such. Unbounded, unfathomable and unanalyzable, it calls man to an indwelling participation in its mystery. Human being cannot respond to it as a mind seeking rational understanding, nor as an emotion seeking feeling, nor, even, as a will seeking activation. The only response that nature requires is an ontological one: the harkening of being human to its ground—participation in the mystery of nature and existence.

As can be seen from its quasi-theological overtones, arcology taps the cosmogonic dimension. But the very shape of Soleri's city belies its authentic understanding of the cosmogonic. A visualization of Soleri's urban plans demonstrates its forfeiture of cosmogonic resonance. Arcologies will be massive mega-cities, self-contained and separated from each other by vast stretches of unurbanized land. These tracts will be given over to a variety of agricultural and recreational uses. Nature, however, as a concrete presence will be there only for observational purposes: real participation, indwelling and communication with it, will be outlawed since the city is the authentic domain of man. By miniaturizing, complexifying, and imploding human nature, Soleri succeeds in repicturing nature as somehow standing outside and opposing itself to human being. Nature is there but only in abstract form, represented as a type of energic fury to be tamed, contemplated, or drawn upon whenever energy supplies run down.

Thus *The City in the Image of Man* is really an image of energy (material but somehow divine) transformed from a state of inchoate unconsciousness to a more refined and therefore more sacred state—namely, that of directed force seeking its self-divinization. The anthropocentric exaggeration is obvious, but the abandonment of nature as the crucible of being human requires remarking. One of the consistent messages of technology has been the suggestion that humankind probably does not need direct contact with nature. Technological expertise is sufficient to develop, construct, and fill out an environment suitable for human being. Representations of nature, derived from valid representational thinking, are the equivalent of concrete immersion in natural processes. The arcological vision endorses this viewpoint and anchors its truth by linking it up with a cosmological and religious interpretation of man and nature.

It is this enthronement of the artifical that defines the meaning of technological religion. As Mircea Eliade convincingly points out, religious man saw nature as a revealing process that intermittently manifested zones of the sacred.[11] These theophanies uttered forth the presence of the mystery within natural events. What we find in Soleri's arcological vision is the opposite: the sacred spots are now nodes of civilization, entirely man-made, irrupting out of the plane of nature. Nature is abandoned, and man begins the effort of divinizing himself and his products.

Whitehead once defined religion as "what a man does with his solitariness."[12] Soleri's arcology suggests how technology will utilize that impulse. Human solitude is to be reaffirmed through the gathering of humankind into fortresslike centers that underscore the rift between man and nature. Solipsism enters through the backdoor of the house of energy since it reduces the basic level of human experience to the exchange of energy. It is this reductionism, this loss of lived experience, that is the price to be paid for cosmologizing technology. Urban existence, to be sure, may very well be improved through Soleri's arcological designs, but the improvements are at the level of efficiency, economy, and maintenance.

Earlier, the cosmogonic meaning of mystery as the "withdrawn" was alluded to. Arcology is a union of building and thinking. It omits the purpose of such a union—dwelling. The conclusion to this paper centers on that concept, for dwelling in the mystery is the homecoming of man.

BEING-AT-HOME AND DWELLING-ON-THE-EARTH

What is most threatening in Soleri's arcology is the way in which it surreptitiously combines concrete human experience and abstract scientific rationalism. Though fundamentally different, these realms are united in a single cosmology. As a result, what is distinctive to both is lost, and a confused amalgamation arises, blurring a fundamental fact. Human consciousness is *qualitatively* different from energy as it is scientifically understood. It constitutes a unique realm bearing in itself its own modes of understanding. As Edmund Husserl has shown, consciousness has its own structure and meaning and cannot be reduced to another level without losing its self-defining characteristics.[13] Consider some of Husserl's findings on the nature of human consciousness:

> Human consciousness is always personal; that is to say, consciousness is always "mine" and can never be reduced to an impersonal domain.

> Human consciousness constitutes a domain that is real, lived, and concrete. It is a *field of experience* that establishes meanings rather than information or data.
>
> Human consciousness is *intentional*. Consciousness is always *consciousness-of*. To be aware is to be pointed toward the world and permeated with its meaning.

As personal, as a field of experience, and as intentional, human consciousness is not to be taken as an abstraction but as a mode of dwelling-on-the-earth. To be human is to establish a realm of significance within which human being finds its place.

Though they differ fundamentally in their ways of achieving their goals, cosmology and cosmogony share a common purpose. They both seek to make sense out of the fundamental polarity of the world: man and earth. It is this fact—that man is on the earth—that requires understanding. Cosmology achieves its end by reducing all phenomena to a univocal level of explanation. Cosmogony retains lived human experience as the foundation of meaning. Let us see what such a retention can achieve when faced with the issue of man and earth.

Human being always seeks a place to be. This place is the locus of its being and has always been called home. To-be-at-home is the desideratum of the human heart, and history is but one long narrative of that search. Our age has seen the loss of place become a commonplace; in fact, we have a term for it—alienation. To be the stranger, the alien, and the orphan is a central motif of our time. Homecoming has become such a need that it stands out as the lure of the age. What does it mean to-be-at-home? It is to have a place within which human consciousness can uncover and develop meanings that gather into a unity of experience the diverse and manifold significations of being human. The home is a place with space, and the space of that place must be sufficient to maintain integrity in the face of the conflicting demands of human existence. Home is the housing of lived human experience in all its diversity so that a unified meaning is embodied and made incarnate.

If homecoming is the need of human being, what of the earth? It is important to note that we speak not of land but of earth. Land is a modern term, whereas earth has within it the ancient ring of lived experience. *Earth* comes from the old saxon term *earden*, which means "to dwell." Dwelling means to stay for a while, to gather together, to settle in the way in which a foundation settles and thereby sustains a building. To be earth is therefore to dwell. Man as *Homo* is related to *humus*, earth, for he dwells on the earth. Earth and man are inseparable for they are intimates: being-at-home is dwelling-on-the-earth.

A cosmogonic thinking of these issues does not, therefore, separate man from the earth, nor does it reduce human existence to a reactive level in the history of energy. Opposing itself to Soleri's arcological vision, it quite literally settles itself in the relationship spanning man and earth. It can do this because it affirms human consciousness as valid for its own ends. Cosmogony does not require the reduction of human experience to another level; it sees in the history of human consciousness sufficient strength to maintain meaning in the face of the struggle between man and earth. Cosmogony, phenomenologically understood, respects the ability of human consciousness to live with nature, not oppose it. There is no need to withdraw from the scene of man's interaction with nature and reconstitute human being on another level. The personal, experiential, and intentional structure of human consciousness suffices to ground being human on-the-earth and at-home.

The difference between urban dwellings looming up like skyscrapers isolated from the earth and dwellings that cling to Earth's face is more than visual. Such a separation symbolizes the thrust of technological thinking. To think technologically is to pro-voke: nature is seen as standing open to provocative inquiry, an examination that elicits desired responses from an appropriately stimulated earth. Provocation as a form of truth seeking is the basic gesture and comportment of technology. Soleri's cosmology justifies such provoking in the name of esthetogenesis and the semidivine character of energy.

Cosmogonic thought, as we have seen, does not provoke answers; rather it remains on the level of the ancient lived meanings of the phenomena in question: man and earth. In so doing, it e-vokes further meaning not with an eye toward gaining control but with a view toward settling more deeply within the being of the experience. Refusing all the justifications of provocative thought—the subject-object dichotomy, reification of beings, abstract objectivation of entities—evocative thought calls forth the concealed experiences that lie hidden in the ground of man and nature. By trusting the realm of human consciousness as a fit and viable medium of disclosure, it secures meanings that touch deeply on the ultimate matter of human homecoming. For to dwell on the earth is to participate in mystery.

It is this primal confrontation between lived human experience and scientific rationalism that enjoins the conclusion to this paper.

In the end, it is a question of whether human being is sufficient to its own end. Or must man, in order to become fully self-conscious, leap beyond that realm and view himself as something other than human being?

TECHNOLOGICAL COSMOLOGY OR PHENOMENOLOGICAL COSMOGONY

What are the gains and losses of Soleri's arcology? The profits are impressive. Urban dwelling in its trend toward entropic chaos will be turned around, and a more rational, better organized, and more efficient system will take its place. Also, if the quasi-theological cast of Soleri's thinking is accepted, mankind will move in a more self-consciously evolving direction. Aesthetic qualities will become more important since the unitary aspect of arcology will prevent individuals from blighting the whole. Problem solving will become easier since an integrated system will replace the present scattered entity that is called a city. In sum, the gains of arcology lie along the line of master-planning efficiency.

What is lost? The chief casualty is the being of being human, that irreducible field of experience that has so far disclosed some of the meaning of the encounter between man and earth. What Soleri's thought threatens to do is to make it impossible for human beings to think of their connection with the earth in anything other than abstract terms. Existential meaning is dropped in favor of abstractions such as energy, evolutionary development, and divine self-realization.

It is, of course, the confused admixture of scientific and theological abstractions that is so enticing in Soleri's thought. Provocation as a way of thinking, and abstraction as a way of being, required a certain softening effect. Otherwise, the harshness and bleak quality of such a world view would be discouraging. Its promise of distant salvation notwithstanding, Soleri's arcology exacts too high a price. Ontological resonance would be replaced by cosmological explanation; and the ancient and universally felt themes of cosmogony—strife, revealment, and the meaningful disclosure of the void—would be cast into oblivion.

Great danger lies in the possibility of forgetting the worth and weight of being. The word *forgetting* is used deliberately. It is not possible to replace being human with another being. To be sure, one can define the essence of man in such ways as to eliminate any reference to being. We have such abstractions as Marxist Man, Rational Man, and Empirical Man. But insofar as all these abstractions become concrete, they immediately *are*, and that is mode of being and no longer an abstraction. Thus, one can only "forget" his being; he cannot have it removed from him through redefinition.

Such forgetfulness is at the bottom of the issue of technology. It is not a question of Luddite hatred of the machine nor a puritanical love of hard labor. And by no means does the danger of technology lie in its potential for political usurpation. Losing touch with the realm of being is what lurks in technology.

Cosmology inevitably turns being human away from the domain of being by reason of its emphasis on the rational and the intellectual. But because of the ineffectuality of speculative thought, such unbalanced images were heretofore kept in check. Nothing that Plato thought in terms of his cosmology ever came to concrete fruition. The situation is different in the matter of technology. Here an abstract world—a cosmology—can produce results that intimately touch the lives of human beings. Through technology the delay between thought and action has been overcome. There is no gap between thinking a provocative thought and its translation into action. Thus, not only a world view arises but a concrete *world-in-itself* is created and shows itself. It is there to be touched, felt, and experienced. Cosmological technology becomes technological cosmology and thereby gives real birth to itself. Self-conceiving and self-propagating, it is capable of convincing being human that it is real, and the question of being becomes an abstraction.

Once such a position of authority is reached, human consciousness finds itself hard-pressed to resist technology's overture to forget its primal ground of being. Being has fled from the modern world and its departure is so well known that all attempts to raise the question of its absence are regarded as a type of regressive retreat to less sophisticated ages. The real threat of technology is ontological oblivion.

What does phenomenological cosmogony offer in place of Soleri's arcology? By comparison with concrete structural designs, city-planning maps, and systematic overviews, evocative thinking offers little. It does not construct models, nor does it build proto-cities. It does only this: it remains within the realm of lived human experience and asks, "What does it mean to be?" It asks this question concretely, for it sees it as a question of being-at-home and dwelling-on-the-earth. It refuses to reduce being and dwelling, home and earth to another level. More positively, it does not abstract from the question in order to reach a vantage point for analysis.

What, then, does phenomenological cosmogony offer? Simply this: it compels us *to remember*. It recalls us to the earth by evoking for our consciousness the meaning of earth. Remembrance of the connection between dwelling, home, and being human is the gift of being. This gift is given because of the nature of phenomenological thought: it lets lie-forth in its unhiddenness the ontological depth of lived human experience. Thinking, therefore, becomes a mode of thanking: it remembers the moment that gathers together earth and her child, being human.

Whether such recollection, such a gathering together again of the human field of ontological experience, can *do* anything remains questionable. It seems too frail and weak to halt or turn aside the juggernaut of technology. But such thinking does not seek to *do* anything. It is content to remember the being of being human and its ancient roots. Such an act of recall is sufficient, for it brings us back to our dignity as "The Shepherd of Being."[14] As dwellers on the earth we safeguard being; in such stewardship rests our future.

If human beings can remain mindful of being in their being human, technology is no threat. Technology can then become our greatest deliverance. But we must be delivered into the presenting gift of being: without such a dwelling in the mystery of being our homecoming will be in vain.

1. To date Soleri has published two books: *Arcology: The City in the Image of Man* (Cambridge, Mass.: M.I.T. Press, 1970) and *Matter Becoming Spirit* (New York: Anchor Books, 1973). The historian William Irwin Thompson has perhaps done the most to bring Soleri to the attention of the American public. See his "The Individual as Institution: The Example of Paolo Soleri," *Harper's*, November 1972.

2. See Henri Frankfort et al., *Before Philosophy* (Baltimore, Md.: Penguin Books, 1963).

3. See B. F. Skinner, *Beyond Freedom and Dignity* (New York: Bantam Books, 1972), passim. These terms, deliberately taken from the vocabulary of behavioral psychology, testify to the extent to which a human being is now reduced to mechanical models.

4. This understanding of the basic meaning of phenomenology is taken from Martin Heidegger, *Being and Time*, trans. John Macquarrie and Edward Robinson (New York: Harper and Row, 1962), pp. 64 ff.

5. Because of the scattered quality of Soleri's writings, these principles must be culled from an overall reading of his texts. But see, especially, the essays "Function Follows Form," "Simulation and Becoming," and "Topics and Questions on Arcology," in *Matter Becoming Spirit*.

6. Soleri, *Matter Becoming Spirit*, p. 26.

7. The guiding influence for this discussion of technology is Martin Heidegger. See Martin Heidegger, *Vorträge und Aufsatze* (Pfullingen: Neske, 1954) pp. 27 ff.

8. Teilhard's own work *The Phenomenon of Man* (New York: Harper, 1963) is the most available introduction to his thought.

9. See the essay *"Civitate Dei,"* in *Matter Becoming Spirit*, pp. 247-53.

10. See Martin Heidegger, *An Introduction to Metaphysics*, trans. Ralph Manheim (New Haven, Conn.: Yale University Press, 1959), pp. 100-101.

11. Mircea Eliade, *The Sacred and the Profane* (New York: Harcourt, Brace and World, 1959).

12. A. N. Whitehead, *Religion in the Making* (New York: Meridian Books, 1926), p. 16.

13. For an introduction to Husserl's phenomenology, see Richard M. Zaner, *The Way of Phenomenology* (Chicago: Quadrangle Books, 1970).

14. See Martin Heidegger, "The Letter on Humanism," in *Philosophy in the Twentieth Century*, ed. William Barrett and H. D. Aiken (New York: Random House, 1962), 3:251-302.